W9-DGC-988

SPECIAL ISSUE
LAW AND SOCIETY RECONSIDERED

STUDIES IN LAW, POLITICS, AND SOCIETY

Series Editor: Austin Sarat

Volumes 1–2:	Edited by Rita J. Simon
Volume 3:	Edited by Steven Spitzer
Volumes 4–9:	Edited by Steven Spitzer and Andrew S. Scull
Volumes 10–16:	Edited by Susan S. Sibey and Austin Sarat
Volumes 17–33:	Edited by Austin Sarat and Patricia Ewick
Volumes 34–40:	Edited by Austin Sarat

STUDIES IN LAW, POLITICS, AND SOCIETY VOLUME 41

SPECIAL ISSUE LAW AND SOCIETY RECONSIDERED

EDITED BY

AUSTIN SARAT

Department of Law, Jurisprudence & Social Thought and Political Science, Amherst College, USA

ELSEVIER
JAI

Amsterdam – Boston – Heidelberg – London – New York – Oxford
Paris – San Diego – San Francisco – Singapore – Sydney – Tokyo

JAI Press is an imprint of Elsevier

JAI Press is an imprint of Elsevier
Linacre House, Jordan Hill, Oxford OX2 8DP, UK
Radarweg 29, PO Box 211, 1000 AE Amsterdam, The Netherlands
525 B Street, Suite 1900, San Diego, CA 92101-4495, USA

First edition 2008

British Library Cataloguing in Publication Data
A catalogue record for this book is available from the British Library

ISBN: 978-0-7623-1460-7
ISSN: 1059-4337 (Series)

For information on all JAI Press publications
visit our website at books.elsevier.com

Printed and bound in the United Kingdom

08 09 10 11 12 10 9 8 7 6 5 4 3 2 1

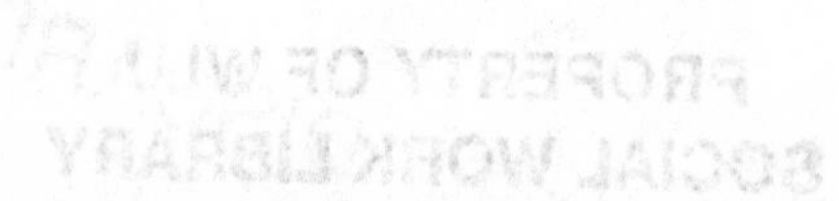

CONTENTS

LIST OF CONTRIBUTORS

Eve Darian-Smith	Law and Society Program, University of California, Santa Barbara, CA, USA
Patricia Ewick	Department of Sociology, Clark University, Worcester, MA, USA
Jonathan Goldberg-Hiller	Department of Political Science, University of Hawaii, Honolulu, HI, USA
Rosemary Hunter	Kent Law School, Eliot College, University of Kent, Canterbury, Kent, UK
Michael McCann	Department of Political Science, University of Washington, Seattle, WA, USA
Sally Engle Merry	Department of Anthropology, New York University, New York, USA
Adelaide H. Villmoare	Department of Political Science, Vassar College, Poughkeepsie, NY, USA
Richard Weisman	Law and Society Program, Division of Social Science, York University, Toronto, Canada

EDITORIAL BOARD

EMBRACING ECLECTICISM

Patricia Ewick

ABSTRACT

Since its emergence as a field of study, law and society scholarship has grown to encompass an array of disciplines, perspectives, methods, and political orientations. A consequence of this disciplinary hypostatization has been to produce a scholarly goulash which, while at times nourishing, now faces the dual dangers of institutional fracture and intellectual incoherence. The aim of this essay is to map a way to embrace the eclecticism that characterizes the field and yet avoid the dangers of dilettantism and to cultivate the interdisciplinarity its founders envisioned without sacrificing a sense of shared purpose or abandoning the possibility of collectively producing a better understanding of law.

"An eclectic is always losing arguments. One lacks the closed-mindedness necessary to treat others' positions with the same contempt they so easily display for one's own."
–Andrew Abbott (2001)

"In this gaudy, all-licensed supermarket of the mind, any idea can apparently be permutated with any other."
–Terry Eagleton (1999)

Special Issue: Law and Society Reconsidered
Studies in Law, Politics, and Society, Volume 41, 1–18

ISSN: 1059-4337/doi:10.1016/S1059-4337(07)00001-4

INTRODUCTION

Last March I was asked to comment on Marianne Constable's remarkable book Just Silences (2005) at the annual meetings of the Law, Culture and Humanities Association at Syracuse Law School. After each of the three readers delivered her comments, a lively and engaged discussion ensued among the audience, the readers, and the author. It soon became apparent that in that room of approximately 50 people I was the only sociologist and perhaps (on this point I am unsure) the only person who would identify as a social scientist. I was particularly conscious of that distinction since much of the discussion focused on the dangers of sociological ways of knowing law.

The discussion followed from Constable's text. Just Silences is an indictment of modern law, what Constable describes as law of technique, a law that deals in what it construes to be fungible resources and the ordering of life on the basis of instrumental rationality. Modern law organizes its practices around market-based logics and the devolution of power to private and quasi-public organizations trained in the skills of accounting, evaluation, and management. But it is not just modern law that attracts Constable's disdain. She argues that the various projects of modern law are enabled, or underwritten by, a "*socio*-logic" that prevails in the everyday operation of law and government. In short, the techniques of knowing, arranging, predicting and so forth that animate modern regimes of governmentality are provided by sociology.

Constable claims that the sociological failure to understand justice – the real subject of her analysis – is a result of the blindness of sociology to anything that is not social; to its refusal or inability to imagine ways of living and being that are not socially constructed; and thus, and most importantly, to the sociological insistence on the contingency of justice. According to Constable, constitutive theories of law and justice seem to posit an unreal, apparent, spurious world; and, even more objectionably they posit a world of contingency in which justice is not necessarily connected to law and thus could be anything, or, for that matter, *nothing*.

For my part on that day, I defended sociology, social constructivism, and the idea of contingency, although I am not sure I persuaded anyone in the room. But my point in recalling this experience is not to reiterate that defense. I describe this encounter because it illustrates a general process in interdisciplinary knowledge formation that Abbott (2001) calls fractalization, the process of creating a distinction and then repeating it within itself. In this case, dichotomies that are used to distinguish (and divide) scholars (e.g., empirical vs. interpretivist, realist vs. constructionist) come to reassert themselves *within* the constructed divisions. To paraphrase Abbott, if we take any group of law and society scholars and lock them in a room, they will eventually divide into the more empirical and the more interpretivist. But, if we separate those two groups and lock each group in a room, they will come to argue and divide over the same issue. For instance, among those of us who call ourselves empiricists, some are highly quantitative (relying on statistical analysis of so-called hard data) and others more qualitative (using ethnographic data or open ended interviews), thus recapitulating within the category of *empirical* socio-legal scholars the larger distinction drawn among all socio-legal scholars.[1]

I recalled Abbott's model as I was listening to the discussion at Law, Culture and Humanities. After having spent most of my career opposing my more positivist, realist colleagues (e.g., criminologists, survey researchers, and those who practice the dark art of regression analysis) on the subject of the social construction of reality and the contingency of social life, I found myself challenged by those on the *other side* of the epistemological spectrum: interpretive, hermeneutical scholars of law. For one group (my more positivist colleagues), I was too interpretive and too committed to the ideas of situated and emergent knowledge; for the positivists' epistemological other (my friends at Law, Culture and Humanities), I was *also* too interpretive, and too committed to situated and emergent knowledge. It seemed as though I had been locked in a room with my realist colleagues for most of my career. On that day, I found myself locked in an entirely different room with a different group. But there was no escaping it: I was still up against the wall.

I would not be surprised if most of us within law and society have had similar experiences, simply because we hang out with an extraordinarily diverse crowd. Since its emergence as a field of study, law and society scholarship has grown to encompass an array of disciplines, perspectives, methods, and political orientations. The initial coupling of social scientists (predominantly sociologists) and law professors has expanded to include all species of social science disciplines, as well as humanistic fields such as literature, film, and history. Its initial goal of producing empirical studies of law in action has enlarged to include interpretive and hermeneutic analysis of texts. Over the years, leaders of the field have sponsored the ideal of using legal studies to make the world a better place (Handler, 1992), have cautioned us to resist the pull of the policy audience (Sarat & Silbey, 1988), and exhorted us to once again take up political activism (Munger, 2001). Even the concept of law – and therefore the subject of all of this inquiry and activism – has become virtually boundless. Law is now understood to be everywhere and to be manifest in pretty much anything.

A consequence of this disciplinary hypostatization has been to produce a scholarly goulash which, while at times nourishing, now faces the dual dangers of institutional fracture and intellectual incoherence. The aim of this essay is to map a way to embrace the eclecticism that characterizes the field and yet avoid the dangers of dilettantism and to cultivate the interdisciplinarity its founders envisioned without sacrificing a sense of shared purpose or abandoning the possibility of collectively producing a better understanding of law.

In its relatively short life, a surprising number of well-researched histories or retrospectives have been written about the origins of the field and its development in the first few decades. I do not intend to extend or revise that accepted history, although I will draw upon elements of it for purposes of illustration. In assessing, or reconsidering, law and society as a field, I will offer a sociology of (law and society) knowledge formation. It is my aim that such an account will illuminate both where the field has been and where it is likely to be in the future.

KNOWLEDGE FORMATION AND TRANSFORMATION IN LAW AND SOCIETY

The dominant and generally accepted theory of scientific knowledge formation is the Kuhnian model wherein periods of normal research are punctuated by abrupt, "revolutionary" shifts in paradigms and the adoption of new questions, methods, and standards. The scientific revolution is sparked by conflict within the community, resulting in a widespread sense among practicing scientists that the old paradigm can no longer effectively address relevant questions or reconcile anomalies. The transition from a paradigm in crisis to a successor paradigm (from which a new tradition of normal science can emerge) is not a cumulative process. The change is revolutionary in that it requires a conversion on the part of practicing scientists. Kuhn characterized this new vision as more than simply a shift in how they see the world; it entails more than a recontextualization of data within a new framework. Consequent to such a revolution, "[s]cientists do not see something as something else; instead they simply see it" (1970, p. 85).

This new vision is achieved through the destruction of the older paradigm. Textbooks, the principle conduit for educating each generation of scientists, are rewritten without mention of the displaced paradigm. This collective "forgetting" thus destroys the evidence that there *was* a revolution. Rather than recounting the incommensurability of the old and new paradigms, the process of change is represented to be *exactly what it is not* – the seamless and progressive accumulation of better knowledge.

It is fairly obvious that this model does not describe the process of knowledge formation in the social sciences, or even less so in an interdisciplinary field such as law and society scholarship (Kuhn, 1970, p. 15). For one thing, we rarely forget. Each new generation of scholars reads the classics; each publication rehearses the approaches it will amend, reject or debunk; and every 20 years or so we write retrospectives such as this.

Indeed, 20 years ago, Sarat and Silbey (1987) explicitly enjoined us from such Kuhnian forgetting. In their self-described "sociology of the sociology of law," Sarat and Silbey depicted the origins of law and society as critical and reformist. But they cautioned us to avoid the smugness that comes with being a successful challenger: beware lest our challenge become the new orthodoxy.

> Although critics first struggle to make room for a new understanding, they, in their enthusiasm, push this understanding from the margin to the center; they seek to make it *the* understanding and thus, in spite of their critical stance, they objectify and reify what was, in its origins, the product of a reformist desire. The critical bite that comes from challenging a dominant paradigm often gets lost when the new vision becomes accepted and taken for granted, and is no longer at the margins but now functions as its own center. (p. 166)

Read one way, the dynamic that Sarat and Silbey imagined and aspired toward was, like Kuhn's, one of periodic renewal as dominant paradigms are displaced by erstwhile marginalized ways of knowing largely carried by a new generation of scholars. But Sarat and Silbey added a critical proviso to the Kuhnian dynamic. Their prescribed antidote for the reification of categories of thought is to avoid the "forgetting" that Kuhn describes as part of the paradigm shift within natural sciences. (Sarat and Silbey characterize it as a "self-deception" rather than "forgetting.") Law and society scholarship should not, they cautioned, "elide its own sources, deny its own history and location, and speak as if there were no perspectives" (1987, p. 172). And they would have it that "in the next two decades of our association's life, our own critical efforts might themselves become the orthodoxy that a new generation would have the temerity to try to save from its own self-deception."

Two Decades Later …

Written almost exactly 20 years ago, we are now in a position to ask whether Sarat and Silbey's vision for law and society has been fulfilled. Has the field we know of as law and society avoided the insistent tug of the conventional, the institutionalized and the disciplined? I think that the answer to that question would be that, to a large extent, it *has* been realized. In the past two decades, the association has grown and diversified. It has generated an abundance of perspectives, methods, research questions, and even new associations, such as the aforementioned Law, Culture and Humanities and the newest kid on the block, Empirical Legal Studies (ELS), each devoted to distinctive approaches to the study of law.

Indeed, rather than periodic revolutions displacing an old orthodoxy with a new orthodoxy, law and society scholarship seems to have developed through a process of expansion and accretion. Orthodoxy can only be attained through exclusion and maintained through silencing. I think that is fair to say that, at least compared to most unidisciplinary fields, this has not occurred. This may be because law and society lacks, or perhaps has successfully avoided, the sort of exemplars around whom conflicts can emerge, crises ensue and revolutions erupt. Kuhn claims that – "the tradition-shattering [of scientific revolutions] complements the *tradition-bound activity of normal science*" (1970, p. 6). By contrast, in law and society there is not much to shatter or revolt against.

The expansion of paradigms and projects may also be a result of a deliberate and laudable plan to be intellectually inclusive and diverse. In the past decades, Law and Society Association (LSA) has extended its reach internationally in order to attract more non-U.S. members. It has also sponsored at least three joint international meetings. Although not entirely successful in this regard (Mather, 2003), LSA has shown public commitment to the goal of inclusiveness. The Graduate Student Workshop and the Summer Institute provide institutionalized egress to young colleagues and their presumably new and sometimes radical ideas. Finally, the Association does not screen papers for the Law and Society Association annual meetings. It thus denies itself a powerful gatekeeping mechanism used by most professional associations for "disciplining" their members. For whatever reason, the result of this accretion, whether deliberate or not, is an ever-expanding menu of perspectives, methods and theoretical exemplars.

In expressing their fears and hopes, Sarat and Silbey may have overstated the role, and thus the danger, of tradition in law and society scholarship. In a more recent overview of the field, Sarat seems to agree. "In the postrealist era that is emerging today, law and society research appears eclectic and non-cumulative. It is neither organized around a single central insight nor an agreed-upon paradigm" (2004, p. 8). In fact, to the extent law and society scholarship is currently experiencing a crisis, it does not seem to be a crisis of orthodoxy. Indeed, some would say it is the exact opposite problem: the center does not hold because there is no center. Sarat goes on to observe that:

> Today while law and society research and scholarship is vibrant and vital, the field is experiencing a period of pluralization and fragmentation. There is no longer a clear center of gravity nor a reasonably clear set of boundaries. Important scholarship proliferates under the banner of law and society even as that designation loses its distinctiveness. (p. 8)

To what extent, then, has law and society scholarship come to resemble what Terry Eagleton characterized as, "the gaudy, all license supermarket of the mind?" Has law and society has become *too eclectic* for its own good?

Before addressing these questions, it is necessary to take stock of some trends in theoretical, epistemological, and methodological socio-legal research. Law and society did not end up with such a diverse (some would say fragmented) menu of methods, foci, or theoretical orientations by chance. In part, it was, as I have suggested above, a result of a deliberate institutional strategy. It was also a consequence of a typical pattern of knowledge formation in which disciplinary ideas presented in an interdisciplinary forum are rapidly appropriated, recontextualized and transformed. This process is what seems to have occurred when, to rely on my earlier account, I confronted the limits of my comfortable social constructivism and found myself arguing, not about the social construction of *reality,* but rather about the *reality* of social constructions. We can read the history of law and society as conforming to this dynamic of fractalization.

According to Garth and Sterling (1998), LSA was founded when legal realists challenged legal formalism. The realist challenge was based on the insistence that, given the indeterminancy of law, legal knowledge must be more than doctrinal and must include empirical studies of law in action. This challenge within the legal academy coincided with a small group of (at least initially) sociologists who, marginalized by orthodox sociology's drift toward quantitative, analytic approaches and by "the precarious position of law within sociology," defected from the ASA and established the LSA. The marriage of legal realists and social scientists thus brought together two groups distinguished from the orthodoxy of their respective home disciplines and intent on constructing an interdisciplinary study of law and society.

But, as with most marriages, this coupling has endured its own share of conflicts, accommodations, reconciliations, and sometimes divorce. The division that has most consistently characterized law and society has been that between academic disciplines and law. Garth and Sterling note in their history of law and society that law professors and socio-legal scholars brought very different social and intellectual capital to the enterprise. And, in the competition between these two types of expertise, Garth and Sterling conclude that the law has emerged the winner.

> The field that was constructed tilted in favor of law. It may have been possible in the 1950s to imagine that sociology or another social science would be able to gain ascendancy over law in providing the expertise and experience in state governance, but by the late 1960s it was clear that law had reformed – incorporated enough social science to regain its status and relevancy. (1998, p. 461)

The law thus "simultaneously repels and absorbs the social science" (p. 462). A consequence of this process is the relative devaluation of the social scientist, if not the social science. Having absorbed their distinctive methods and theories, the legal academy spurned disciplinary socio-legal scholars for precisely that which was appropriated from them.[2]

Despite this tilting toward law, according to Silbey's analysis of articles published in the *Law & Society Review* from 1966 to 2000, the field has been moving toward the increasing representation of a broader array of methods (2000, p. 863). While the use of survey research methods has remained relatively constant, historical and comparative work have grown. In light of this diversity, LSA has been characterized by well-documented conflicts between those who champion an empirical approach to the study of law (with affinities toward the behavioral, quantitative, and structural) and those who sponsor interpretive approaches (with affinities toward the textual, qualitative, and cultural). The drift toward methodological diversity has moved LSA toward a position where (somewhat like myself last spring) it is, for some, too qualitative and for others not qualitative enough. Those within the latter group who have adopted a more explicitly cultural and humanistic approach have emigrated toward LCH. On the other hand, the Association's waning commitment to more orthodox social scientific methods has created an audience for the more quantitative approaches employed by ELS.

The creation of these associations (and journals) dedicated to legal scholarship has provoked some measure of consternation, wariness, and self-examination among law and society scholars (viz this paper/volume). In its short life, ELS in particular has accumulated considerable intellectual capital and plenty of buzz. One measure of its emerging ascendance in the broader field of "law and movements" is the wariness that has been expressed by established law and society scholars as to what ELS is exactly, and, more importantly, what it represents for disciplinary (sociology of law, anthropology of law, etc.) or interdisciplinary (law and society) socio-legal research. For instance, in a recent newsletter of the Sociology of Law Section of the American Sociological Association, Section Chair, Mark Suchman asks, "What then should be our stance toward this new movement? Part of me ... welcomes this development and hopes that the sociology of law can find a seat on the ELS bandwagon." Later, however, Suchman advises caution, "because in clambering aboard the ELS bandwagon, we may be tempted to leave behind many of the trappings that identify us as sociologists" (2006, p. 13).

The "quantitative turn" (toward ELS) and the "qualitative turn" (toward LCH) seem to have led to an identity crisis of a sort for law and society. Sitting precariously outside of the law schools, robbed of their exclusive claim to empirical social science and their rightful claim to interpretive cultural studies, LSA feels itself on the brink of losing definition or purpose, and appears to be experiencing what Sarat characterizes as a "crisis of self-understanding" (2004, p. 8). To avoid such a crisis, LSA may be tempted to stake out a position for the sole purpose of occupying new or exclusive ground. LSA might dedicate itself to a renewed empiricism or commit to a thorough-going interpretivist methodology. I think that such a solution would be a mistake insofar as it would necessitate a retreat from the eclecticism that has sustained socio-legal research for the past few decades. Instead of ceding the empirical/realist/quantitative ground to ELS, or the hermeneutic/interpretivist ground to LCH, law and society should continue to borrow and appropriate from both as a way to generate new knowledge.

Let me offer an example of this process – and its productive capacity – in the context of recent socio-legal research. Twenty years ago there was scant reference to or use of the role of narrative in social studies of law. Kreiswirth (1992) traces the narrativist turn in the human sciences to the 1980s and credits Hayden White with being the first and most significant theorist of narrative to ignore disciplinary and methodological boundaries. In making this turn, empirical and social scientifically leaning scholars appropriated the concept of narrative from their more interpretive and textually oriented colleagues (initially, outside of law and society) and went on to conduct empirical analyses of how narratives work in legal settings. (Similar appropriations and mediations occurred in other "human sciences," such a psychology, experimental science, education, and philosophy, to name a few). Whereas literary and semiotic scholars of narrative had been traditionally more interested in the features of narrative (the "how" of narrative), the social scientific appropriation added a new question for narrative: "why" and "with what consequences" does narrative operate in social interaction (Cobb, 1997; Ewick & Silbey, 1998; Engel & Munger, 2003; Fleury-Steiner, 2002; Sarat, 1993)?

As with most fruitful cross-disciplinary borrowings, the flow of concepts and methods was not one-way. Inspired by what others make of our ideas, we often reappropriate them. So it was that the more literary/linguistic studies of narrative "moved away from the predominantly semiotic concerns, on the one hand, and the predominant disciplinary orientations (literary/linguistic) and objects of inquiry (literary fictional narratives – novels), on the other … to human activities and meanings that may only problematically be labeled texts: the psychoanalytic dialogue, social dramas, and the phenomenology of temporality" (Kreiswirth, 1992, p. 632). It was the serial recontextualization of narrative as something that occurs within social interaction, and of social interaction as something that is constituted by narrative, that transformed its significance for social scientists and their literary/linguistic counterparts. In law and society, this process of borrowing ended up producing a rich body of research about the role of narrative in producing legal culture.

The irony in this process, as Abbott notes, is that "[t]his perpetual recontextualization forces each newly triumphant position to recognize that it has omitted central matters of concern or that … it is itself now representing what it thought it had defeated" (Abbott, 2001, p. 18). Of course, this irony (and the burden it imposes) constitutes the most often overlooked value of interdisciplinarity and eclecticism. According to Abbott, disciplines correct each others absurdities. The more we are confronted with other ways of knowing, the more we confront the deficiencies in our own.

The theory of fractalization is not just a descriptive model of knowledge formation. It is also prescriptive. In many ways, the aspirations of LSA from its founding has been to cultivate this process of division, overlap, borrowings (or thefts) through its deliberate embracement of interdisciplinarity. Of course, interdisciplinarity carries with it some problems. For instance, a common assumption of contemporary philosophers of knowledge is that knowledge is validated through a community of knowers. One of the curses of interdisciplinary fields is not being able to take that community for granted. There is always the possibility of miscommunication, and consequent to that, the burden of translation.

But the necessity of translation, if it is honored, is also a blessing. The need to take stock of others ideas and find ways of expressing our own in a variety of contexts abets understanding and accelerates the process of correction. We are less likely to become captive of our own assumptions. We are made acutely aware of our own perspectivalism and the need to reconcile our ideas with those we encounter. And out of the reconciliation something new and worthwhile may emerge. To reiterate, I would argue, that law and society should confront and embrace intellectual eclecticism. But that in doing so we should proceed cautiously, and, as always reflexively, toward a type of eclecticism that avoids on the one hand dilettantism (an unprincipled mélange) while avoiding orthodoxy, on the other.

TOWARD A PRINCIPLED ECLECTICISM IN LAW AND SOCIETY RESEARCH

Historically, eclecticism refers to the doctrine of selecting or choosing according to pleasure. When eclecticism first appeared as a philosophical school in 2nd century BC, it was an expression of the realization that absolute truth was humanly unattainable. If a single absolute truth did not exist, or could not be apprehended by humans, then a composite truth – one accountable to pleasure or pragmatic usefulness – could be constructed instead. In the 19th century, eclecticism experienced a renewed prominence among philosophers. Victor Cousins, the doctrine's leading advocate at the time and, by chance, the director of the Ecole Normale Superieure and Minister of Public Instruction, claimed that eclecticism was the only method open to philosophers. "Each system," he wrote, "is not false, but incomplete, and in reuniting all incomplete systems, we should have a complete philosophy adequate to the totality of consciousness." The principle aim of the eclectic is not then to reveal the truth, but to engage in critical selection from a variety of existing systems of thought to produce, like any good pragmatist, a truth that is "adequate" to the task at hand.

It is not surprising that eclecticism should be adopted as an ideal by law and society, or, for that matter, much contemporary scholarship – often under the guise of "interdisciplinarity." Some of eclecticism's central epistemological tenets are highly compatible with anti-foundational and post-positivist views regarding the naïve pursuit of truth, views that have become more or less non-controversial in the past few decades. Similarly, the eclectic's rejection of disciplinary ways of knowing sits easily with the contemporary rejection of canons, conventions and disciplinary dogma (Schneider, 1998). Finally, eclecticism's endorsement of selecting and juxtaposing elements from different systems of thought anticipates the playfulness and inventiveness of much post-structural scholarship.

Despite these strengths, eclecticism as an epistemological foundation carries a lot of pejorative weight. In part, the term often inspires contempt because it is mistakenly confused with dilettantism, an approach to knowledge that is to some extent enabled by eclecticism but not identical to it. The connotations of amateurism and triviality that attach to dilettantism are not a necessary part of eclecticism. Eclecticism can be intellectually rich, nuanced, and complex. On the other hand, because eclecticism lacks a systematic character, which could be used to assess and invalidate facile knowledge claims, the dilettante can get away with a lot before he is finally uncovered.

A very different objection to eclecticism was recently articulated by Joan Wallach Scott (2005). Scott denounced eclecticism, not for lending cover to the dilettante, but rather for inadvertently preserving the ascendancy of conventional disciplines. While eclecticism is often associated with innovation and pleasure, Scott makes manifest some of its less obvious conservative consequences.

> What I am against is the notion, implied in the uses of eclecticism I have cited, that we are no longer foregrounding conflict and contradiction in our work, no longer subjecting the foundational premises of our disciplines or, for that matter, our era to rigorous interrogation, no longer asking how meaning is constructed and what relations of power it supports, but instead applying so many useful methods in a common empirical enterprise in which even radical insight is presented simply as new evidence and the conceptual foundations of disciplinary practice are left safely in place. Eclecticism … connotes the coexistence of conflicting doctrines as if there were no conflict. (p. 116)

According to Scott, while the eclectic may escape having to conform to a powerful orthodoxy, the freedom is purchased at the price of not being able to successfully challenge that orthodoxy. Its patchwork of theories, concepts and methods ends up being too conciliatory to be in competition with anything and, by refusing to compete head to head with conventional disciplinary knowledge, eclecticism often ends up forfeiting the game. The fact that ELS is not as eclectic as LSA may explain ELS's current ascendancy within law studies. Whereas LSA employs an array of empirical and interpretive methods, ELS's nearly exclusive use of conventional quantitative social science methods and its tacit commitment to the transparency of language and meaning position it well to launch a credible challenge to the orthodoxies of legal scholarship.

Scott sees eclecticism as particularly dangerous in the present time in which the discourse of eclecticism ("fair and balanced," "intellectual diversity") has been appropriated by a conservative vanguard intent on purging the academy of so-called politics through the insistence upon objectivity ("the new empiricism"). On face of it, dilettantism and orthodoxy are two very different problems dogging the eclectic. But in the real politick of scholarship, where the *charge* of dilettantism (if not the reality) often serves as the trump card of convention, the two ideas act in cahoots to give eclecticism a bad rap.

A third problem with eclecticism is in determining what questions should drive our research. What methods would yield the best evidence? What theoretical models would most productively make sense of that evidence? In most conventional disciplinary fields, prevailing paradigms determine the questions, methods, and theories that scholars employ. In the absence of such external disciplinary constraints, what then organizes and authorizes the choices we make? One troubling possibility for eclecticism is that, as external determinants retreat, individual inclinations and interests drive the choices that are made. I suspect the fear of such intellectual narcissism troubles those who resist eclecticism within LSA. Like them, while I have nothing against pleasure, or novelty or unconventionality, I cannot endorse any of these principles as a model of knowledge formation. What, then, should animate our choices, if not disciplinary orthodoxy or individual pleasure?

I propose that we accept and even embrace eclecticism as a productive way of generating knowledge but, that in order to do so, we must abandon pleasure for a principled eclecticism that would avoid dilettantism or orthodoxy or the incoherence that narcissism would produce. The proposed principle upon which selections are to be made draws upon the model of fractalization described above and, in particular, to the idea embedded in this model that knowledge is neither produced in a linear and progressive march toward truth, nor, the result of a contest between simple binary oppositions. Rather knowledge emerges in fits and starts as scholars explore the empty spaces between the fractal divisions, appropriating and recontextualizing that which has been "borrowed." It entails not only a skepticism of own claims to knowledge but an awareness that any way of knowing is always relational and opposed to some other way, and that this opposition occurs, and thus changes, over time. Most important, as the oppositions that emerge in scholarship become institutionalized (in disciplines, associations, schools of thought) and bounded, empty, unexplored spaces of knowledge necessarily emerge. The philosopher of science Michael Polanyi in *The Tacit Dimension* noted that scientists are only able to critically appraise the work of others in their own or a closely related field. This fact, taken to extreme, produces such empty spaces of knowledge. By contrast, to the extent that scholarship is produced in "chains of overlapping neighborhoods," then even the "most widely separated branches" are effected by and come to rely on each others work.

Silbey (2000) claimed that this model of "overlapping neighborhoods" is precisely the process through which socio-legal studies came to be among the earliest fields to develop a cultural approach to studying social institutions.

> I surmise that this theoretical advance in understanding the cultural dimensions of law, and theorizing about culture itself, may have happened because of the intense, perhaps difficult but nonetheless intersecting, conversations concerning particular legal phenomena among lawyers, psychologists, anthropologists, historians, political scientists, economists, and sociologists. In other words, while multidisciplinarity may make sociolegal studies a "fuzzy set," it seems to me ... that the softness in its borders, or perhaps because of the porous borders, sociolegal scholarship has produced a body of durable and sound observations about the way the law works. (p. 871)

The fruitfulness of interdisciplinarity suggests an approach to collectively producing a better understanding of the law. This approach entails an attentiveness to and a willingness to borrow from our fractal others. Such a principled eclecticism would afford the pleasure that comes from juxtaposing elements of thought and method that have been excluded in order to create something new, but not just for the sake of novelty or creativity. The selections should derive from a commitment to examine all that is left out by the logic of exclusion upon which conventional knowledge operates. It is precisely this logic of exclusion that underwrites this principled eclecticism. What are the questions, the "unthought categories of thought that delimit thinking (quoted in Waquant page 40)" that our or any other approach obscure? Harding called this "strong objectivity" (1991), Bourdieu, called it "reflexive sociology," Sarat and Silbey referred to it in their call for "critical traditions." Our own scholarship should thus contain the elements of its own unsettling, or, as Aristotle wrote of tragedy, "the unraveling of the plot must occur within the plot."

It encourages us to transgress conceptual hierarchies we construct, question the integrity of own constructs (by acknowledging the traces of our own handiwork in constructing them in the first place), and to apply new methods to old questions. As a collective project this approach holds greatest promise for producing deeper understanding of law. It does so because it disrupts the models of stable "schools" or perspectives wherein scholars labor in isolation from one another: quantitative empiricists in one room, ethnographers in another, semioticians in another, and so forth.

And so I return to my experience at Law, Culture and Humanities last spring. Out of the exchange, I realized that Constable's charge that socio-legal scholars have been silent on justice is accurate. As she noted, for most socio-legal scholars the notion of power has served as the conceptual understudy of justice. There are several reasons for this displacement. One obvious explanation is that power, as a concept, is more compatible with the methods and epistemology of social science. For instance, Garth and Sarat (1997) have noted that. "While avoiding discussions that directly address justice, most law and society researchers have no such qualms about the concept of power. One reason is an assumed academic division of labor. The study of power is relatively easy to frame as legitimate social science." Whereas, power seems ubiquitous and robust, justice seems rare, fragile, and elusive. Power leaves a mark: it maims, it diminishes, it injures, and it can be known by the trail it leaves. In short, power avails itself of being observed, recorded and measured. Justice, by contrast, is not so easily known or reckoned. Justice demands that we make a judgment about the value of something: its justness; its fairness; its truth. Studying justice requires that we leave the presumptive value-free realm of social science. To avoid such epistemological exile, the idea of justice is often avoided. By focusing on the operation of power as the proxy for justice, law and society researchers thus avoid wading into the murky value-laden waters of moral philosophy or social policy.

Constable's challenge was to reconsider the way in which sociological approaches to the study of law have too often accepted the idea of the social construction of reality as applying to virtual every human activity, save our own (Woolgar & Pawluch, 1985). In so doing, Constable claims, we do more than render justice silent, we may create the conditions that obliterate it (the socio-logic of modern law). To the extent that the conflation of justice with power is an effect of that particular "logic of exclusion" inherent in empiricism, her challenge presents an opening for the principled eclecticism I am sponsoring and an incitement for a sociological study of justice.

Willing to see our plots unravel, principled eclecticism invites us to abandon our affinities in search of new ways of seeing and knowing. Doing this requires a measure of humility and receptivity to changing one's ideas, rather than simply entertaining the ideas of others. As Frank Munger points out, "Sometimes interdisciplinary is taken to mean, 'I can do two things,' rather than entering into a dialogue or listening to a point of view that pulls you to a different place."[3] To be an eclectic, or at least to take advantage of the insights eclecticism allows, we need to be uncertain, skeptical and (as if the contempt of others were not sufficient) a bit contemptuous of our own truths.

NOTES

1. In his essay, "The Taboo of Virginity," Freud (1997) wrote of what he called the narcissism of small differences. The phrase refers to the tendency for groups (ethnic, religious, or, say, academic) to target their most vehement distain on others who are, by most objective measure, most like them. The following joke illustrates this tendency.

> *I was walking across a bridge one sunny day, and I saw a man standing on the edge, about to jump. I ran over and said: 'Stop. Don't do it.' 'Why shouldn't I?' he asked. 'Well, there's so much to live for!' 'Like what?' 'Are you religious?' He said: 'Yes.' I said. 'Me too. Are you Christian or Buddhist?' 'Christian.' 'Me too. Are you Catholic or Protestant?' 'Protestant.' 'Me too. Are you Episcopalian or Baptist?' 'Baptist.' 'Wow. Me too. Are you Baptist Church of God or Baptist Church of the Lord?' 'Baptist Church of God.' 'Me too. Are you original Baptist Church of God, or are you reformed Baptist Church of God?' 'Reformed Baptist Church of God.' 'Me too. Are you Reformed Baptist Church of God, reformation of 1879, or Reformed Baptist Church of God, reformation of 1915?' He said: 'Reformed Baptist Church of God, reformation of 1915.'I said: "Die, heretic scum," and pushed him off.*
>
> –Joke from Owner's Manual

One might imagine rewriting the joke in the context of my experience at LCH, "I was attending a conference one day last spring when someone asked me whether I study law on the books or in practice?" ... "Using quantitative or interpretative methods?" "Employing a realist or constitutive perspective?" And so on, right up to the push.

2. The relevance of social science, or more specifically sociology, to postmodern governance is a matter of some disagreement. Sarat (2004) sees the influence of sociology declining in an age when the reformist or activist state withers and is replaced with more calculative and dispersed sites of regulation. Others, including Constable (2005), see sociology (at least the data gathering and analytic practices of sociology such as surveys and prediction based on inferential statistics) as central to new forms of governance. The apparent contradiction may disappear if we differentiate sociology qua profession from sociology qua technique. It may be that the latter has been appropriated from sociologists, who are left with little to offer either the legal academy or the various experts who govern.

3. Personal correspondence, September 2006.

ACKNOWLEDGMENTS

I would like to thank Austin Sarat, Lee Cuba, Frank Munger, and Susan Silbey for their helpful comments on this essay. In addition, I thank the anonymous reviewers for their critical reading and suggestions.

REFERENCES

Abbott, A. (2001). *Chaos of disciplines*. Chicago, IL: University of Chicago Press.

Cobb, S. (1997). The domestication of violence in mediation. *Law and Society Review*, *31*, 397–440.

Constable, M. (2005). *Just silences: The limits and possibilities of modern law*. Princeton, NJ: Princeton University Press.

Eagleton, T. (1999). In the gaudy supermarket. *London Review of Books*, *21*(2), 3–6.

Engel, D., & Munger, F. (2003). *Rights of inclusion*. Chicago, IL: University of Chicago Press.

Ewick, P., & Silbey, S. (1998). *The common place of law*. Chicago, IL: University of Chicago Press.

Fleury-Steiner, B. (2002). Narratives of the death sentence: Toward a theory of legal narrativity. *Law and Society Review*, *36*, 549–579.

Freud, S. (1997). *The taboo of virginity. Sexuality and the psychology of love*. New York: Touchstone.

Garth, B., & Sarat, A. (1997). Justice and power in law and society research: On the contested careers of core concepts. In: *Justice and law in sociolegal studies* (pp. 1–18). Northwestern University Press.

Garth, B., & Sterling, J. (1998). From legal realism to law and society: Reshaping law for the last stages of the social activist state. *Law and Society Review*, *32*, 409–471.

Handler, J. (1992). Postmodernism, protest, and the new social movements. *Law and Society Review*, *26*, 697–732.

Harding, S. (1991). *Whose science? Whose knowledge: Thinking from women's lives*. Ithaca, NY: Cornell University Press.

Kreiswirth, M. (1992). Trusting the tale: The narrativist turn in the human sciences. *New Literary History*, *23*, 629–657.

Kuhn, T. (1970). *The structure of scientific revolutions*. Chicago, IL: University of Chicago Press.

Mather, L. (2003). Reflections on the reach of law (and society) post 9/11: An American superhero. *Law and Society Review*, *37*, 263–282.

Munger, F. (2001). Inquiry and activism in law and society. *Law and Society Review*, *35*, 7–20.

Sarat, A. (1993). Speaking of death: Narratives of violence in capital trials. *Law and Society Review*, *27*, 19–58.

Sarat, A., & Silbey, S. (1987). Critical traditions in law and society research. *Law and Society Review*, *21*, 165–174.

Sarat, A., & Silbey, S. (1988). The pull of the policy audience. *Law and Policy*, *10*, 97–168.

Schneider, U. J. (1998). Eclecticism rediscovered. *Journal of the History of Ideas*, *59*, 173–182.

Scott, J. W. (2005). Against eclecticism. *Differences: A Journal of Feminist Cultural Studies*, *16*, 114–137.

Silbey, S. (Ed.) (2000). *Law and society review*, *34*, 859–872.

Suchman, M. (2006). Empirical legal studies: Sociology of law, or something ELS entirely? *AMICI: Newsletter of the Sociology of Law Section of the American Sociological Association,* p. 13.

Woolgar, S., & Pawluch, D. (1985). Ontological gerrymandering. *Social Problems*, *32*, 214–227.

DR. STRANGELOVE (OR: HOW I LEARNED TO STOP WORRYING AND LOVE METHODOLOGY)☆

Michael McCann

ABSTRACT

This chapter derives from the movie Dr. Strangelove *cues for exploring questions about the quest for methodological insularity and purity in socio-legal research. Steven Lukes' classic three-dimensional model of power provides an intellectual focus for the core exploration of relations between epistemology and data generation, the two key elements that we usually identify with methodology. The discussion culminates in an affirmative argument for the value of approaching methodology as jazz, the creative popular music that grounds reliable, humane sense in Kubrick's movie and provides an apt analogy for much of the leading scholarship in the LSA tradition.*

☆I write this chapter for our graduate students at the University of Washington – past, present, and future. I benefited greatly from commentary on earlier drafts by many scholars, including: Stuart Scheingold, William Haltom, Gad Barzilai, Katherine Beckett, Rachel Cichowski, Angelina Godoy, Steve Herbert, George Lovell, Jamie Mayerfeld, Joel Migdal, Arzoo Osanloo, Mark Weitzenkamp, Cesar Rodriguez-Garavito, David Engel, Jeff Dudas, Lisa Miller, Jon Goldberg-Hiller, Susan Sterett, Helena Silverstein, John Gilliom, and an anonymous reviewer for this book.

Special Issue: Law and Society Reconsidered
Studies in Law, Politics, and Society, Volume 41, 19–59

ISSN: 1059-4337/doi:10.1016/S1059-4337(07)00002-6

> Now look boys, I ain't much of a hand at makin' speeches. But I got a pretty fair idea that something doggoned important's going on back there. And I got a fair idea of the kind of personal emotions that some of you fellas may be thinking. Heck, I reckon you wouldn't even be human beings if you didn't have some pretty strong personal feelings about ... (methodological) combat. But I want you to remember one thing, the folks back home is a countin' on ya, and by golly we ain't about to let 'em down. Tell you somethin' else. This thing turns out to be half as important is I figure it just might be, I'd say that you're all in line for some important promotions and personal citations when this thing's over with. That goes for every last one of you, regardless of your race, color, or your creed. Now, let's get this thing on the hump. We got some flying to do.[1]
>
> – Major T.J. "King" Kong, *Dr. Strangelove*

> I am not sure but that methodology is a little like religion. It is something we need everyday, but something which we are irresistibly impelled to think and talk about, but regarding which we never seem to reach a definite conclusion. Each one, if he is clever, works out something adequate for his own use, but the general principles remain unsettled ...
>
> – Thomas Cooley, 1930, cited in McCann, 1996, p. 457

> Why should the bomb be approached with reverence? Reverence can be a paralyzing state of mind.
>
> – Stanley Kubrick, 1964, interview

> My breakthrough moments always seemed to come when I left the lesson plans ... My grandfather didn't seem to worry that he was making it up as he went along, and I try not to either.
>
> – Bela Fleck, NPR interview[2]

INTRODUCTION

Themes

This chapter addresses two themes that have, in my view, proved foundational to the rich tradition of interdisciplinary law and society research. The first theme is the *analytical focus on power*, and especially on inequalities of power that law sustains, restrains, contests, and sometimes transforms. This theme is particularly interesting for me as a political scientist, although in my view law and society research has devoted rather *more* explicit and sophisticated attention to questions of unequal power than does scholarship in my home discipline, and especially in the subfield of public law. Second, I call attention to the notable socio-legal tradition of crafting *new and original research questions, designs, and methodologies.* Methodological diversity and innovation have been hallmarks of law and society scholarship, and this marks another one of the reasons why I and many others long ago became interested in Law and Society Association (LSA). The virtue of the legacy is not just its openness to different approaches, but its celebration of creativity and improvisation in imagining the very enterprise of research. The interdisciplinary intellectual tradition of law and society research has been as inventive in the forms of research as in the substantive questions it poses.

The Contentious Context: A Provocative Analogy

This chapter reflects on both of these themes, but my primary point of departure and focus is the latter topic concerning methodological inclinations. *In short, this chapter reconsiders familiar methodological modes for interrogating power in an effort to deconstruct and challenge the power of methodological obsession itself in professional academic life.* I am moved to this topic for lots of reasons, but at least in part because a palpable rift attributed largely to methodological differences has developed over recent years among law and society scholars. In some ways, this schism follows from the very success of LSA in attracting scholars from so many different academic disciplines, thus contributing to an ever-proliferating diversity in methodological orientations. It thus seems ironic that increasing theoretical diversity and openness in LSA has been attended by the intensifying perception of schisms drawn along simplistic binary lines of methodological inclination. Readers of this chapter no doubt are familiar with the usual litany of imagined clashes, including quantitative vs. qualitative, behavioral vs. interpretive, experimental vs. ethnographic, rigorous vs. non-rigorous, and hard science vs. soft science or non-scientific methods.[3] These divisions long have been deep within the social science disciplines, but such depth of tension strikes me as relatively new in the interdisciplinary study of law and society.[4]

Perhaps the most palpable sign of this division is the recent development of separate interdisciplinary socio-legal associations defined by methodology, each with its own conferences and journals.[5] One group has been bound by commitments to cultural studies drawing on humanities traditions and largely eschewing scientific claims; the other has congregated colleagues who are committed to quantitative social science and mostly undertake statistical empirical studies of social behavior.[6] Generally, these groups are differentiated by their separate, specialized conception of "appropriate methodologies," although many readers will already note in that claim the problem of collapsing techniques for generating and analyzing data with their underlying epistemological and theoretical foundations, a point that is developed further in the following pages.[7]

In the spirit of intellectual play, my discussion builds on a loose, very imperfect, but hopefully provocative analogy between this rift in LSA and the satirical take on the Cold War offered by Stanley Kubrick's hilarious 1960s movie *Dr. Strangelove*. The ostensible methodological fissure in LSA is, after all, mostly a sort of cold war punctuated by occasional hot clashes, with détente sustained by an informal non-aggression pact and various efforts by leaders of different groups to promote parity in organizational resources and to preach mutual tolerance as the keys to coexistence in the same multi-disciplinary professional sphere. In the movie, the seemingly rational logic of mutually assured destruction ultimately fails when a rogue U.S. Air Force general authorizes dropping a nuclear bomb on the Soviet Union, which in turn detonates a Russian "doomsday machine," the ultimate technology without mind or conscience that obliterates the civilized world. The parallel that most interests me, though, is how the fixation with specific forms of technology potentially can – as expressed artistically through various sexual and gendered connotations about power, fetish, and sheer craziness – subvert good sense, practical professional norms, meaningful dialogue, and creative action. In particular, the obsession with purity as a source of potency is a theme hammered repeatedly in the movie. As General Ripper is quoted after issuing "the code" for attack, "God willing, we will prevail in peace and freedom from fear and in true health through the purity and essence of our natural fluids. God bless you all." The very danger of sustained contact with the alien Communist rivals, Ripper declares, is that it will "sap and impurify our precious bodily fluids."

The movie thus probes a familiar paradox, one that haunts academic research. On the one hand, methodologies are important technological means that humans construct to advance the rational pursuit of normative ends. We thus think of methods as normatively "neutral" and apolitical, as humanly crafted techniques intended to serve independently derived values and purposes. Such techniques are celebrated for ensuring systematic rigor and well-defined standards of reasonableness for professional action. As the Empirical Legal Studies blog playfully proclaims, "Bringing Methods" is a way to discipline "Our Madness." On the other hand, methodological techniques of data production and analysis are not value-free, but rather they inherently implicate and instantiate many types of epistemological and ontological premises or values.[8] Like all purposive, moral, or religious discourses, methodologies express certain intrinsic, foundational ways of knowing that generate contending allegiances and become normative ends in themselves that drive human action. It follows, moreover, that methodologies often become inescapably tied to particular patterns of professional practice and privileged position.[9] Quests for instrumental effectiveness and moral superiority become fused, perhaps confused, in institutional practice, sometimes causing individuals to go "a little funny in the head" and organizations to go awry.[10] Major Kong's famous speech, quoted at the start of this chapter, captures this point as well. Dr. Strangelove's erratically sadistic drive for technical superiority, Ripper's mad obsession with purity, and General Buck Turgidson's adolescent lust for the bomb each underlines further the theme that methods can be a source of madness far more than modernist mythologies recognize.

My appropriation of this theme here allows me to inquire about whether the increasing intellectual fixation on equating methodological specialization and purity with intellectual potency is similarly misguided and unproductive among socio-legal scholars. Like Kubrick, my venture imagines a possible scenario that is undesirable, but I make no effort to link this imagined potential trajectory to specific people, statements, and events in LSA. The goal is to stimulate thought and discussion about the relationship between ends and means in socio-legal scholarship, not to identify demonstrable sins or sinners.[11] I instead stick to my key thematic inspiration from the movie: how the lure of technical purity and superiority of method can impede creative thought, undermine good sense, subvert good intentions, divert organizational energies, and generate unproductive conflict. Indeed, the movie brilliantly satirizes how the pull of technology can become a fetish potentially detrimental to cogent analysis, meaningful dialogue, and humane action.

The scale of implications for the fictional movie vision and real academic life are, of course, incomparable. It would be absurd in the extreme to liken the implications of academic fads to nuclear holocaust, which Kubrick brilliantly underlines with black humor. Buck Turgidson's chilling lines are worth recalling on this point: "Mr. President, I'm not saying we wouldn't get our hair mussed. But I do say … no more than ten to twenty million killed, tops. Uh … depended on the breaks." At the same time, we should recognize that the stakes in the methodology wars are not inconsequential for individual academic careers. Institutional hiring, advancement, awards, grants, graduate student devotees, and the like all are affected by these battles, which invests such goods with some passionately experienced significance. As Kong puts it in the movie, "important promotions and personal citations" are at stake.[12]

Finally, I profess at the outset that my primary goal in the chapter is not to produce greater peace among scholars nor to promote a more stable coexistence among diverse scholars in LSA. Those may be laudable goals in academic politics and international policy-making alike, but they are not my motivations here. I do not seek to preclude all fighting in the intellectual war room.[13] In fact, my contentious argument may well add to strained relations. But I do view the tendencies to common scholarly identification along divergent lines of methodological conformity and the pursuit of methodological purity as potentially detrimental to the unique interdisciplinary quest and character of the law and society community. Such identification is likely to obscure the more complex and important challenges of crafting epistemological clarity while discouraging innovation, serious debate, and creative synthesis in research design. Retreat into like-minded academic clusters threatens to privilege intellectual insularity, encourage misplaced confidence in our limited ways of knowing, and reward repetition of familiar research modes regardless of their merits. The risks are not, as in nuclear war, rapid death to masses of fellow citizens, but rather the slow demise of the critical exchange necessary to innovative thought. The commitment to purity may produce more conceptual rigor mortis than rigor if scholars increasingly interact with and produce research primarily for those who already agree with their first principles. As I see it, this is as true for humanities-oriented scholars who spurn scientific conventions as for social scientists, for post-positive culturalists and interpretivists as much as for behavioral positivists. In short, methodology is an odd, unproductive foundation for organizational investment and rivalry, one that often deserves the parody that outsiders to academic professions find easy prey.

The fact that the LSA was born in the same year (1964) as the movie *Dr. Strangelove* was released thus strikes me as potentially ironic. Has the association's founding fusion of commitment to well-grounded empirical inquiry, intellectual creativity, cross-disciplinary dialogue, methodological bricolage, and political progressivism – the historically apt antidotes to Kubrick's nuclear nightmare – succumbed to the technological righteousness, professional specialization, and concomitant ideological insularity that Kubrick long ago satirized as insane? Has LSA divided along lines of specialization familiar in the disciplines rather than transcended them by nurturing a truly interdisciplinary or trans-disciplinary identity? Not really, in my view, at least not yet. But I hope that the outrageous analogy at least creates an opening for the more subtle, measured reflection about our intellectual legacy, current trends, and possible fates that follows.

A Preview of the Analysis

The remainder of this chapter will explore the contours of this logic. I have chosen to develop the argument by focusing on different approaches to analyzing or interpreting "power," the substantive theme earlier recognized as highly salient in law and society scholarship. I use the three-dimensional conceptual scheme devised by sociologist Steven Lukes (1974, 2005) some thirty years ago as a starting point to formulate my key points about the complex, indeterminate, often confused relationship between two dimensions of methodology – between *techniques of data generation/manipulation* and fundamental *epistemological premises*, between the conventions we use for evidencing manifestations of power and the modes of imagining what we mean by the concept of "power." The subsequent section then builds on the lessons of that inquiry. My point is not that methodology does not matter, nor is it that the quest for rigor is futile. Quite the opposite: I suggest that we must resist the potent pull toward methodological purity in order to adequately develop supple, effective, well-crafted methodological approaches that help to make sense of power's many faces in social organization. Lusting for methodological insularity, purity, or superiority is the opposite of taking methodology, much less interdisciplinarity, seriously. Specifically, I argue for greater humility about the promises of specific methods to help us know our topics, for the value of commitments to multi-methodological inquiry, and for studies that integrate different epistemological groundings and craft diverse methodologies accordingly. In short, I celebrate scholarship that defies easy categorization, spurns methodological purity, and revels in creative synthesis or at least juxtaposition of different approaches to addressing unusual questions. These virtues are what once drew me to much law and society scholarship, and it is a legacy that merits respect and understanding. Along the way, I raise a variety of other related conceptual issues and offer many examples from the canon of law and society scholarship to illustrate my more affirmative points.[14]

A THREE-DIMENSIONAL MODEL OF POWER: METHODOLOGICAL IMPLICATIONS

On Power

Steven Lukes' slim 1974 volume, *Power: A Radical View*, was a landmark contribution to social theory. My brief discussion here cannot begin to capture the originality and complexity of his analysis, to assess its considerable intellectual impact, or to address its constraints, conundrums, and confusions. I do not even try. My aim instead is to use his conceptual analysis as a starting point and organizational scheme for thinking about the relationship between epistemologies of power and techniques for investigating those different ways of thinking about or knowing power. In short, I shamelessly exploit his work for my own ends and, in the process, often depart from and even invert some of his theoretical positions.

It is worthwhile, however, to offer at the start a few general comments about Lukes' project, which recently was expanded to address new currents of social theory over the last several decades (2005). His initial study focused on the dynamics of social domination and inequality, and especially on the many ways that hierarchical power relations induce or enforce quiescence from subaltern subjects. Lukes' primary orientation to power thus is relational in character and focused on forms of constraint; he outlines a conception of "power over" that presumes asymmetry and inherent conflict of interests (see Lukes, 2005, p. 64). All the three dimensions of power that he explores thus are grounded in "the same underlying conception of power, according to which A exercises power over B when A affects B in a manner contrary to B's interests" (Lukes, 1974, p. 30).

Lukes recognizes in the reissued volume that his initial angle was "narrow" and presumed a simplified model of binary power relations, focusing on a conflict between groups defined as dominant and subordinate along singular, seemingly clear lines. The legacy of neo-Marxist class theory, and especially Gramsci's conception of hegemony, is unmistakable in this regard, even though Lukes devotes few words to those influences. This initial framework excludes other plausible approaches to power, including power as a "resource to be distributed" and power as an "enabling or productive force" (Allen, 2005). Lukes wrestles with these other approaches to power, and especially with Foucault, in his updated volume (2005). The limits of his framework are not crippling for my purposes here, however, for many socio-legal scholars similarly focus on how law figures into structures of domination and the complex constraints placed on subaltern groups, whether demarcated simply or complexly. Indeed, Lukes' fundamental question about how power constrains, channels, limits, co-opts, absorbs and diverts or directs subjects – and especially ordinary people with few resources and little status – in ways that sustain injustice is at the heart of much socio-legal scholarship. I will offer specific examples of well-known socio-legal studies in the following pages illustrating the various dimensions of power that he offers.

Finally, it is worth noting that Lukes says very little directly about my primary theme regarding the relationship between epistemology and methodology, although in many ways his entire book can be viewed as very much about this topic. Again, my discussion ranges beyond and at times even against the grain of his thinking. I have been helped along the way, though, by John Gaventa's 1980 volume attempting to implement Lukes' three-dimensional model interrogating "power and powerlessness" in a small Appalachian coal-mining town. Gaventa directly faced the fact that "there are methodological difficulties" involved in operationalizing the ambitious model (1985, p. 25). How do we study what does not happen? How do we falsify claims about non-action? How do we demonstrate unarticulated or latent interests? Can we find relevant counterfactuals? Gaventa effectively labors to show that these challenges are "surmountable." Part of his answer is conceptual clarity in framing the questions and assumptions specific to each dimension of power, and part is methodological flexibility; both parts require lots of work. But some ground must be covered before we get to that argument.

The One-Dimensional Approach

Lukes begins with the most simple and familiar dimension or conception of power. This "one-dimensional view of power involves a focus on *behaviour* in the making of *decisions on* issues over which there is an observable *conflict* of (subjective) *interests*, seen as express policy preferences, revealed by political participation" (2005, p. 19). He links this approach to the pluralist analysis advanced by political scientist Robert Dahl (1961) and his students, where the key question is "who governs," and the answer largely turns on who participates and has the resources to wield influence in policy-making venues (see Gaventa, 1980, pp. 13–14). The perspective tends to presume, I might add, a model of relatively autonomous, self-directed actors who intentionally seek various ends through strategically rational behavior, thus imparting a strong "methodological individualism" to most versions of this approach. Moreover, there is a pronounced commitment to determining the relative *causal* significance of actors on their context or of contextual factors (e.g., organizational and monetary resource distribution) on the capacity of actors. These latter two features align the first dimensional model easily with traditional behavioral study as well as with various game theoretic or microeconomic models of interaction. In short, power is envisioned as demonstrable causal influence, with causality largely understood as linear, direct, unidirectional, and measurable. A strong current of positivist epistemology generally drives the emphasis on observable action and conflict.

This type of inquiry into power is very common among socio-legal scholars. Indeed, it is difficult to undertake study of human interaction without wandering into this explanatory realm to some degree, asking "who acts?", "who prevails?", "to what effect?", and "why?" The approach is very often identified by law and society scholars with an "instrumental" conception of law's power or action, and it is heavily linked to the legacy of legal realism. One can think of many examples. The longstanding interest of law and society scholars in "access to justice" and individual legal mobilization has raised many relatively straightforward questions about who mobilizes law, what factors affect that mobilization (or lack thereof), what accounts for the escalation or dropping of grievances at various points in disputing processes, and what factors determine the effectiveness of such mobilization actions against adversaries (e.g., Black, 1973; Miller & Sarat, 1980–1981; Zemans, 1983). Specifically, for example, why do low income people mobilize law less to redress their many legal grievances (Curran, 1977)? Many later studies of legal mobilization typically include elements of such instrumental analysis in various degrees as well.

Another tradition of instrumental analysis concerns institutional impact, often focused on legal implementation capacities and processes. Some scholars focus again on the inegalitarian implications of "who governs" in implementation processes (Melnick, 1983; Kelman, 1981; Coglianese, 2001) or official non-compliance with or resistance to legal governance (Muir, 1967; Dolbeare & Hammond, 1971; Wirt, 1970). A related body of scholarship has explored the potential power of law to deter individual criminal action (Piliavin, Gartner, Thornton, & Matsueda, 1986; Matsueda, Kreager, & Huizinga, 2006). Yet another tradition of studies regarding the impact of U.S. federal court decisions has relied heavily on the direct, linear conceptions of causal influence that Lukes characterizes in the one-dimensional model of power (Rodgers & Bullock, 1972; Rosenberg, 1991; Donohue & Heckman, 1991). The relative (in)capacity of the Supreme Court to prevail over other branches of national government also poses similar questions framed in similar terms (Dahl, 1957; Casper, 1976).

The examples from socio-legal research are potentially endless. Rather than offer more examples, though, I turn to the important issue of methodology. One does not need a comprehensive survey to recognize the wide range of methodological techniques – conventions for data generation, retrieval, and organization – that have been mobilized to address one-dimensional power relations. Studies by law and society scholars run the gamut of data-gathering conventions addressing one-dimensional causal approaches to power. For example, studies of Supreme Court decision-making range broadly, including attitudinal explanations drawing on elaborate big-N databases (Segal & Spaeth, 1993); rational choice frameworks mixing formal modeling with a variety of quantitative and qualitative case study data (Epstein & Knight, 1998); wholly qualitative case study narratives by historical institutionalists (Clayton & Gillman, 1999); interview intensive studies of court personnel (Perry, 1991); multi-method studies of legal support networks (Epp, 1998). However different the techniques of data generation, all these studies are interested in explaining fairly straightforward questions about what causes and constrains judicial behavior or judicial impact on other actors. We see the same diversity of methodologies in looking at the impact of courts on social relations. Gerald Rosenberg's landmark study of judicial impact and capacity to secure compliance uses a wide range of methodologies and types of data in one large study (1991).

The very fact of diversity in methodological techniques among and within studies is evidence that there is no deterministic relationship between theoretical or epistemological foundations of methodology and conventions of data production; one-dimensional power can be theorized in different ways and evidenced by different types of data. "There is no single correct method of causal analysis," agrees Ian Shapiro (2005, p. 41). Indeed, this fact of pervasive diversity suggests that scholars generally find value in each of many methodological approaches, and there is no compelling reason for deeming any particular mode of data generation as inherently superior. That said, big-N statistical studies, and especially sophisticated forms of regression analysis, are more common in studies at this level of power than for other dimensions. The reason will become even more evident in subsequent pages, but suffice it to say that empirical models of observable conflict and linear causal factors among rational, relatively autonomous subjects are far more amenable to such statistical methods than are other, more complex models of power and subjectivity.[15] In other words, the lure of the one-dimensional model of power and subjectivity often is less its intrinsic theoretical or epistemological integrity than its amenability to formulaic methodological operationalization. And to the extent that this is the case, we witness one way in which methodological capacity, elegance, and purity can drive, rather than just neutrally serve, scholarship. We will return to this theme shortly.

The Two-Dimensional Approach

The second dimension of power derives from E.E. Schattschneider's (1975) classic insight that lack of action or ineffective action by various people may reflect less their personal failures than "the suppression of the options and alternatives that reflect the needs of non-participants ... Whoever decides what the game is about also decides who gets in the game" (p. 105). This was the foundational understanding on which Bachrach and Baratz (1970) constructed their "second face of power," which in turn was appropriated and developed by Lukes. Its core insight, to quote Schattschneider again, is that "... (a)ll organizations develop a mobilization of bias' in favour of the exploitation of certain kinds of conflict and the suppression of others. Some issues are organized into politics while others are organized out" (cited in Gaventa, 1980, p. 9). The reluctance to express grievances, or apparent quiescence, thus may not reflect affirmative consensus about the status quo or inability to recognize core interests so much as realistic recognition on the part of the disadvantaged that change may not be possible or worth the costs of effort.

Lukes emphasized that this second face, or dimension, of power was initially grounded in a critique identifying important limitations of the one-dimensional model, including especially the latter's focus on observable decision-making behavior amidst a context of demonstrable conflict. The second dimension instead is attentive to "non-decisions" and inaction that result from exclusions of participants and their issues or anticipated negative consequences from the subaltern population's potential actions. These exclusions or anticipated negative consequences can take many forms (force, sanctions, manipulations, deceptions, biased treatment, procedural barriers, unequal resource distribution) and include informal as well as formal, rule-oriented features of institutionalized activity. And it is the "organization of bias" sewn into social and political institutions, processes, and routines that is the focus of most study in the second dimension. This approach still gives considerable attention to instrumental action by rational social agents, but it suggests a more complex, dynamic conception of contextual influence at work in cognitive processes as well as socially conditioned (i.e., "constituted," and hence not autonomous) subjectivities. Indeed, many subsequent scholars interested in agenda setting, framing practices, and social movement struggles have developed process-based understandings of this second level to include feedback loops, multiple causality, and dialectically interacting forces that relax, even defy, the strict assumptions of positivist linear causal models. At the same time, however, it is critical to remember that Lukes viewed the second dimension of power as building upon and supplementing rather than supplanting the first dimension in the aggregative two-dimensional model.

Not surprisingly, a great deal of socio-legal scholarship has directly or indirectly addressed the second dimension of power. For example, Stuart

Scheingold (1974), drawing on the important scholarship of Murray Edelman, demonstrated how the "myth of rights" at once lured Americans to value certain principles while discounting others, to privilege certain ways of addressing grievances while ignoring others, with both diversions supporting status quo inequalities. Joel Handler's (1966) earlier important work critiquing new property ideals was grounded in recognition that our proprietarian legal tradition facilitates economic independence for some people and organizations that make legal action realistic while rendering it strategically unrealistic for dependent others such as the welfare poor. Perhaps the most brilliant and influential study in this mold was Marc Galanter's (1974) *Why the 'Haves' Come out Ahead.* Galanter's argument about differences between "one-shotters" and "repeat players" in civil disputing was a classic demonstration of mobilized biases in law. Not only do organized repeat players tend to prevail in civil disputing due to one-dimensional power advantages of wealth, expertise, and status, Galanter suggests, but their ongoing engagement in various types of disputes enable them to shape the very rules of law in ways that favor systematically their position and interests over time relative to one-shot disputants.

Much other literature on disputing follows suit. Mather and Yngvesson's (1980–1981) discussion about how legalization of conflicts by disputants, third parties, or audiences can either narrow or expand the terms of the contest is a classic second dimension analysis. Laura Beth Nielsen's recent study (2004) of citizen responses to street harassment likewise shows how aggrieved women and minorities remain largely quiescent because of the perceived biases or unresponsiveness of the legal system. At a broader group-based level, Gad Barzilai's studies of minority politics in Israel illustrates how the individualistic thrust of liberal legal rights talk renders legal mobilization by non-dominant communities either unattractive or ineffective, demonstrating yet another mobilized bias of law (2004). Stephen Daniels and Joanne Martin have explicitly built on agenda setting theory to demonstrate how the anecdote-infused "rhetoric of reform" has been "organized into politics," while social science evidence about civil disputing and juries has been "organized out" (1995). A long tradition of studies regarding social movement litigation has similarly demonstrated how courts and law generally have narrowed activists' substantive agendas and tactics into manageable, "co-opted" terms (Kessler, 1990; Edelman, Erlanger, & Lande,1993; Coglianese, 2001; Eskridge, 2001), while others have argued how well organized and funded legal activists in turn have at times influenced the agendas of high courts (Lawrence, 1990; Epp, 1998). Indeed, just about all socio-legal study to some degree has worked to expose the mobilized biases and constraints of law in responding to both discrete grievances and promoting status-quo hierarchies.

Again, we can witness many methodological techniques of producing data in this second dimensional research, although the balance of qualitative study to quantitative study tends to be weighted more toward the former than in one-dimensional studies. One important reason is that the relaxed or qualified approach to causality and the common focus on inaction or non-decisions renders positivist premises and statistical regression models for sorting out discrete variables less useful. Some studies of institutional bias have drawn on quantitative analysis, but they tend to be out-numbered by qualitative case study based on analytic narratives. At the same time, critical exchanges about specific analytical ventures often highlight the clash between assumptions and techniques in first dimension studies that are less relevant at the second dimension. To what extent, and in what aspects, can mobilized bias be studied as a matter of strict causality, and especially through statistical measures? This question has been prominently debated, for example, between analysts of top-down judicial impact, who often use positivist models of causality to study "indirect" as well as "direct" effects of judicial decisions, and scholars of legal mobilization who urge relaxation of strong causal arguments in making sense of reform litigation processes initiated by subaltern populations in two-dimensional terms (Rosenberg, 1992, 1996; McCann, 1994, 1996).[16] Debates about the merits of quantitative vs. qualitative techniques and other matters of technical convention (case selection, etc.) often are involved, but these often only obscure the more fundamental debates about basic epistemological premises.

The Three-Dimensional Approach

The third dimension of power goes far beyond the other two dimensions, although it is important to emphasize again that Lukes intends the former to build on the latter in aggregative fashion. What is new in the third dimension is recognition that the human subject may not only be inhibited or diverted from pursuing his preferred interests, but his quiescence or conciliatory actions may reflect various forces "influencing, shaping or determining his very wants" (1974, p. 23). This focus thus variously directs attention to: the "study of social myths, language, and symbols;" the "social construction of meaning and patterns;" forms of mass communication and information control; patterns of socialization and "internalization of … values, beliefs, or rules of the game;" the psychological processes of subject identity formation; and the development of subject "consciousness" – all forces that sustain subordination and hierarchical order in an organized life (Gaventa, 1980, pp. 15–20). Studies of this third dimension very self-consciously transcend the confining individualistic and behavioral premises of other two approaches. It thus "offers the prospect of a serious sociological and not merely personalized explanation" (Lukes, 1974, p. 38). And, finally, in emphasizing sociological processes of subjectivity formation as well as latent conflicts that may not be observable, discussions of power in the third dimension are further removed from reliance on the logic of causality.[17]

Lukes' demarcation of the third dimension arguably represents his most original and important contribution. His debt to Gramsci and other neo-Marxists who highlight ideology, consciousness, and hegemony again is clear. Moreover, Gaventa later showed how the approach links up well with scholarship by Murray Edelman and others on "symbolic politics" and "deep" agenda setting theory. It also is relevant to note the applicability and appeal of these ideas for the huge movement in interpretive theory that grew in the decades following publication of Lukes' volume.

At the same time, subsequent trends in social theory posed significant challenges for Lukes' model. For one thing, Lukes' suggestion that people have objective interests that they can fail to recognize or act on generated much critical debate. Gaventa (1980) and Lukes (2005) each provide spirited defenses of the conceptual move, and many other types of theorizing could be mobilized as well for their position (Pitkin, 1972, pp. 253–256; Shapiro, 2005, p. 32), but most contemporary scholars have remained skeptical. Second, and more interesting, some scholars have debated how the contributions of Michel Foucault and his followers do or do not fit into Lukes' (and Gaventa's) scheme. Specifically, how does the latter, who tends to agree that third dimensional power is widely dispersed and diffuse, address "power/knowledge" that "is everywhere, not because it embraces everything, but because it comes from everywhere" (1978, p. 93)? Lukes addresses this issue at length in his revised edition, arguing that Foucault's bold argument about the decentered character of positive constitutive power is radically overstated and that Foucault himself abandoned or modified his strongest claims in his later theory, while a more reasonable version of Foucault's argument fits and adds to Lukes' theory. Other scholars see in Foucault a more formidable challenge to Lukes and suggest that the former should instead be viewed as offering a "fourth dimension" of power analysis. This is an important debate, but it is not critical to my analysis here, for many socio-legal scholars are interested in the questions that Lukes poses, regardless of how they do or do not situate Foucault in the mix.

Finally, Lukes' third dimension poses a host of methodological challenges. How do we demonstrate interests that are not expressed and conflicts that are not observable? How do we probe and demonstrate citizen consciousness, identity, and thought processes? Gaventa (1980 p. 27) takes this challenge head-on at the levels of general theory, research design, and research interpretation. I noted earlier that he views the challenges as formidable but "surmountable." His general proposal involves "… going outside of the decision making arenas and carrying on extensive, time-consuming research in the community in question … to discover through their experiences, lives, conditions, and attitudes, whether and by what means power processes" work (p. 27). His empirical study itself is almost entirely qualitative, combining a vast array of techniques that include in-depth interviews, archival research, news media assessment, and various other quasi-ethnographic tools. While some scholars have used traditional quantitative methods such as attitudinal surveys and opinion polls to probe the third dimension, most scholars – especially in the interpretive camp – find these of little use for understanding the complex ways that cognition, consciousness, and identity of subjects are socially constructed. As Pitkin (1972) puts it, citing Peter Winch, understanding human action or inaction "means, consists in, 'grasping the point or meaning of what is being done or said. This is a notion far removed from the world of statistics and causal laws; it is closer to the realm of discourse and to the internal relations that link the parts of a realm of discourse' " (p. 254).

We need not look far to find a great deal of socio-legal scholarship that explores law's manifestations and influence at the third dimension. Scheingold's classic study – published in the same year as Lukes and drawing on other scholars such as Edelman and Geertz working at similar levels – of the "myth of rights" that at once "beguile" the American citizenry and provide discursive resources for political mobilization provides a classic study at this level (1974; see also Milner, 1986). The entire tradition of legal mobilization studies that developed in subsequent decades arguably focused much of its attention on third dimension questions, building on and contributing to the "interpretive turn" in scholarship. Following upon questions about "legal meaning" framed in early behavioral scholarship (Miller & Sarat, 1980–1981; Mather & Yngvesson, 1980–1981), a litany of studies by prominent socio-legal scholars (Merry, 1990; Yngvesson, 1993; Sarat, 1990; Ewick & Silbey, 1998; Greenhouse, Engel, & Yngvesson, 1994) used in-depth interviews and various quasi-ethnographic methods to explore the "legal consciousness" of ordinary citizens, including especially the least powerful subjects in modern American society. Bumiller's (1988) original analysis of the paralyzing psychological effects of embracing anti-discrimination rights likewise fit right into the third model. All of these studies looked at the ways in which legal norms and conventions shape subject consciousness and identity, contributing variously to conformity, contestation, and resistance (Ewick & Silbey, 1998; Engel, 1998). A new generation of scholars has followed this lead in exploring "civil rights" consciousness through highly interpretive approaches (Engel & Munger, 2003; Fleury-Steiner & Nielsen, 2006; Lovell, 2006). At the same time, studies of group based and social movement legal mobilization have refined and extended Scheingold's initial approach to include focus on legal consciousness and meaning making (Hunt, 1990; McCann, 1994; Silverstein, 1996; Brigham, 1996).

Another major trend, inspired by the interpretive turn in the humanities, has directed attention to the power of law in popular culture and power of popular culture in shaping legal practice. The most systematic social scientific versions of such study have focused on how political discourses about law in the mass media have saturated civil society, shaping the fears and legal expectations of subjects in mass society. Perhaps the best known of such work is in the area of criminal justice (Scheingold, 1984; Beckett, 1997), although studies of mass media production of knowledge about civil law also have won attention (Daniels & Martin, 1995; Galanter, 1998; Haltom & McCann, 2004). Other scholarship, often influenced by Foucault, has focused on the discursive norms, practices, and policy logics of legal elites within criminal justice bureaucracies (Simon, 1994; Herbert, 1996) and society at large (Garland, 2002). Finally, study of legal constructions in popular texts such as movies, novels, TV shows, and the like have proliferated, many associated with the Law, Humanities, and Culture group.

Most of this literature fits the epistemological premises and methodological expectations of third dimension power relations outlined by Lukes and Gaventa. The research tends to be directly or indirectly critical of behavioral approaches, of the commitment to assessing relative causality, of the limitations of methodological individualism, of core premises about autonomous rational subjects, and of reliance on quantitative techniques of data gathering. At the same time, while some of this research admirably comports with Lukes' entire three-dimensional framework, much of it can be, and has been, subjected to criticism on the basis of Lukes' ambitious approach. For one thing, an exclusive focus on "meaning" can diminish or obscure broad-ranging attention to the role of social context in shaping citizen subjectivity and cognition. In Lukes' terms, much study of the third dimension simplistically rejects rather than builds on first and second levels of power, with their attention (strictly or loosely) to behavior, causality, and the like. Indeed, the widespread practice of reporting findings about legal consciousness of subjects or the meanings of various cultural texts often is attended by a relative suspension of scholarly analysis about the sociological factors that contributed to the production, circulation, and significance of various norms, values, or conventions. This tends either to leave unexplored the sources of meaning that are not evident to subjects themselves or to grant free reign for the interpretive researcher to impute such patterns based on theory alone, ungrounded in empirical research (Shapiro, 2005, p. 33). As Ian Shapiro has argued, this trend among interpretivists and culturalists arguably represents as much a conceptually simplistic evasion of grounded social analysis as the narrowly confined projects of behavioralists who inquire only into one-dimensional power relations (2005). The pathologies of methodological purity can afflict scholars who restrict themselves to any one of the three dimensions of analysis alone.

Moreover, the fixation on third dimensional interpretive concerns alone can produce analysis which is disingenuous. After all, it is virtually impossible to ignore issues of behavior, overt conflict, and causality in social analysis.[18] I frequently underline this point for graduate students by assigning a representative text in which the "interpretivist" author in the opening pages boasts of rejecting causal analysis, and then leading the students through the litany of implicit causal claims and behavioral observations that the same author makes in subsequent pages. Disavowing causal factors rarely leads to ignoring them; it instead provides the author only a weak rationalization for not doing so in explicit, rigorous, systematic ways. Finally, research cast entirely at the third dimension of power can easily divorce itself from conventional techniques associated with more formal methodologies commonly employed in first or second dimension studies yet relevant to the study at hand. For example, studies of selected social texts (movies, novels, TV shows, etc.) often pay little attention to legitimate questions about why those texts matter, what they represent generally beyond themselves, and why they should be considered as important or worthy of attention. In short, they circumvent very relevant questions about case selection, sampling bias, and generalizability of findings that most positivist methodologies take seriously. Interpretive scholars no doubt sometimes think through these issues and can offer good answers or at least caveats, but often studies dismiss such concerns as a result of rejecting positivist or related commitments and retaining fidelity to pure interpretive conventions.

Summary

The preceding discussion of Lukes' provocative inquiry about multiple dimensions of power has underlined several important themes. First, core conceptual or epistemological premises of general methodological approaches do not determine which specific techniques of data gathering are appropriate, especially regarding quantitative or qualitative data, even though there is a substantial connection between different theoretical frameworks for understanding power and the tools chosen to evidence them. It follows that most debates over methodology turn primarily on underlying epistemological issues rather than strictly on matters of data gathering techniques, although the latter may receive most of the attention or become shorthand for deeper differences. Much ordinary academic discourse tends to be quite confused and confusing about these distinctions.

Second, methodological disagreements often reflect and nurture tendencies to focus narrowly on one or another epistemological dimension of analyzing power rather than embracing the complex, aggregative, multi-dimensional approach urged by Lukes and Gaventa. As the latter scholars would have it, attention to any one dimension alone represents a highly limited and misleading foundation for analyzing human relations.[19] First dimensional approaches tend to simplify reality by confining attention to behavior by rational individuals in contexts of expressed competition or conflict, thus ignoring or dismissing the intersubjective discursive practices, cognitive processes of meaning production, and constructed identities of subjects at stake. By contrast, interpretive studies limited to the third dimension of power typically explore the latter themes, but they slight attention to the loosely causal or sociological dimensions of contextual influence and instrumental activity that figure into specific relationships. Each approach captures important aspects of power relations but also is simplistic and misleading. As Shapiro (2005) has put it, each side – both pure behavioralists and interpretivists – flirts with its own flight from reality into methodological specialization, obsession, and myopia.

My argument about these dynamics so far has been largely deductive and speculative, as I have intentionally avoided citing specific examples of the trends that I find problematic. Even if I were to cite specific examples, moreover, I have not developed data demonstrating that there is a marked, significant trend in these directions among socio-legal scholars. My point here is not to lament that these tendencies have grown to a large degree among law and society scholars but, like the director Kubrick, to envision a dramatic scenario of what could happen, if the pressures and inclinations of methodological specialization and tribal segregation among groups of scholars continue to grow. Increased methodological insularity and myopia does seem a plausible outcome from the emergence of separate associations, conferences, and journals organized along methodological lines. And where two sides organize for the sake of preserving purity and technical superiority, General Ripper proclaimed, "there will be only one course of action open: total commitment." The result will not be that we all are carried away on a thrill-ride to oblivion. But something important in our research community is likely to be lost.

APOCALYPSE, NOT: TOWARD AN AFFIRMATIVE METHODOLOGICAL VISION

I do not actually believe that LSA is collapsing either organizationally or intellectually any more than Stanley Kubrick actually expected in 1964 that the entire world soon would go up in a chain of mushroom clouds. But I want to go further than Kubrick, whose brilliant fictional drama's success above all turned on its capacity to provoke sustained nervous laughter.[20] In short, the remainder of this chapter will develop a more affirmative way of thinking about methodology that transcends the pathological inclinations toward insularity hinted in previous pages. In some ways, this argument outlines my own personal vision about research. But I developed this vision through thinking about the implications of Lukes' (and Gaventa's) arguments for the requirements of compelling interdisciplinary scholarship[21] as well as reflecting on the scholarship in the law and society research tradition that has most inspired me. I thus cite along the way examples of work that represent the virtues that I enumerate, the antidotes to obsessions with technological purity and potency that were at the heart of the doomsday fantasy that I have imagined by way of analogy to *Dr. Strangelove*.

The Ambiguous Power of Methodology

It is important, above all, to affirm that methodology can be a powerful force. This is true in two senses. On the one hand, professional identity, status, and affiliation often turn on differential methodological commitments. This type of methodological power can become fetishistic when insulated from alternative forms of knowledge and made a discrete object of desire. This power of methodological allegiance is neither necessary nor particularly desirable. On the other hand, scholars who resist professional tribalism and purism should appreciate the ways that concern for methodology actually can improve our academic research efforts. We usually think that methodology matters because it disciplines our research through fidelity to proven principles, conventions, and techniques that systematically govern our selection, production, and processing of data. In this sense, methods should elevate our research activity over less sophisticated, slipshod ways of knowing. But I would add a second different if closely related feature – in short, that methodology can provide a powerful resource for inspiring a sense of *trust* from our readers. When we take methodology seriously, we work hard to be credible, to show that we reflected very deeply about our core questions and research designs, that we thought through alternative arguments, questions, and forms of evidence, that we anticipated objections and did the best we could to address them in consistent fashion. In this sense, methodology represents a noble aspiration that can never be fully achieved.[22]

Charles Tilly's recent book *Why?* (2006) is helpful on this point. He argues that giving reasons is a relational act, by which he means that providing explanations aims to build, sustain, and sometimes rebuild relations with specific groups of others. Developing and displaying our methodological maneuvers is just such an act of good faith directed specifically to our professional colleagues, who in turn will judge us by our efforts. I may be naïve, but I regularly tell graduate students that the particular methodologies that they employ matter far less than the sincerity and effort that they make to demonstrate their serious efforts to be systematic. If you do your best to develop a rigorous approach, I suggest, most other scholars are likely to treat the endeavor respectfully, even if it does not fit their preferred styles or commitments. This message may reflect a bit of wishful thinking, but it has been generally confirmed by what I have witnessed among law and society scholars over several decades. Such relational good faith has been an important part of what has made our intellectual community special.[23]

In making this case, I emphasize again taking a larger view of methodology, one that places emphasis on the basic epistemological premises of the research project as well as on the specific techniques that are employed to evidence that project. This view assumes that every project uses techniques that are inherently imperfect, limited, selective, and biased. One does not have to be a zealous post-positivist to recognize that we cannot neutrally or fully apprehend reality as it is, but rather we can understand only through the constructed conventions of language and related cognitive techniques or tools. Of course, we should debate the contributions of specific techniques and freely critique scholarship that transgresses sound principles, consistency, or good sense in choosing and implementing techniques. But this focus should be secondary to the expectation of clearly articulated and consistently executed epistemological claims about how we know the world, how we imagine power in social relationships, and the like. After all, our studies can be no better than the questions we pose. An elegant, careful, data-rich study of an unclear premise or trivial question achieves little. By contrast, a weak or thin empirical study of a well-conceived and important question at least can provoke more and better research. Coherence and consistency in both articulating core conceptual or epistemological foundations and matching our techniques of data production to them should be the first order of our commitments about methodology. As noted earlier, we often confuse criticism and judgment about the latter with the former, and that confusion does not serve us well. One reason why this confusion matters is that continuous generation of good questions depends on relaxing the grip that both specific epistemologies and evidentiary techniques can place on our critical imagination.

On Methodological Humility and Interdependence

Taking methodology seriously in these ways requires a fair amount of humility about what we attempt and achieve, or even can achieve, as researchers. We must remember that every way of seeing is a way of not seeing; every epistemology and technique of data generation obscures even as it reveals. Particular methodologies can refine a particular lens but not overcome the limits of that specific lens and the standpoint of the viewer. That is, I think, why methodological purists of all sorts evade discussion about epistemology, about basic premises regarding how we know – because the infirmity, the instability, the "unsettled" character (see opening Cooley quote) of the conceptual ground on which all techniques are built quickly becomes apparent upon direct reflection. As such, claims about the intrinsic superiority (or inferiority) of particular methodologies, whether positivist or post-positivist, behavioral or interpretivist, experimental or ethnographic, should not be taken seriously; indeed, they should be viewed as the opposite of taking methodology seriously. The sometimes heard claim that "I have the facts and others just have opinions" is as misguided as are the obsessive, patriotic rants equating purity with potency by Buck Turgidson or General

Ripper in *Dr. Strangelove*. Indeed, those in the movie – like Mandrake, Muffley, and Kisof – who display humility about the limits of knowledge and fragility of communication again are reviled and disobeyed by the "psychotic" military leaders who defy the former's authority. An avid aversion to certain methodologies (like positivism) reflects a similar type of quest for purity, which can be especially disastrous when it licenses rejecting the challenges of methodological rigor altogether. That inclination is akin to rejecting the goal of technological improvement because of reservations about the dangers specifically of nuclear power. Both show how methodological fetishism can make us "go funny in the head," as President Muffley put it in the movie.

Again, critical exchanges about the care or wisdom in implementing particular techniques or matching techniques to epistemological principles are fair game in academic "shooting wars." But claims of harnessing the superior technological form are hardly warranted, at least until one of our colleagues shows that the perfect and complete study is possible.[24] Moreover, such presumptuousness is hardly consistent with the commitments to democratic equality, social justice, and respect for others that most of us proclaim. As Tilly (2006, p. 180) shows and Kubrick demonstrates, claims of superior forms of esoteric knowledge or technological purity are inherently elitist, hostile, and demeaning; they evade engagement, discourage dialogue, and erode relations of trust and understanding among differently oriented scholars, contradicting our commitments to solidarity in causes of understanding injustice and promoting justice.[25]

Finally, humble respect for the promises, challenges, and limitations of methodology can help us to realize how much we need and benefit from the alternative ways of knowing enacted by our colleagues. I do not offer here a weak argument for tolerance, as tolerance encourages passivity in the face of insularity and myopia. It is the evasive recourse of those who defend thin versions of methodological pluralism or *multi-disciplinarity*.[26] Rather, following David Engel (1999), I offer a "strong argument in favor of the proposition that we as law and society scholars are mutually dependent on one another" (p. 14). Because every individual mode of study is selective, confined, and doomed to distortions that accompany its illuminations, our best shot for understanding lies in the connections, interstices, and aggregations among different ways of knowing. As Engel (1999) urges, we should not think of different methodological approaches on a continuum, except unless that continuum is a Mobius strip, a continuously progressive, twisting loop that has no inside or outside. "Each approach now seems closely related to the others; they are additive, not alternative" (p. 13).

Linear models of causal power capture certain dimensions; literary approaches sensitive to ambiguity, irony, and contradictions in meanings capture other dimensions. As Lukes urged, they together provide a more complex set of understandings that far transcend the potential of any one-dimensional model alone. It stands to reason that we learn more by taking each approach seriously and by facilitating respectful, engaged dialogue among approaches rather than in evaluating one as intrinsically more worthy than the other. Moreover, as Engel again notes, contact among different methodological approaches can be a source of creative synthesis and new insights. "Our field is enriched by the growing variety of forms and approaches, for each new approach at one level signals new possibilities at other levels, and each insight obtained through one mode of investigation suggests new issues to pursue using other modes of investigation" (p. 15). What is brilliant scholarship, after all, but such new, unexpected syntheses of previously unconnected ways of knowing joined to a fascinating substantive question?

All these premises or norms, I might add, are reinforced by the exposure to multiple methods and especially interdisciplinary engagements commonplace in LSA research. It is not difficult to identify the rich, complex legacies of studies constructed over time on related subjects by scholars from different espistemological standpoints. By contrast, sequestering ourselves in familiar circles of like-minded researchers is unlikely to moderate one-dimensional narrowness or to promote such catalytic encounters, juxtapositions, and fusions.

Jazzing It Up: Toward Multi-Methodological Studies

I want to push the argument further, however. Rather than just underlining the potentially complementary and catalytic effect of methodological diversity *among* socio-legal scholars, I want to make the case for methodological diversity *within* single projects. By this, I again do not mean just a diversification in the routine employment of quantitative and qualitative, experimental and ethnographic, data gathering techniques, although that surely is a part of my call. My more ambitious challenge instead is for studies that explicitly integrate and balance different epistemological approaches to the subject at hand. This follows quite directly from Lukes' three-dimensional model of power, which is aggregative in character. My reading of Lukes' model, and the powerful empirical study generated by Gaventa, suggests that focus on any one dimension alone is inadequate, while studies that integrate all three analytical dimensions – with their different epistemologies and ontologies – of power at once provide a more ambitious and potentially satisfying endeavor.[27] Gaventa's own empirical study led the way in facing the many challenges at stake and illustrating the rich array of payoffs. His study integrates historical, instrumental, institutional, ideological, and other dimensions into a complex narrative full of rich data as well as complex, comparative analysis. He shifts back and forth between different levels with great dexterity, and the overall final product is profound, compelling, and insightful. Most readers seem to agree that he wins great trust that he has not only conducted his empirical investigation exhaustively, utilizing a variety of appropriate techniques, but he worked extremely hard to imagine power at multiple epistemological levels, to integrate insights of different kinds, and to produce a complex yet accessible account of how unequal power works in a small Appalachian coal-mining town (see Shapiro, 2005, pp. 42–49).

Such complex, multi-dimensional work has long been encouraged by many scholars in the social sciences, so I claim little originality for my exhortation. The promises of such broadly multi-epistemological and multi-methodological study are many. For one thing, if all approaches are limited, selective, and distorted, integrating multiple dimensions into a single study can at least offset some of measure of that myopia. We need to be both hedgehogs and foxes, balancing the strengths and weaknesses of different ways of knowing; we can never see human reality in all its complexity, but we can see more complexly and variously than from a single vantage point.[28] Moreover, as noted above, integrating seemingly different ways of knowing is often the source of creativity, of intellectual innovation. As Pitkin (1972) urges, "(o)ur need is for forms of social and political study that can do full justice to the complexity of action, that are not doctrinaire ... but open, inventive, observant, flexible ..." (pp. 285–286). In short, we should not be content just to develop singular approaches that engage and complement different approaches by others; we should strive to pack different angles of vision into each of our studies. Finally, the commitment to multiple epistemological standpoints and approaches is likely to be a sound antidote to the dangers of methodological myopia, obsession, and fetishism for purity discussed earlier. Commitment to integrating plural epistemologies should help us retain a clearer grasp on the problematic illusions about methodology generally.

I venture to offer a familiar metaphor for this supple approach to methodology – that of improvisational jazz music. *Dr. Strangelove* again is suggestive in this regard. Kubrick uses music very sparingly and selectively in the film. One motif is humorously ironic juxtaposition, as illustrated in the opening scene featuring a quasi-erotic exchange between one plane fueling another (think mother and child) while the sentimental pop song "Try a Little Tenderness" plays in the background; another is the final scene of nuclear apocalypse with the equally sentimental, wistful "We'll Meet Again" providing stark contrast.[29] A second motif is the use of the familiar civil war tune "When Johnny Comes Marching Home"[30] that plays whenever the scene shifts to the B-52, at once underlining the mindless patriotic conventions driving the madness along with the irony that these soldiers would not be coming home. About a quarter of the way into the film the use of music becomes even more subtle and creative, however. Captain Mandrake, struggling to retain some grounding in common sense against Ripper's stiff obsessions with esoteric jargons and codes, finds a radio on the base playing "civilian jazz," thus providing him evidence that the nation is not under nuclear attack and a counter-attack is unwarranted. Kubrick cuts back and forth between Mandrake drawing on jazz to support his sane pleas at the base and Major Kong in a B-52 obsessively preparing to deploy his weapon while the morbidly patriotic "Battle Hymn of the Republic" intones. "Please sit down. And turn that thing off!", Ripper finally roars at Mandrake, refusing to process an alternative source of lyrical knowledge that makes a lie of his pure conviction and codes. "There will be only one course of action open: total commitment ... I thought I issued instructions for all radios on the base to be impounded."

Kubrick's dramatic intentions here are clear. In short, jazz provides a creative form of knowledge in the movie, the well-grounded and supple antidote to the one-dimensional, repetitive musical knowledge that is propelling the whole military industrial complex to catastrophe. Interviews with Kubrick and commentary by reviewers[31] support an expansive interpretation of jazz as an apt analogy for the style of research methodologies that I celebrate here. For one thing, any good jazz player must master the primary forms and logics as well as techniques of music, beginning with multiple genres of Western classical music but often including all types of world music. These basic conventions provide the foundation on which the musician builds and "plays," in the classic sense explored by Piaget, allowing even that conventions may be knowingly discarded, challenged, and violated as well (e.g., atonal jazz). Second, a good jazz player must integrate multiple levels of knowledge at once, including chord structure, scales, harmonic logic, rhythm, tempo, and technique; blues-based jazz generally shifts these dimensions from which players "take off" only rarely within a song, while other forms of jazz transition among these various dimensions continuously, often concurrently. To be an accomplished jazz player, one thus must not only master the fundamentals of form and routinely "cite" the canon by playing classic tunes or familiar licks recounted from earlier artists or standards, but one must experiment within an ever-expanding range of stylistic variations on elements of form and canonical themes. Finally, while some jazz players prefer to play solo, most prefer playing live in combos, for that is were the excitement of dynamic interaction, of exchanging styles and creative turns, takes place. Jazz traditions encourage individual players to engage and humbly honor other contributors, both those concurrently on the same stage and those many others identified with the broader historical jazz tradition. In sum, jazz is a well-grounded and highly disciplined mode of inventive, flexible, integrative performance developed through engagement with forms and techniques endorsed by a sophisticated interpretive community.

Jazz thus becomes my metaphor for sophisticated, creative, multi-dimensional, impure, even openly transgressive but still rigorous socio-legal methodology.[32] It is the methodological temperament that best seems to fit the designs of those who imagine law and society scholarship as a *trans-disciplinary* aspiration. The law and society tradition is full of wonderful examples that represent ambitious efforts along these lines. I can quickly list a number of classic books that to a notable extent represent this tradition: Stuart Scheingold (1974, 1984) *The Politics of Rights* and *The Politics of Law and Order*; Jonathan Simon (1994) *Poor Discipline*; Yves Dezalay and Bryant Garth (1996) *Dealing in Virtue*; David Johnson (2001) *The Japanese Way of Justice*; Malcolm Feeley and Edward L. Rubin's (1998) *Judicial Policy Making and the Modern State*; Austin Sarat (2001) *When the State Kills*; Lynn Mather, Craig McEwen, and Richard Maiman (2001) *Divorce Lawyers at Work*; Gad Barzilai (2003) *Communities and Law*; Kitty Calavita's (2005) *Immigrants at the Margins*; Jon Gould (2005) *Speak No Evil*. Each of these studies not only draws on diverse types of data, but each integrates multiple levels of analysis (epistemologies) regarding power and subjectivity, at least implicitly paralleling the type of study to which Lukes and Gaventa point. Perhaps the most impressive example of all, in my view, is Sally Merry's (2000) majestic *Colonizing Hawai'i*. The book blends very sophisticated understandings of culture and colonialism into a complex analysis of power that seamlessly integrates instrumental agency, institutional structure, and constitutive understandings of subjectivity with an enormous variety of data, producing a richly innovative, insightful, inspiring volume. Of course, all of these examples are books, and most are big books at that.[33] But multi-methodological study is possible within article-length format.[34] David Engel's widely known essay "The Oven Bird's Song" (1984) does it all, fusing attention to instrumental, institutional, and ideological dimensions of power into a single provocative essay, a classic in the field.[35]

Engagement and Distance

Finally, I add a few words on classic issues regarding the tension between distance and engagement in our research. Traditional social science has highly valued distance, both geographic and cognitive, of scholars from their subjects. The idea is to promote data collection and interpretation that is independent of, and hopefully more sophisticated than, that possessed by the subjects whom we study. Methodology, and positivism in particular, is valued for playing a role in disciplining knowledge gathering and inferences, insulating the researcher from contaminating partiality or over-determination by presumptive normative or theoretical biases. Distance and disinterest are commonly equated with objectivity. There are many epistemological problems in this quest for an Archimedean point, including the fact that we researchers cannot ever escape the selective, biased lenses through which we see the world.[36] Equally problematic is that distance from subjects and their context removes researchers from access to local knowledge, from information and understandings that may be critical to making sense of social relations, while at the same time inviting ungrounded abstract theory to impute alien causal mechanisms.[37] Just how much should we trust the interpretations of a scholar who spends all her time poring over statistical data at a computer in an academic office, far removed from the lives, motivations, and actions of people she claims to be studying? Conversely, direct engagement with the subjects and context of study – say, through ethnography, participant observation, or other interview-intensive qualitative methods – promises access to local knowledge and subjects' worlds of meaning, but risks undermining independent analysis of subjects' motives or of contextual influences or implications to which the subjects are relatively unaware. Moreover, highly discretionary personal interactions of researchers and subjects permit a great deal of "loading" and fixing in data seeking and interpretation. In short, research that is "up close and personal" can be blinded by its own affinity with the expressed interests of subjects or the researcher's own personal causes.

My unremarkable point is that multi-dimensional methodological studies offer the possibility of balancing the advantages of both distance and engagement. While we should stop far short of expecting to produce a complete check and balance on limited knowledge, the effort to integrate different levels of analysis can be productive. One classic model of such study routinely begins with a large-N statistical portrait of certain patterns in correlation among variables, followed up by several in-depth case studies that add additional qualitative data regarding local meanings, practices, and contextual contingencies that are less amenable to standardized measures (see, for example, Ginsburg, 2003). Efforts to balance macro-, meso-, and micro-level analysis, or different dimensions of power as demonstrated by Lukes, represent other familiar strategies. In short, there are many ways that different epistemologies and techniques can be combined to diversify the standpoints of researchers, see through multiple lenses, and balance the goals of both distance and engagement.

I add two other less conventional arguments along this line. First, and perhaps most controversial, such multi-methodological approaches can be especially useful for scholars who self-consciously develop research agendas grounded in their own personal engagements and commitments to politics. In my view, one of the most welcome features of the law and society tradition has been a relative openness to research that aims to build on and advance political causes of particular disadvantaged or oppressed groups to win justice or increase social welfare. Indeed, the original thrust of LSA was to harness the many tools of social science to legal realism in ways that might increase the capacity of law to advance justice and the social good. Faith in social engineering through legal reform waned in the latter part of the twentieth century, but commitments to justice continued to drive many intellectual currents – critical legal studies, critical feminism, critical race theory, and more recently various global justice advocates, to name a few – that have long played a prominent role in LSA.[38] This type of overt merger of politics and scholarship has generally been accorded less approval in the more scientifically inclined disciplines, but it has provided a badge of honor for many socio-legal scholars, one of the reasons for discipline-weary scholars to seek refuge in LSA.[39]

One reason why this tradition of more overt political engagement has produced highly respected research, I would suggest, follows precisely from the methodological diversity and creativity displayed in much law and society scholarship. Again, when multiple standpoints and types of data support a line of analysis, there is more reason for trust that the interpretive argument is not simply driven (or over-driven) by political values or identifications and thus merits substantial respect even by those who do not share the commitments of the author. Indeed, multi-epistemological analyses are more likely to resist the often implicit, unacknowledged theoretical and political biases that attend each particular methodology alone (see Lukes, 2005, p. 63). Hence, I would propose that methodological jazz has contributed to the very best traditions of politically engaged scholarship seeking to win trust and credibility in the LSA tradition.

Second, and finally, effective political engagement relies on effective communication. One of the endemic problems for sophisticated academic analysts, whether employing single-epistemological or multi-epistemological approaches, is in translating our typically complex, data rich, and often esoteric treatises into terms that mass publics – from students to journalists to policy-makers to ordinary consumers – can understand. Indeed, our rich traditions of potentially relevant research often have remarkably little impact beyond our professional colleagues (Haltom & McCann, 2004). "(O)n the whole, social science's technical accounts stay within the academy, unheard by the general public," Tilly has observed, and I suspect the same is true for most critical scholarship in the humanities traditions as well (Tilly, 2006, p. 177). I thus echo Tilly's recent exhortations for scholars to supplement their specialized academic studies with versions of "superior stories" that render more accessible and credible the core points and themes of our research for broader public consumption (pp. 175–180). This not only promises to increase our capacity as publicly engaged intellectuals to influence the world beyond, to enhance the "sociological imagination" of our fellow citizens and to challenge the madness that often triumphs in other insulated regions of specialized activity such as satirized in *Dr. Strangelove.* But injecting that "human element" of common sense, as General Turgidson called it, also provides another check on the obsessions for methodological purity and pull of arcane fads that frequently drive academic life. If we scholars cannot make our findings sound plausible in ordinary language, as accessible and lyrical as the jazz we hear on the radio, it might just mean that we have, in Shapiro's apt words, taken "flight from reality" (2005).

CONCLUSION

Divisions over preferred methodologies have grown in the LSA during recent years, but they have produced at most a temperate Cold War. Although signs of withdrawal into insular organizational activity are palpable, patriotic gore produced by overt rivalries has been limited.

Moreover, I happily note that I have encountered only a few colleagues in either camp whose methodological fetishes remind me of Ripper, Turgidson, or the mad scientist Dr. Strangelove. Indeed, even though I cannot claim to know what goes on in these methodologically specialized conferences and related exchanges, I would not be surprised to find only meager evidence supporting my concerns. To be honest, I have encountered many splendid examples of scholarship from each of the different methodological camps in the recent period. Likewise, while there may be some relationship between the increased attention to technical purity and withering of overt political discourse at LSA meetings that troubles some of us, the latter trend probably reflects more the greater size, diversity, and anonymity of association membership, the larger national context of political malaise, generational change, and other such factors. At the same time, the sounds of intellectual jazz can be heard everywhere, especially in the Collaborative Research Networks, the International Research Collaboratives, and other less formal groups organized around substantive themes. As I see it, increasing levels of comparative, transnational, and global study have made the improvisational approach endorsed here all the more relevant, the methodological equivalent of world music. In fact, increased exchanges from scholars and activists from around the world are making such a posture not only desirable, but almost unavoidable. And, finally, I take it as a good sign that LSA officers are unlikely to insist that I post on this chapter the same type of disclaimer that the U.S. Air Force imposed on Kubrick's apocalyptic film.[40]

But I do nevertheless find in recent trends reason for reflection. The concern is not, I want to underline, the individual choices of scholars about the methodologies that they employ in their research and teaching. I have no interest in telling other individuals how to conduct their research, much less in arguing that any one mode is superior to another. Indeed, that is precisely the type of inclination that I am challenging. Intellectual jazz is not the best style for everyone or every project; many scholars continue to produce excellent research by reliance on traditional methodological and epistemological frameworks. My aim, then, is not individual conversion so much as revitalization of respect for some of the most distinctive traditions and commitments in the LSA. I wonder whether the development of separate methodological sub-groups will: endorse misleading analytical categories associated with methodology; reinforce the perception that scholars must choose from two (or more) opposing methodological traditions and align themselves with either of two (or possibly more) intellectual tribes; discourage scholars from appreciating the many independent, supple, creative approaches to research that have been advanced by the LSA legacy; and, perhaps most important, divert attention away from the important substantive questions we ask and novel themes we study, such as those concerning unequal power and the possibilities of social justice. These developments could, in short, change the character and influence of LSA as a uniquely creative, diverse, even disruptive intellectual community in ways that many of us would, and should, lament. This impact probably would be most felt by graduate students and junior scholars who look to LSA as a source of intellectual guidance and professional support for independent research, but it no doubt would also be manifest in many other spheres of professional decision-making and practical power.

So how might we imagine the appropriate response? The standard response is an appeal to increased tolerance for diversity in methodologies. This is the modest "big tent" vision of *multi-disciplinarity*, familiar in LSA presidential speeches. The problem is that this posture hardly discourages, and actually would encourage, methodological insularity, with different players choosing to perform in separate rings largely for their own specialized audiences. It does little to promote dialogue and innovation. A second response might be the "stronger" vision of *interdisciplinarity* encouraged by David Engel, wherein we socio-legal scholars commit ourselves to respecting and valuing the interdependency that we all share among our differential methodological approaches. In this mode, we might each continue to go our separate ways, but we would view our own projects more humbly and understand the importance of learning from others and developing our work in ways that build on and speak to scholars whose research is cast in very different forms. This approach greatly values serious dialogue, and I have heartily endorsed this prescription.

But I have also gone further in suggesting yet a third response, one that affirmatively celebrates experimentation with the complex rhythms of intellectual jazz improvisation in our scholarship. This posture urges us to transcend reverence for familiar methodological models and fashion new synthetic approaches that are highly innovative in form as well as in the substantive questions we ask. Such a spirit can be found in much previous socio-legal scholarship, and it constitutes one of the most exciting dimensions of the LSA tradition. It seems essential to the aspiration for trans-disciplinarity in law and society research, especially in an increasingly globalized context.[41] We have our own versions of Miles, Monk, Trane, and Fleck, and my hope is that their inspiration is not lost amidst the patriotic rhythms that urge methodological alliance or purity. Following that muse offers one way by which we might together learn to stop worrying and love methodology.

NOTES

1. The word "nuclear" was deleted at the point of the ellipses, and "methodological" is inserted in its place, thus appropriating the movie text to make the point of the chapter.

2. Bela Fleck is the leader of the phenomenally creative, eclectic, boundary-breaking jazz quartet, The Flecktones, who have been nominated for over twenty Grammies and won in eight different categories.

3. I do not include a third methodological camp – that of rational choice, game theory, and related methods grounded in microeconomics – in this discussion. This is in part to contain the length of my discussion, but mostly because this research agenda has been rather less prominent in LSA than in the disciplines.

4. The familiar argument that recent tensions reflect differences *among* the disciplines gathered under the LSA tent thus are misleading. Not only are these methodological tensions rampant *within* many social science disciplines, but much of the recent organizing around methodology has been led by law school scholars largely outside the social sciences and humanities disciplines, while yet other leaders have actually bolted from their home disciplines to declare methodological conversion.

5. Some may object that these new associations are not officially, intentionally, or significantly connected to LSA. But these points do not contradict my premise that these developments, whatever their intent, will surely affect LSA, quite possibly in ways that I enumerate at the end of the chapter.

6. For the Association for the Study of Law, Culture, and theHumanities, see http://www.utexas.edu/cola/conferences/lch/index.php?path[0]=main. The other is the Empirical Legal Studies group. http://www.elsblog.org/. Each has its own website, conferences, and journal.

7. Some non-positivist cultural analysts go further in expressing disdain for methodology itself, as if the attempt to be careful, rigorous, systematic, disciplined, and coherent itself is mad. I address this later.

8. Consider Pitkin (1972), "What social scientists do is not, of course, any concept-free observation of events among human beings, but an attempt to fiddle with the concepts we already have in such a way to make them scientifically usable. That has meant the invention of new, technical concepts, the attempt to confine work to those concepts which seem "realistic" or "factual," the use of "operational definitions," and the attempt to redefine familiar concepts in such a way to make them realistic, factual, or scientific. The effort has not been spectacularly successful ... Technical terms still reflect our conceptual system ... Terms that appear realistic or factual turn out to be grammatically as complex as any "value word" ... And the attempt to redefine familiar terms to make them scientific is subject to vicissitudes of its own" (p. 275).

9. Fay's compelling analysis (1987) shows how logical positivism is no less political and normative than positions grounded in critical challenge to existing institutional structures (see also Shapiro, 2005).

10. This is how President Mandrake explains the deployment of the bomb to Dmitri Kisof, the Soviet premier.

11. In the terms of Lukes (1974) discussed below, my analysis consciously deemphasizes the first dimension of instrumental power, and focuses far more on

second and third dimensions of power in the LSA academic community. In short, this chapter is primarily about professional ideology and organizational practice. The overall chapter also balances analytical with normative concerns, although I remain perplexed by the conventional distinctions implied by use of these terms in much professional discourse.

12. Many readers of early essay drafts urged me to include a sociological analysis of how methodological claims shape and express struggles over unequal professional power in and beyond LSA. This endeavor is sensible, potentially valuable, and tempting. However, I have concluded that this approach does not fit or advance, and may actually obfuscate, my specific concerns in this chapter.

13. My comment invokes one of the most famous funny lines in the film: "Gentlemen, you can't fight in here. This is the War Room!"

14. My approach thus reverses Kubrick's in one way. Where he focused the screenplay on satirizing mad individuals and practices while downplaying sane alternatives, I avoid lampooning any specific persons but do point to examples of works that might serve as antidotes to ideological obsessions with methodology.

15. The "technology required is easily within the means of even the smallest nuclear power. It requires only the will to do so," says Dr. Strangelove about the inviting fetishism of technical power.

16. The debate between Rosenberg and me arguably demonstrated the simplistic obsessions and purist assumptions that I critique here. Rosenberg strongly defended causal analysis, while I rejected it in favor of process-based views of power, implicitly merging second and third dimensional approaches of Lukes. However, our dichotomous framings of our approaches obscured how we each integrate different levels of power analysis and diverse methodological premises in our studies. In short, we each were guilty of a sort of purist posturing that magnified some differences in our actual studies but obscured others.

17. Pitkin (1972) is useful on this point in discussing ordinary language theory. "Our concepts of action require explanation in terms of motive and reasons rather than causes …" (p. 253).

18. As Shapiro (2005) notes, "studying the evolution of ideologies while ignoring causal questions is not possible. We should be unsurprised, therefore, to discover … substantive work (that) is laced with implicit causal claims and assumptions" (p. 35). This claim about causality seems overdrawn, in my view, but the general thrust of the statement merits attention.

19. See Michael Pollan's brilliant editorial (2007) demonstrating how the "ideology of nutritionism" fueling contemporary American obsessions with obesity isolates individual nutritional elements at the expense of examining their interactions and more holistic understandings of diets and health. His target was normal natural science, but the argument has implications for any one-dimensional approach to empirical inquiry and analysis.

20. "The greatest message of the film is in the laughs. You know, it's true. The most realistic things are the funniest," Kubrick related in an interview (Tabriz, 2005).

21. The attentive reader will note that I have been using the term "interdisciplinary" in relatively unproblematic ways up to this point. I will complicate this characterization in subsequent pages.

22. In this sense, it is through the public act of representing our methodologies that we discipline ourselves. The very anticipation of having to explain and defend

our processes of inquiry in order to be considered trustworthy imposes structure and method on the research and interpretative process.

23. I am quite familiar with the claim of some positivists that fidelity to sound methodological principles provides an alternative to having to trust the scholar. This strikes me as an untenable premise of the natural science model. That interpretive scholars sometimes seem equally comfortable assuming that trust of readers is given and need not be won by the author's rigorous attention to method strikes me as equally untenable, however. "Proof," the cerebral but dramatic play by David Auburn (and movie by John Madden), is an interesting meditation on these and other related themes. Not only does the play draw clear links between methodological purity and madness, but it raises questions about whether elegant techniques can either succeed in analyzing human relations or eliminate the need for trust among scholars.

24. Ian Shapiro offers this advice (pp. 197–198): "One of the worst features of methodological disagreement ... is the propensity for protagonists to compare the inadequacies of one method with the adequacies of a second, and then declare the first to be wanting. Since all methods have limitations and none should be expected to be serviceable for all purposes, this is little more than a shell game. If a method can do some things well that are worth doing, that is a sufficient justification for investing some research resources in it. With methods, as with people: if you only focus on their limitations you will always be disappointed."

25. In *Dr. Strangelove*, the two figures who seem most sane and reasonable display a general suspicion of technological obsession and humility about the difficulties of understanding and communicating. That both of them, RAF Captain Lionel Mandrake and President Merkin Muffley, are clearly identified as feminine (consider their names), mild-mannered, and impotent "perverts" is an important part of the sexual and gendered logic of the film. Such portrayals again should provide scholars some reason for introspection about their own languages and associations regarding methodological prowess.

26. I assume familiarity with the distinctions between disciplinary, multi-disciplinary, interdisciplinary, and trans-disciplinary modes of study (see Van den Besselaar & Heimerikis, 2001).

27. "Dimensions of power and powerlessness may be viewed as interrelated and accumulative in nature, such that each dimension serves to re-enforce the strength of the other" (see Gaventa, 1980, pp. 20–22, 256).

28. This virtue is often equated with the practice of "triangulation" (see McCann, 1994, pp. 16–17), although I have become disenchanted with the mechanical natural science logic of that analogy.

29. "We'll meet again, don't know where, don't know when/But I know we'll meet again, some sunny day ..."

30. On the many potentially relevant meanings of this song, see http://lcweb2.loc.gov/cocoon/ihas/loc.natlib.ihas.200000024/default.html and http://en.wikipedia.org/wiki/When_Johnny_Comes_Marching_Home.

31. Kubrick was a jazz drummer when young, specialized in photographing jazz players in his initial career, and remained a jazz enthusiast throughout life. He is well known for his creative use of both classical and jazz music to advance substantive themes in all of his movies. Moreover, many commentators have likened the production of the movie *Dr. Strangelove* itself to improvisational jazz in the ways

that I suggest here, an analogy that Kubrick himself encouraged in his repeated suggestion that making movies is more like making music than other artistic endeavors. Consider, for example, the parallels to my analysis in an extended essay on Kubrick by Adam Uhlich (2002): "The jazz photos show a side of Kubrick that is less discussed, the spontaneous, musical side ... A photo of a trumpet player feels three dimensional, as if the instrument and its master reach beyond the lens and into the very lives of the viewer. You can hear the music and feel the movement in this still frame, and the sense of life being lived (as opposed to the sense of life *having been* lived in the 'pose' photographs) is extraordinary. This image, and the many others like it, presuppose the musical interludes in Kubrick's films that recreate these feelings of presence. It is in these moments of musicality, of the physical and psychological dance of characters and setting, where Kubrick's movies come most alive." It hardly seems a stretch to argue that Kubrick's own cinematic jazz aimed to offer an antidote to the narrow methodical madness he perceived in the modern military industrial complex.

32. For a parallel discussion of the jazz metaphor, see Silbey (2003). Howard Becker (1998) also invokes jazz in his wonderful book on research techniques and philosophy, *Tricks of the Trade*.

33. As far as I know, most of these scholars have played little role in the recent methodological Cold War, a fact that underlines my basic point.

34. A parallel objection can be raised that this challenge raises a high bar for which many scholars have inadequate training. But jazz can be learned while very young, after learning just some basic chords and scales; my neighborhood piano teacher has 8-year olds playing jazz within a couple of months of starting lessons. No one begins as a master jazz player; rather, one can learn elementary jazz with the basics and continue to learn and experiment with new repertoires and levels of sophistication throughout life. That is what makes it fun, a fulfilling art as well as a science.

35. The book that I co-authored with William Haltom, *Distorting the Law* (2004), explicitly develops a three-dimensional approach to power closely paralleling Lukes and Gaventa. My earlier book, *Rights at Work*, implicitly but very consciously builds on these same models, although in less playful ways. *Java Jive (2002)*, which I also co-wrote with Haltom, also integrates the three-dimensional approach of the book into a single essay.

36. "This much, however, seems clear: at least our talk about the world is conventionally delimited. Whether or not what we see is objectively there, whether or not there is any objective reality to see, what we say or think discursively about it must be said or thought in language. And that means in saying it, we must introduce assumptions and implications built into our language ... This strongly suggests, finally, that the interdependence of words and the world, the determining and limiting role of concepts on what is perceived as reality, will generally be most intensive with respect to human, social, cultural, and political things." Moreover, "our conceptual system depends both on what we have learned to say and on what we have experienced, and both these dimensions expand as we learn and grow." (Pitkin, 1972, pp. 111, 114–115).

37. Distance from research sites and subjects is implicated in one of the most common problems in quantitative research – the reliance on poor statistical indicators to serve as proxies for independent causal variables.

38. My claim here is not that scholars in all of these movements produced rigorous, well-designed empirical research, but they did encourage socio-legal research framed by novel questions and openly committed to goals of social justice.

39. A fair number of socio-legal scholars have increasingly lamented the retreat from more direct political engagement, both individually and collectively, in LSA over recent decades. Whether this alleged retreat is at all related to the increase in growing obsessions with methodological purity would be an interesting thesis worth considering, but space does not permit it here.

40. "It is the stated position of the United States Air Force that their safeguards would prevent the occurrence of such events as are depicted in this film. Furthermore, it should be noted that none of the characters portrayed in this film are meant to represent any real persons living or dead."

41. The applicability of these ideas for comparative and transnational research deserves far more extensive attention than I can devote here. Indeed, if space permitted, I would add much more about comparative research design grounded in extensive local knowledge of different social contexts (see Merry, 2006).

REFERENCES

Allen, A. (2005). Feminist perspectives on power. In: *The Stanford encyclopedia of philosophy* (Winter Edition), Edward N. Zalta (ed.), URL = http://plato.stanford.edu/archives/win2005/entries/feminist-power/

Bachrach, P., & Baratz, M. (1970). *Power and poverty: Theory and practice*. New York: Oxford University Press.

Barzilai, G. (2003). *Communities and law: Politics and cultures of legal identities*. Ann Arbor: University of Michigan Press.

Becker, H. S. (1998). *Tricks of the trade: How to think about your research while you're doing it*. Chicago: University of Chicago Press.

Beckett, K. (1997). *Making crime pay: Law and order in contemporary American politics*. New York: Oxford University Press.

Black, D. (1973). The mobilization of law. *The Journal of Legal Studies*, *2*(10), 125–149.

Brigham, J. (1996). *The constitution of interests: Beyond the politics of rights*. New York: New York University Press.

Bumiller, K. (1988). *The civil rights society: The social construction of victims*. Baltimore: Johns Hopkins University Press.

Calavita, K. (2005). *Immigrants at the margins: Law, race, and exclusion in Southern Europe*. Cambridge: Cambridge University Press.

Casper, J. (1976). The supreme court and national policy making. *American Political Science Review*, *70*, 50–63.

Clayton, C. W., & Gillman, H. (Eds). (1999). *Supreme court decision-making: New institutionalist approaches*. Chicago: University of Chicago Press.

Coglianese, C. (2001). Social movements, law and society: The institutionalization of the environmental law movement. *University of Pennsylvania Law Review*, *150*, 85.

Curran, B. A. (1977). *The legal needs of the public: Final report of a national survey*. Chicago, IL: American Bar Foundation.

Dahl, R. (1957). Decision-making in a democracy: The supreme court as a national policy maker. *Journal of Public Law*, *6*, 279.

Dahl, R. (1961). *Who governs?* New Haven: Yale University Press.

Daniels, S., & Martin, J. (1995). *Civil juries and the politics of reform.* Evanston, IL: Northwestern University Press.

Dezalay, Y., & Garth, B. G. (1996). *Dealing in virtue: International commercial arbitration and the construction of a transnational legal order*. Chicago: University of Chicago Press.

Dolbeare, K., & Hammond, P. E. (1971). *The school prayer decisions: From court policy to local practice*. Chicago: University of Chicago Press.

Donohue, J. J., III., & Heckman, J. (1991). Continuous versus episodic change: The impact of Civil Rights policy on the economic status of blacks. *Journal of Economic Literature*, *29*(4), 1603–1643.

Edelman, L. B., Erlanger, H. S., & Lande, J. (1993). Internal dispute resolution: The transformation of civil rights in the workplace. *Law and Society Review*, *27*(3), 497–534.

Engel, D. (1984). The oven bird's song: Insiders, outsiders and personal injuries in an American community. *Law and Society Review*, *18*, 551–582.

Engel, D. (1998). How does law matter in the constitution of legal consciousness? In: B. Garth & A. Sarat (Eds), *How does law matter?* Evanston, IL: Northwestern University Press.

Engel, D. (1999). Making connections: Law and society researchers and their subjects. *Law and Society Review*, *33*, 3–16.

Engel, D., & Munger, F. (2003). *Rights of inclusion: Law and identity in the life stories of Americans with disabilities*. Chicago: University of Chicago Press.

Epp, C. (1998). *The rights revolution: Lawyers, activists, and supreme courts in comparative perspective*. Chicago: University of Chicago Press.

Epstein, L., & Knight, J. (1998). *The choices justices make*. Washington, DC: CQ Press.

Eskridge, W. N., Jr. (2001). Channeling: Identity-based social movements and public law. *University of Pennsylvania Law Review*, *150*, 419.

Ewick, P., & Silbey, S. (1998). *The common place of law: Stories from everyday life*. Chicago: University of Chicago Press.

Fay, B. (1987). *Critical social science: Liberation and its limits*. Ithaca: Cornell University Press.

Feeley, M. M., & Rubin, E. L. (1998). *Judicial policy making and the modern state: How the courts reformed America's prisons*. Cambridge: Cambridge University Press.

Fleury-Steiner, B., & Nielsen, L. B. (2006). *The new civil rights research: A constitutive perspective*. Burlington, VT: Ashgate-Dartmouth Press.

Galanter, M. (1974). Why the 'Haves' come out ahead: Speculations on the limits of legal change. *Law and Society Review*, *9*, 95.

Galanter, M. (1998). An oil strike in hell: Contemporary legends about the civil justice system. *Arizona Law Review*, *40*, 717–752.

Garland, D. (2002). *The culture of control: Crime and social order in contemporary society*. Chicago: University of Chicago Press.

Gaventa, J. (1980). *Power and powerlessness: Quiescence and rebellion in an Appalachian valley*. Urbana: University of Illinois Press.

Ginsburg, T. (2003). *Judicial review in new democracies: Constitutional courts in Asian cases*. New York: Cambridge University Press.

Gould, J. B. (2005). *Speak no evil: The triumph of hate speech regulation*. Chicago: University of Chicago Press.

Greenhouse, C. J., Engel, D. M., & Yngvesson, B. (1994). *Law and community in three American towns*. Ithaca, NY: Cornell University Press.

Haltom, W., & McCann, M. (2004). *Distorting the law: Politics, media, and the litigation crisis*. Chicago: University of Chicago Press.

Handler, J. (1966). Controlling official behavior in welfare administration. *California Law Review*, *54*, 479–510.

Herbert, S. (1996). *Policing space: Territoriality and the Los Angeles Police Department*. Minneapolis: University of Minnesota Press.

Hunt, A. (1990). Rights and social movements: Counter-hegemonic strategies. *Journal of Law and Society*, *17*, 309.

Johnson, D. T. (2001). *The Japanese way of justice: Prosecuting crime in Japan*. New York: Oxford University Press.

Kelman, S. (1981). *Regulatory America, regulatory Sweden: A comparative study of occupational safety and health regulation*. Cambridge, MA: MIT Press.

Kessler, M. (1990). Legal mobilization for social reform: Power and the politics of agenda setting. *Law and Society Review*, *24*, 121–144.

Kubrick, S. (1964). Dr. Strangelove (Or: How I Learned to Stop Worrying and Love the Bomb).

Lawrence, S. E. (1990). *The poor in court: The legal services program and supreme court decision making*. Princeton: Princeton University Press.

Lovell, G. (2006). Justice excused: The deployment of law in everyday political encounters. *Law and Society Review*, *40*, 283–324.

Lukes, S. (1974). *Power: A radical view*. London: Macmillan.

Lukes, S. (2005). *Power: A radical view* (2nd ed.). New York: Palgrave Macmillan.

Mather, L., McEwen, C. A., & Maiman, R. J. (2001). *Divorce lawyers at work: Varieties of professionalism in practice*. Oxford University Press.

Mather, L., & Yngvesson, B. (1980–1981). Language, audience, and the transformation of disputes. *Law and Society Review*, *15*(3/4), 775–822.

Matsueda, R. L., Kreager, D. A., & Huizinga, D. (2006). Deterring delinquents: A rational choice model of theft and violence. *American Sociological Review*, *71*, 95–122.

McCann, M. W. (1994). *Rights at work: Pay equity reform and the politics of legal mobilization*. Chicago: University of Chicago Press.

McCann, M. W. (1996). Causal versus Constitutive explanations (or, on the difficulty of being so positive ...). *Law and Social Inquiry*, *21*, 457–482.

Melnick, R. S. (1983). *Regulation and the courts: The case of clean air*. Washington, DC: Brookings.

Merry, S. E. (1990). *Getting justice and getting even: Legal consciousness among working class Americans*. Chicago: University of Chicago Press.

Merry, S. E. (2000). *Colonizing Hawai'i: The cultural power of law*. Princeton: Princeton University Press.

Merry, S. E. (2006). *Human rights and gender violence: Translating international law into Local justice*. Princeton: Princeton University Press.

Miller, R., & Sarat, A. (1980–1981). Grievances, claims, and disputes: Assessing the adversary cultures. *Law and Society Review*, *15*(3–4), 525–566.

Milner, N. (1986). The dilemmas of legal mobilization: Ideologies and strategies of mental patient liberation. *Law and Policy*, *8*, 105–129.

Muir, W. K. (1967). *Prayer in public schools: Law and attitude change*. Chicago: University of Chicago Press.

Nielsen, L. B. (2004). *License to harass: Law, hierarchy, and offensive public speech*. Princeton: Princeton University Press.

Perry, H. W. (1991). *Deciding to decide: Agenda setting in the United States supreme court*. Cambridge, MA: Harvard University Press.

Piliavin, I., Gartner, R., Thornton, C., & Matsueda, R. L. (1986). Crime, deterrence, and rational choice. *American Sociological Review*, *51*, 101–119.

Pitkin, H. F. (1972). *Wittgenstein and justice*. Berkeley: University of California Press.

Pollan, M. (2007). Unhappy meals. *New York Times*, online ed. 1/28.

Rodgers, H. R., Jr., & Bullock, C. S., III. (1972). *Law and social change: Civil Rights laws and their consequences*. New York: McGraw-Hill.

Rosenberg, G. (1991). *The hollow hope: Can courts bring about social change*. Chicago: University of Chicago Press.

Rosenberg, G. (1992). Hollow hopes and other aspirations: A reply to Feeley and McCann. *Law and Social Inquiry*, *17*, 761–778.

Rosenberg, G. (1996). Positivism, interpretivism, and the study of law: McCann's *Rights at Work*. *Law and Social Inquiry*, *21*, 435–456.

Sarat, A. (1990). '… The law is all over': Power, resistance and the legal consciousness of the welfare poor. *Yale Journal of Law and the Humanities*, *2*, 343.

Sarat, A. (2001). *When the state kills: Capital punishment and the American condition*. Princeton: Princeton University Press.

Schattschneider, E. E. (1975). *The Semisovereign people: A realist's view of democracy in America*. Himsdale, IL: Dryden Press.

Scheingold, S. A. (1974). *The Politics of rights: Lawyers, public policy, and social change*. New: Yale University Press.

Scheingold, S. A. (1984). *The politics of law and order*. New York: Longman.

Segal, J. A., & Spaeth, H. J. (1993). *The supreme court and the attitudinal model*. New York: Cambridge University Press.

Shapiro, I. (2005). *The Flight from reality in the social sciences*. Princeton: Princeton University Press.

Silverstein, H. (1996). *Unleashing rights: Law, meaning, and the animal rights movement*. Ann Arbor, MI: University of Michigan Press.

Simon, J. (1994). *Poor discipline: Parole and the social control of the underclass, 1890–1990*. Chicago: University of Chicago Press.

Tabriz, S. G. (2005). *The worlds of Herman Kahn: The intuitive science of Thermonuclear War*. Cambridge: Harvard University Press. Quotations from the book featured in this came from the excerpted text online: http://apertp://www.strategypage.com/moviereviews/default.asp?target=Dr.%20Strangelove%20Or:%20How%20I%20Learned%20To%20Stop%20Worrying%20And%20Love.

Tilly, C. (2006). *Why? What happens when people give reasons … and why?* Princeton: Princeton University Press.

Uhlich, S. (2002). Stanley Kubrick. http://www.sensesofcinema.com/contents/directors/02/kubrick.html

Van den Besselaar, P., & Heimerikis, G. (2001). Disciplinary, multidisciplinary, interdisciplinary – Concepts and indicators. http://hcs.science.uva.nl/usr/peter/publications/2001issi.pdf

Wirt, F. M. (1970). *The politics of southern equality: Law and social change in a Mississippi county*. Chicago: Aldine.

Yngvesson, B. (1993). *Virtuous citizens, disruptive subjects: Order and complaint in a New England court*. New York: Routledge.

Zemans, F. K. (1983). Legal mobilization: The neglected role of the law in the political system. *American Political Science Review*, *77*, 690–703.

PRECEDENTS OF INJUSTICE: THINKING ABOUT HISTORY IN LAW AND SOCIETY SCHOLARSHIP

Eve Darian-Smith

ABSTRACT

In this essay I discuss how law and legal precedent present a false or eschewed construction of the past. The Chicago Haymarket Riot in 1886 and the subsequent trial of eight rioters in Spies vs. People *provide a dramatic illustration of the lasting consequences of privileging some historical narratives and silencing others. Occurring as it did at the dawn of the "Red Scare," the miscarriage of justice in* Spies vs. People *acts as a landmark precedent in a tradition within the United States of extra-judicial lawlessness that stretches from this case through 100 years of labor turmoil, two World Wars, McCarthyism, the Cold War, and up to the current War on Terror. Moreover, these instances of lawlessness and extra-judicial activity, while not written into legal records, nonetheless resurface again and again to form patterns of behavior that amount to what I call precedents of injustice, and which I argue are as integral to law as any formal legal precedents. By way of conclusion I urge all sociolegal scholars to remain attentive to the wider historical contexts which over time are repeatedly silenced through the institutionalized legal processes of denial and forgetfulness.*

Special Issue: Law and Society Reconsidered
Studies in Law, Politics, and Society, Volume 41, 61–81

ISSN: 1059-4337/doi:10.1016/S1059-4337(07)00003-8

Modern western law appears to float above the melee of human experience and historical specificity. As a body of knowledge and mechanism of power, law presents itself as an objective, autonomous, and universal entity, outside of localized context and temporal meaning. In the past, law's claim to being ahistorical allowed it to transcend national borders and be applied by colonial regimes to a variety of cultures and political systems, in turn violating and oppressing local systems of control. Today, these dangers continue to be very real given that the economic might of the United States and the west often leads toward a myopic vision of law and a readily asserted belief in its universal application. Such assertions ignore the cultural specificity of western legal concepts, and prevent people appreciating that, analogous to past colonial periods, in a global political economy Anglo-American law is not always transportable, transferable, or translatable across political landscapes and religious communities.

In a sense, I have written this essay to serve as a warning to the dangers of disconnecting law from historical context. This is not a new or original idea, but one that seems to need constant reiteration.[1] My general argument is that in order to counter the ahistorical construction of the rule of law, sociolegal scholars have to be ever vigilant in recovering and reattaching historical context to otherwise sterilized legal processes and precedents. Of course, some sociolegal scholars – particularly those trained as historians and anthropologists – are very attentive to history. And, for instance, the USA Law & Society Association makes great efforts to promote legal history with an annual prize awarded in this research area. My aim here is not to chastise law and society scholars for their lack of attention to the importance of history. Rather, given the drive by the legal system to silence or forget the historical conditions in which law is created, and that this silencing is typically affirmed through law school education[2], my hope is to underscore the importance of history in all sociolegal scholarship so that as a field of inquiry it can remain critical, insightful and, above all, relevant to real world affairs.

My first aim is to demonstrate that law and legal precedent privilege some historical narratives and silence others. Law's history, as I discuss below, presents a false or eschewed construction of the past. The Chicago Haymarket Riot in 1886 and the subsequent trial of eight rioters in *Spies vs. People* provide a dramatic illustration of the lasting consequences of privileging some historical narratives and silencing others. By drawing on the Haymarket Riot, and then linking this past case to subsequent events up to the current War on Terror, I hope to show how law eviscerates from public record and memory particular traces of historical content. This evisceration is important to acknowledge given that it plays a role in shaping our current abilities to think and imagine. In short, exploring events such as the Haymarket Riot demonstrates that understanding present social contexts requires also capturing larger historical contexts that shape the present.

My second aim is to focus specifically on some of the details that are left out of official legal records. The Haymarket Riot and subsequent cases show that instances of lawlessness and extra-judicial activity informing legal decision-making in these instances, while not written into legal records, nonetheless resurface again and again to form patterns of behavior that amount to what I call precedents of injustice. The Haymarket Riot and trial involved extra-judicial prosecution of mainly German foreigners protesting exploitative labor conditions. I argue that the conservative backlash to the anti-laissez-faire sentiment expressed by the Haymarket rioters fits a pattern of historical conditions that accompany extra-judicial prosecutions throughout the history of the United States. Occurring as it did at the dawn of the "Red Scare," the miscarriage of justice in *Spies vs. People* acts as a landmark precedent in a tradition of extra-judicial lawlessness that stretches from this case through 100 years of labor turmoil, two World Wars, McCarthyism, the Cold War, and up to the current War on Terror. These events underscore the patterns of injustice and repetitious nature of lawlessness that are an integral part of our legal system.

Of course, the Haymarket Riot and other cases referred to here are dramatic examples of unlawful activity. That being said, I believe there are many more precedents of injustice in existence that are not as spectacular, and hence more easily covered up by law and ignored or forgotten by society. One only has to think of the vast range of racially motivated violence and practices of discrimination that have been almost entirely written out of the text of law.[3] The danger in ignoring these precedents of injustice, I suggest, is that it precludes us from seeing the larger structural inequalities and political contexts that are silenced and written out of our prevailing legal system. In short, disconnecting law from historical context prevents us from fully understanding law in the United States for what it is – a site of constant struggle and negotiation over what constitutes "legitimate" social, cultural, political, and economic interests at any one moment in time (see Sarat, Garth, & Kagan, 2002). In the current phase of 21st century US imperialism, this understanding remains highly significant in order to counter a widespread public discourse that Anglo-American law is both a model and commodity, easily disconnected from its cultural moorings and transportable to countries overseas.

LAW'S HISTORY

As has been argued by Austin Sarat and Thomas Kearns, the historical narratives produced through law are not comparable to the "facts" of history. Rather, a focus on law's history examines "law for the way it uses and writes history as well as for the ways in which it also becomes a site of memory and commemoration" (Sarat & Kearns, 1999, p. 2). In this essay I am concerned not so much with law as a site of memory and remembrance, but with law as a mechanism for deliberate amnesia and forgetfulness. What I am interested in recovering are the precedents of injustice that are silenced and written out of the text of law, but yet periodically resurface over time at particular moments of perceived crisis and threat. By precedents of injustice I am referring to precedents of particular action and behavior that typically justify illegal activity or are in fact illegal, and form the larger historical context in which formal decisions are reached. In this way, precedents of injustice form part of the structural conditions for decision-making, and I argue, play as a significant role in our legal system as the use of formally recorded precedents evoked under the doctrine of *stare decisis*.

The importance of history is not simply looking at the past to glean lessons or authority for the present – though there are moments when examining how those in the past confronted the difficulties and challenges of their times provide insights and instruction for contemporary issues. However, I would argue, as have others, that the greater value of historical insight is more subtle and deeper than is usually appreciated by those simply seeking lessons from the past. Historical narratives are intrinsically bound up with the parameters of the human imagination, and inform and shape community capacity to think and behave in certain ways (see Halbwachs, 1980; Lowenthal, 1985; Bal, Jonathan, & Spitzer, 1999). This is because historical narratives operate at both conscious and unconscious levels in the form of cultural memory, shaping human experiences and the ways individuals think about themselves in the world and the way we as scholars understand that world. Paul Connerton in his influential book *How Societies Remember* summed up this point by stating:

> our experience of the present very largely depends upon our knowledge of the past ... And we will experience our present differently in accordance with the different pasts to which we are able to connect that present. Hence the difficulty of extracting our past from our present: not simply because present factors tend to influence – some may say distort – our recollections of the past, but also because past factors tend to influence, or distort, our experiences of the present. This process, it should be stressed, reaches into the most minute and everyday details of our lives. (Connerton, 1989, p. 2)

An appreciation of the interwoven forces of past and present in the making of peoples' everyday communal reality is a fundamental reason why law and society scholars should and do care about history. This appreciation is important both in studying the here and now, and in thinking about how as a society we have come to be. It is significant to remember that throughout the 19th and 20th centuries, certain narratives of American exceptionalism, frontier romanticism, and triumphant capitalism were privileged over other narratives such as racial discrimination and economic exploitation of minorities and women. As the historian Ernest Renan observed over a century ago, "Forgetting, I would even go so far to say historical error, is a crucial factor in the creation of a nation" (Renan, 1882, 1990, p. 11). My point is that law's history played, and continues to play, a critical role in providing a logic of reason that helps US society commemorate and at the same time forget certain historical realities.

LEGAL PRECEDENTS AND "PRECEDENTS OF INJUSTICE"

Within Anglo-American law, the value of history is most obviously evident in the doctrine of *stare decisis* and the use of precedent. A precedent is when a *ratio decidendi*, or the rationale or principle of a case, is evoked in subsequent cases as a source of authority. "Precedents are prior decisions that function as models for later decisions" (MacCormick, 1997, p. 2; Summers, 1997, p. 378). While some theorists argue precedents are necessary to provide legal rules with predictability, stability, and legitimacy, others scholars caution against it because it in practice can "pre-judge" subsequent cases that appear to have analogous circumstances.[4] Whether viewed positively or negatively, precedent is a fundamental feature of common law systems. As the legal realist Karl Llewellyn remarked in his classic introductory text for law students, *The Bramble Bush* (1930):

> the lawyer searches the records for convenient cases to support his point, presses upon the court what it has already done before, capitalizes the human drive toward repetition by finding, by making explicit, by urging, the prior cases ...

However, as Llewellyn further noted, precedent does not mean that lawyers and judges slavishly apply prior legal principles to new circumstances.

Rather, legal professionals selectively manipulate the use of precedent according to the outcome desired. Argued Llewellyn:

> What I wish to sink deep into your minds about the doctrine of precedent is that it is two-headed. It is Janus-faced. That it is not one doctrine, nor one line of doctrine, but two, and two which, applied at the same time to the same precedent, are contradictory of each other. That there is one doctrine of getting rid of precedents deemed troublesome and one doctrine for making use of precedents that seem helpful. That these two doctrines exist side by side. That the same lawyer in the same brief, the same judge in the same opinion, may be using the one doctrine, the technically strict one, to cut down half the older cases that he deals with, and using the other doctrine, the loose one, for building up with the other half. Until you realize this you do not see how it is possible for law to change and to develop, and yet to stand on the past. (Llewellyn, 1951, pp. 64–69)

Much has been written about the theory, interpretation, and application of precedents in common and civil law systems, and whether adherence to precedent is merely persuasive or obligatory according to its application in different branches of the law (MacCormick & Summers, 1997; Siltala, 2000). In the context of this essay, I am not interested in the technicalities of administering legal precedent, but rather how the doctrine functions as an explicit instance of the law eliciting, distilling, and reifying one set of historical facts or story from a case in an effort to create an official version of the truth (see Sarat & Kearns, 1999, pp. 4–6). Legal precedent, by its essential nature, requires the denying of competing narratives, historical incongruities, and the wider contextual considerations in which the original case was determined. Through the process of recording and creating authoritative texts, the doctrine is used to cut away the messy everyday lived experiences of people, simplify facts to a principle, and legitimate and venerate one interpretation of the past (Darian-Smith, 2004, p. 555). And this veneration has real consequences. As sociologists Nicolas Pedriana and Robin Stryker have argued, "In short, values and language of prior law combine symbolic politics with state coercive power to create opportunities and constraints on later interpretation and mobilization of law by both state and societal actors" (Pedriana & Stryker, 1997, p. 642). In this way, the mechanism of legal precedent which explicitly strips from law all context, historical or otherwise, can be understood as an instance of both law's limits and its power.[5]

However, as we all know, people experience the past in a variety of different ways. Surrounding any event are multiple stories circulating and at times competing to present a definitive version of "truth." And in some cases, if not all cases, it is the silenced histories, unrecognized and unrecorded in law, that nonetheless create patterns and models and in some cases opportunities for future legal action (see Constable, 2006). I have been calling these "precedents of injustice" – precedents of particular action and behavior that were in fact essential in extracting the original rationale of the case itself, and which set up the necessary conditions for applying the formal legal precedent in subsequent cases. Following this line of argument, I suggest that precedents of injustice, despite being written out of legal records and text, should be considered an integral part of our legal system. As sociolegal scholars, I believe one of our responsibilities is to remain attentive to what is written out of the legal text, and what over time is repeatedly silenced through the institutionalized processes of denial and forgetfulness.

THE HAYMARKET RIOT OF 1886

One such precedent of injustice can be found in the case of *Spies vs. People* which followed the Chicago Haymarket Riot in early May in 1886. This riot and trial are remembered each year around the world on May 1 as an important moment in the history of achieving the eight-hour work day and rights for the working class. It is considered a day of pride in organized labor's capacity to fight back against laissez-faire interests, and a day of tribute for the many people who throughout the 19th and 20th centuries gave their lives in an effort to secure equality for mostly poor and oppressed sectors of society.[6] In Chicago in May, 1886, the riot resulted in a bombing that killed police, a reign of terror and torture, and a trial which resulted in the public hanging of four working class men and the suicide of another.

Because May Day is such a politically and socially significant date in all developed western countries (except the United States which I will explain below), when teaching US college students I was not prepared for students' blank stares when I asked them what 1st of May meant to them. The result was the following exchange.

> **Instructor to class:** Today is May 1st – Does this day mean anything to you in terms of rights or politics or even religion? Do you associate anything historically important with this date – anything at all?
>
> **College student**: I know, I know – it's important because when you are driving a plane and it's about to crash, you call out May Day, May Day!

I reeled out of class incredulous and amazed, in search of some explanation for my students' total lack of appreciation for the significance of the day. And what I discovered only served to heighten my general sense of alarm. After doing some basic research I discovered that in the United States there has been considerable effort and resources put into obliterating the general historical circumstances of the Haymarket Riot from public records and popular memory. This is because the Haymarket rioters, and their demands for an eight-hour workday, represented a bitter battle between labor and capitalism and demonstrated the lengths 19th century business leaders were willing to go to protect their largely unfettered rights to make profits. This included the manipulation of the law, denial of due process, use of racial profiling, abuse of extra-judicial authority, and the manufacture of facts in order to prosecute and condemn the leaders of the movement. These gross injustices were written out of the legal records, though publicly acknowledged by the Governor who pardoned the indicted men seven years after the trial.

The facts of the Haymarket Riot have been recorded in a number of historical accounts.[7] May 1, 1886, was designated the start of a nationwide strike calling for the eight-hour workday and it is estimated that around the country perhaps half a million workers, of "all colors and nationalities," joined in the public demonstration. In Chicago, 80,000 workers marched peacefully down Michigan Avenue led by two prominent anarchists, August Spies and Albert Parsons. Chicago had a reputation for being a city full of anarchist organizations, and among the city's large population of immigrants from Poland, Germany, Bohemia and elsewhere there were men and women sympathetic to anarchist and socialist calls for labor reform emanating from Europe. Importantly, these activists also proudly declared their atheism which stood against the dominant Christian social ethics of the period.

While Chicago's May Day march was peaceful, two days later the workers' moods quickly changed when a large crowd of lumbermen gathered at the McCormick Harvester plant factory to rally against scab laborers. As the crowd forced the strikebreakers to retreat back into the factory, police were called and shots fired, killing one worker immediately and causing another three to later die of injuries. August Spies had been present at the rally and witnessed the police attack. Without delay he printed off 20,000 circulars, in both English and German, calling for an early morning meeting the following day (May 4) in Haymarket Square to "avenge this horrible murder." At 7.30 am about 3,000 protesters gathered. The speakers, August Spies, Albert Parsons, and Samuel Fielden, addressed the crowd and called them to action against the government. However, as the rain came down the crowds dispersed, leaving only about 200 workers listening to the third speech by Fielden. Mayor Carter Harrison, who had stood listening to the speeches, left the meeting and stopped in at the local police station about half a block away to tell Captain Bonfield to call in the police since the meeting was peaceful and nearly over. However, in direct contrast to the Mayor's orders, Bonfield ordered his 180 men to march into the market, surround the workers, and disperse the crowd. "Seconds later a spluttering bomb flew through the air and exploded in front of the police, killing one instantly and wounding over seventy (Fig. 1). The remaining police regrouped and emptied their revolvers into the panic-stricken protesters, wounding many, at least one fatally" (Foner, 1986, p. 30). A total of 11 people died. No one saw who had thrown the bomb or where it came from. According to George Brown, an eye-witness:

> He [Fielden] started to finish his speech when there was a movement of the crowd, which forced me back and up onto the pavement. From this position I could see over the heads of those in the street, and to my astonishment I saw a great company of police, with their revolvers drawn, rushing into the crowd which parted to make way for them. The captain commanded the meeting to disperse. Fielden leaned forward and said to the officer: "This is a peaceable meeting, and you have no right to interfere." Up to this time there had been no disorder of any kind. Now something occurred on the side of the street farthest from me, and the police captain called out, "Arrest that man," and instantly the police began firing into the people ... something went quite high over my head which looked like a lighted cigar: in the semi-darkness only the lighted fuse showed. This was the bomb. It exploded in the midst of the police. I raised myself up as well as I could in the dense pack of the crowd, and looking past the wagon I saw a confused, writhing, squirming mass of policemen on the ground. (cited in Roediger & Rosemont, 1986, p. 75)

Fig. 1. Depiction of the Haymarket Riot, 1886. *Source:* © Chicago Historical Society.

Fear and hysteria descended over Chicago. Mayor Harrison declared martial law and ordered widespread police dragnets. Julius Grinnel, State Attorney General, advised the police to disregard the law as they made their raids of homes and union offices, and tortured and abused hundreds in an attempt to find incriminating evidence. Thirty-one people were indicted, and eight selected for trial. Of those eight, only two had been present at the Haymarket riot, but all were declared "guilty by association." The men were the following: August Spies, Albert Parsons, Louis Lingg, Adolph Fischer, George Engel, Oscar Neebe, Samuel Fielden, and Michael Scwab. Five were German immigrants, and a sixth a US citizen of German descent. The news media made much of the racist implications,[8] calling the defendants "foreign savages," the "offscourings of Europe" and "the lowest stratum found in humanity's formation" (cited in Roediger & Rosemont, 1986, p. 93).

THE TRIAL OF THE CHICAGO MARTYRS

The trial of the defendants was set for June 21, 1886. Judge Joseph E. Gary appointed a special bailiff to select the jurors, and those selected were managers, salesmen, and businessmen. Another selected was a relative of a police officer who had been a victim of the Haymarket bombing. It was clearly a jury deeply prejudiced against those involved in any form of labor agitation. The defendants were not charged with murder or bomb-throwing, but of conspiracy. As declared by Attorney General Grinnell in his summation:

> Law is on trial. Anarchy is on trial. These men have been selected, picked out by the grand jury and indicted because they are the leaders. They are no more guilty than those thousands who follow them. Gentlemen of the jury: convict these men, make examples of them, hang them and you save our institutions, our society. (Foner, 1986, p. 34)

The jury declared the men guilty and sentenced them all, except Neebe, to death by hanging. The defense appealed, and while the Illinois Supreme Court acknowledged faults in the trial, it also upheld the verdict. A further appeal was made to the United States Supreme Court but the court refused to hear it. The execution date was set for November 11, 1887. Calls for clemency were made by labor movements across the United States as well as from Britain, Germany, France, Holland, Russia, Italy, and Spain. American intellectuals joined the trade unionists in petitioning for clemency, and William Dean Howells, a well known novelist and literary critic called the verdict "the greatest wrong that ever threatened our fame as a nation"

New York Tribune, November 6, 1887. Partly in response to local and worldwide pressure, on 10 November, the day before the execution, the sentences of Fielden and Schwab were converted from death to life imprisonment. The next day, Lingg committed suicide in his cell, and Parsons, Engel, Spies and Fisher were hung. Spies' last words on the scaffold were: "There will be a time when our silence will be more powerful than the voices you strangle today" (Parsons, 1969, title page) (Fig. 2).

Some 7 years later, on June 26, 1893, a day after the Haymarket Martyr Monument was dedicated before 8,000 people in Chicago, Governor John Peter Altgeld officially pardoned the eight defendants. Altgeld declared all eight to be innocent and victims of a biased trial. As argued by one historian since:

> A biased jury, a prejudiced judge, perjured evidence, and extraordinary and indefensible theory of conspiracy, and the temper of Chicago led to the conviction. The evidence never proved their guilt … No valid defense can be made for the verdict. (David, 1936, p. 489)

Fig. 2. The Law Vindicated: Four of the Chicago Anarchists Pay the Penalty of their Crime. Frank Leslie's Illustrated Newspaper. Vol. 65, No. 1679 (Nov. 19, 1887). New York. *Source:* © Chicago Historical Society.

RADICALIZING AND CO-OPTING MAY DAY

The deaths of the Haymarket rioters galvanized an international labor movement as no other previous event had. Two years after the Haymarket affair the International Labor Congress was held in Paris. A year later, on May 1, 1890, the First International Workers Day was held and thousands marched around the world in support of working class demands for an eight-hour day. In London alone it was said that between 350,000 and 500,000 workers marched in what the *Times* reported was the "greatest demonstration of modern times" (*London Times*, May 5, 1890). Frederick Engels, in the preface of the fourth German edition of the Communist Manifesto, enthusiastically wrote of the hundreds of thousands of workers who had demonstrated in so many countries:

> As I write these lines, the proletariat of Europe and America is holding a review of its forces: it is mobilized for the first time as One army, under One flag, and fighting for One immediate aim: an eight-hour working day, established by legal enactment … . The spectacle we are witnessing will make the capitalists and landowners of all lands realize that today the proletariat of all lands, in very truth, are united. If only Marx were with me to see it with his own eyes! (Foner, 1986, p. 55)[9]

A year later, in preparation for May Day of 1891, enthusiasm for the labor movement continued as thousands of workers and union groups planned for mass demonstrations and strikes. The issue of the eight-hour workday was still central to the platform, but by this stage other demands were added such as universal suffrage, freeing of political prisoners, the right to political organization, and the end of colonial oppression. Samuel Gompers, President of the American Federation of Labor, in an interview in *The People*, announced:

> May 1st of each year is now looked upon by organized wage-workers and the observing public as a sort of new Independence Day upon which they will every year strike a blow for emancipation and steadily weaken the shackles of wage slavery. (*The People*, April 26, 1891)

While anarchist and socialist groups involved in May Day activism did use anti-capitalist rhetoric, it was language very much focused on laissez-faire capitalist practices of explicit and overt exploitation that bordered on slavery. May Day marches, for the majority of ordinary people who participated in these events, were seen as public demonstrations that critiqued the status quo by calling for basic rights such as an eight-hour workday, the right to vote, the right to minimum wages, and equal rights for children, women and ethnic minorities. These participants did not want to overthrow the economic and legal system. On the contrary, the majority of the workers firmly believed in law and justice and hence their determination to bring about legal reform.

As mentioned above, while the celebration of May Day gained increasing popularity over the decades among working groups from many countries, in the United States there emerged concerted efforts by those in power to prevent further class organization and what was labeled anti-capitalist agitation. Throughout the early years of the 20th century, it became an increasing economic and political necessity for the US government, as well as industrial and corporate interests, to radicalize the image of the labor movement, distort its agenda, and whip up public opposition against it. This was achieved relatively easily by using the media to underscore the links existing between labor groups and socialist and communist organizations. And since many labor organizers were immigrants and new to the United States, it was easy to fuel nationalist fears of invading foreigners. As early as the 1910s, first President Theodore Roosevelt and then President Woodrow Wilson warned of "hyphenated Americans," who the latter argued, had "poured the poison of disloyalty into the very arteries of our national life. Such creatures of passion, disloyalty and anarchy must be crushed out" (Kennedy, 1980, p. 24).

The government, in cooperation with corporate America, denigrated and denounced labor demands by fueling the growing Red Scare and general fears of Bolshevik activism that emerged in the wake of the Russian Revolution of 1917.[10] The result was a growing distrust of organized labor, which in turn became increasingly militant given the lack of any substantive changes to labor laws. Conflicts, sometimes violent and bloody, occurred between labor activists and governmental agencies throughout World War I and into the 1920s and 1930s, such as the Palmer Raids on the radical left which occurred in the years 1919–1921. With the 1929 stock market crash, which left millions of people unemployed, starving and destitute, the need to quell civic protest intensified further. At the 1930 May Day parade in New York, a crowd of 100,000 gathered to demonstrate "while machine guns appeared on top of low buildings and their muzzles tilted downward to the Square" (Foner, 1986, p. 110).

But the most explicit and systematic silencing of domestic labor demands for just pay and conditions came with the launching by Harry Truman of the Cold War in the late 1940s and the second wave of the Red Scare under McCarthyism. By once again mobilizing fear outward against foreign peoples and their "anti-American" ideologies, the power elite, backed by legal authority, could avoid dealing with structural injustices and the exploitation of minorities and the poor built into the domestic capitalist system. In March 1947, Truman ordered a full-scale "loyalty investigation" and this frenzy to ascertain who was a potential threat to the United States spilled over into legislation regulating labor. Under the 1947 Taft-Hartley Act the power of employers was increased and the power of trade unions further limited. In an explicit conflation of terrorist fears with business interests, the Act forced union officials to swear that they did not have any allegiance with communist ideologies or belong to the Communist Party. Labeling labor movements as communist meant that labor demands could be dismissed. Hence from 1948 on mainstream media in the United States linked May Day to the Communist Party, and in so doing silenced what had become a public demonstration against the structural inequalities leveled primarily at the working class and in particular women and racial minorities.

Athens, Greece; Poland

London, England; Turkey

Fig. 3. Pictures of Mayday Marches from around the World, 2006. *Source: TML Daily*, May 12, 2006, No. 79. http://www.cpcml.ca/Tmld2006/D36079.htm

In 1955, in an explicit move to co-opt May Day, President Dwight Eisenhower declared May 1 to be "Loyalty Day" and in 1958 it was passed by Congress and made into law. The same year, Eisenhower also proclaimed May 1 to be "Law Day" in an effort to "strengthen our great heritage of liberty, justice, and equality under the law."[11] While today very few people actually observe either Loyalty Day or Law Day on May 1, these 1958 proclamations demonstrate the lengths the government was prepared to go in an attempt to rewrite May Day's symbolism in a larger effort to fight both internal and external Cold War threats to the American way of life. Since the 1950s and the decline of the Red Scare, there have been very few May Day labor marches in the United States. While hundreds of thousands of people take to the streets each year on this day around the world and celebrate the courage and achievements of the Haymarket rioters, ironically in the United State, the birthplace of this achievement, the day passes without comment, recognition, or even much media coverage of the annual mass demonstrations around the world.[12] Hundreds of thousands march, but for what reasons we cannot remember (Fig. 3).

PRECEDENTS OF INJUSTICE

What is the significance of the Haymarket Riot and trial for law and society scholars? I have used this rather extreme case in an attempt to underscore how law and legal processes were used to rewrite segments of US history. Moreover, this case suggests that the wider historical contexts in which the trial and the precedents of injustice took place have episodically reappeared in the years since 1886. For despite major efforts to deny or "paper over" the Haymarket affair, the lawless extra-judicial circumstances of the case which included lack of due process, the use of surveillance, torture and coercion, the use of racial profiling, guilt through association, and the manipulation of media and political processes, have resurfaced periodically throughout the 20th and early 21st centuries.

This periodic resurfacing of injustices suggests a greater structural context for the sanctioning of lawlessness. In many ways, the Haymarket Riot and trial stand as a landmark and predecessor to the use of extra-judicial authority evoked in subsequent times of national crisis to combat communism in the late 1910s, during World War II, in the 1950s under McCarthyism, and throughout the Cold War era. More recently, extra-judicial authority has been used to combat Islamic-fundamentalism in the Gulf Wars and in the post 9/11 War on Terror. In all these cases, whether the enemy is labeled an irrational anarchist, godless communist, or Islamic fundamentalist, it is the threat to the American way of life (which often involves a critique of laissez-faire capitalism) that has been consistently used to create an environment of fear and xenophobia and justify lawlessness in the form of extra-judicial prosecution.

Historically, extra-judicial authority is evoked in times of national crisis, war, and threats of terrorism domestically and overseas. It is during these extreme moments that concessions are made for the government to operate outside of the authority of a court, and outside of the usual judicial proceedings required to ensure due process and legal accountability. There is in fact very little direction as to what constitutes appropriate extra-judicial activities and their constitutionality. The Alien and Sedition Acts of 1798 are generally held up as examples of unconstitutional executive power, and were later repudiated. But to this day legal confusion surrounds the topic. This has been most recently evidenced by the Bush administration justifying the stripping of habeas corpus protections from those deemed to be terrorists under the Military Commissions Act of 2006. This justification held despite the Supreme Court decision a few months earlier in *Hamdan vs. Rumsfeld* which found that the federal government did not have authority to set up special military commissions, and that these commissions were illegal under the Geneva Convention and the Uniform Code of Military Justice. A lot more could be said about this use of congressional power to overwrite judicial decisions, and where, in effect, the executive branch "suspends law, or contorts law to its own uses" (see Butler, 2004, pp. 57, 50–100). My point here is that in terms of historical precedent, it seems that accompanying all instances where extra-judicial authority has been used to combat "terrorism" there has also been in evidence elements of the precedents of injustice originally associated with the Haymarket Affair. As noted by one historian, "The rulings in the Haymarket trial have contributed repressive legal precedents which have been used for 100 years" (Ashbaugh cited in Roediger & Rosemont, 1986).[13] Thomas Sullivan, a former United States attorney who has represented detainees at Guantanamo, also refers to this lineage of legal injustices when he writes:

> I believe that if this bill [to redefine US obligations under the Geneva convention] is passed with these habeas-stripping provisions in it, then after I am dead and the members of this Senate hearing are dead, an apology will be made just as we did for the incarceration of the Japanese citizens in the Second World War. (*New York Times*, September 26, 2006, p. 19)

CONCLUDING COMMENTS

In the US, it appears that the use of extra-judicial authority against terrorism is consistently accompanied by instances of abuse of due process, manipulation of media and political processes, and arguably racial profiling and torture as well. This suggests that the precedent for applying extra-judicial authority in times of crisis and terrorism has built within it a precedent of injustice – the first cannot be evoked without reliance upon the second. Being integrally intertwined, both form part of the US legal system. And it's for this very reason that there is a need to silence, write-out, and forget (see Renan above) the historical contexts and wider social details that surround the periodic use of extra-judicial activities in the United States.

Against this process of forgetting, what I have been arguing for is the need to remain attentive to certain elements from the past. One way to do this is by focusing on precedents of injustice as a mechanism to help identify and see historical links and structural connections between particular moments in time. While we rarely think of expressions of lawlessness being connected together these extreme reactions can be interpreted as historical moments when mainstream American society felt in some way threatened or challenged. Together, these instances of lawlessness point to huge systemic and integrally connected structural problems in the US system such as economic exploitation, racial discrimination, and nationalist xenophobia.

The problem is that as a society we need to write these moments of lawlessness as horror stories, as anomalies and aberrations, as one-off events that have no connection to each other. Hence by singling out and blaming specific individuals for the inequities of an exploitative labor market, the case of *Spies vs. People* could neatly side-step and avoid dealing with the underlying exploitative economic conditions being protested. By singling out and blaming specific individuals the legal system operated as an effective mechanism that both denied the historical context of the riot and reconstructed a new history of "foreign terrorism" that could not be seen as structural.

I want to return to the general point of this essay, which is to underscore the importance of the historical past in research that seeks to examine law in the present. If we rely on law's history alone we are left with a non-structural reading of our own past that avoids acknowledging or addressing any underlying structural problems or inequities and preserves the status quo. And it is precisely this process that ensures the conditions in which precedents of injustice will cyclically resurface again and again. However, if we remain ever attentive to recovering forgotten historical contexts and silenced historical narratives it may be possible to paint a fuller picture of the past and draw structural connections between moments of lawlessness. This ability to see links and connections may provide insights into understanding why events such as 9/11 occur, and help us begin to deal with long-standing social injustices that a capitalist system is invested to ignore.

The Haymarket Riot, and the subsequent radicalizing and co-opting of May Day's symbolism by the US government, dramatically illustrates how vulnerable historical narratives are to being reinterpreted and manipulated and the role law plays in this manipulation. The Haymarket Riot and trial shows us the need to recover other histories and truths about the past that have been carefully written out of the text of law, systematically redacted from public record, and effectively erased from collective memory. And the Haymarket Riot and trial have hopefully served as a reminder of the deep significance of historical legacies, and the temporal layering of cultural meaning that frames and informs and constructs current events, experiences, and abilities to think and articulate ideas. By remaining attentive to historical contexts, it may be possible to reveal other precedents of injustice and other versions of truth that lie at the heart of and are integral to the functioning of Anglo-American legal systems. In short, sensitivity to how the past is constructed and what this means for the present is one way toward opening up the field of law and society to questions that we as scholars may not yet be able to imagine or remember.

NOTES

1. "Commentators continue to marvel at the seeming ignorance of the past and the need, once again, to discover the role of social context in shaping what law is and what it does. This role of social context is admitted by all but inevitably neglected by many – especially lawyers – anxious to get on with the 'business of reform'" (Garth, 2006, p. 941).

2. Note, however, the efforts of the New Legal Realism Project at the University of Wisconsin Law School which is trying to combine "diverse social science methods and perspectives" in order to "provide a more encompassing understanding of the dilemmas facing law" (http://www.newlegalrealism.org/); see also the special issue dedicated to the New Legal Realism project in *Law & Social Inquiry* 2006, 31(4).

3. The lawless acts that were allowed to happen within the parameters of the legal system in the case of *Spies vs. People* cannot be disconnected from similar acts of

violence occurring completely outside the courtroom. The violence against immigrant laborers during this period is shadowed by even more extreme extra-judicial or vigilante violence against black Americans in the form of public lynchings. And almost completely written out of the text of the law are an entire series of racially motivated massacres for which very few, if any, convictions are recorded. Examples of this are the Cincinnati Vigilante Riot of 1884 that resulted in the massacre of more than 50 black people, the 20 or more race riots that occurred throughout the Red Summer of 1919, the Tulsa Race Riot of 1921 that killed an estimated 300 black people, the Detroit race riots which claimed 34 lives, 25 of them black, or the Zoot Suit Riots in Los Angeles in 1943 against Latino youths. There are a shocking number of similarly lawless moments that are almost completely missing from both history texts and the text of law.

4. "The German for 'precedent' is *Präjudiz*. Its primary meaning is 'prejudgement,' but is also verges on 'prejudice.' A similar word (*praeiudicia*) was occasionally used by Roman jurists as a description of prior court decisions; as *préjugés*, with the same meaning, it appeared in pre-revolutionary France. Whether taken as 'prejudgement' or 'prejudice,' it carries an implication that is distinctly unpleasant; it suggests that minds have been at least partly closed" (Dawson, 1968, p. xv).

5. Legal precedent, like legal jurisdiction, illustrates the limits of law and at the same time demonstrates its capacity to reproduce itself. As noted by Sarat, Douglas and Umphrey:

> Law confers authority upon itself through these practices. They constitute law, in its own self-understanding, as something other than the naked exercise of power. By staying its power, by limiting its reach and domain, law creates its integrity and efficacy as a system of rules. (Sarat, Douglas, & Umphrey, 2005)

6. Demands for basic worker rights began in the late 1790s before the organization of trade unions. Strikes and protests for the ten-hour workday occurred in 1827 in Boston and Philadelphia, and in 1835 there was a successful general strike in Philadelphia that won advances for wages for pieceworkers and the ten-hour day maximum. This success was diminished by the impact of an economic depression between 1837 and 1841 and work hours returned to 12–14 a day. Struggles continued throughout the second half of the 19th century but were generally ineffective. However, after the Civil Wart there was renewed momentum and labor agitation which coincided with local trade unions becoming more organized and linking up with national labor unions and the first International Workingmen's Association which was founded in 1864. In some cities, legislation was introduced to support the eight-hour workday but these laws were generally not enforced (see Tomlins, 1985, 1993; Foner, 1986, pp. 8–18).

7. A number of books have been written about the Haymarket Riot and its historical significance (see David, 1936; Foner, 1969, 1986; Roediger & Rosemont, 1986; Nelson, 1988). Most recently, James Green (2006) has published an excellent book titled *Death in the Haymarket*.

8. Understandings of racism in this period involved the color of a person's skin as well as a range of factors such as socio-economic status, culture, customs, and

nationality (see López, 1996; Noel Ignatiev's, 1996 book *How the Irish Became White*).

9. Karl Marx died on March 14, 1883, in conditions of extreme poverty. However, Marx's daughter, Eleanor Marx Aveling, was very much involved in these events.

10. In 1919, both the Communist Party and the Communist Labor Party were formed in the United States, and in the following year "over 6,000 men and women were arrested by federal agents, and 556 aliens, though convicted of no crimes, were deported" (Foner, 1986, pp. 92–3).

11. Interestingly, as pointed out by my colleague Tom Hilbink, a few years earlier in 1954 Eisenhower also signed the resolution into law that made the phrase "In God We Trust" the national motto of the United States and the phrase first began to appear on paper currency in 1957.

12. However, May 1st was chosen by immigrant groups in 2006 as the day for a massive general strike across the United States to protest the increasingly harsh penalities against illegal immigrants and heightened security at the US-Mexican border. In the *New York Times*, and other major news media, it was said that the boycott was "timed to coincide with International Workers' Day" which is apparently one of the few known instances of the day being mentioned by this name in the US press over the past 30 years.

13. For a powerful and compelling essay on the links between McCarthyism and the War on Terror see Cole (2005).

BIBLIOGRAPHY

Bal, M., Jonathan, C., & Spitzer, L. (Eds). (1999). *Acts of memory: Cultural recall in the present*. Hanover, London: Dartmouth College, University Press of New England.

Butler, J. (2004). *Precarious life: The powers of mourning and violence*. London, New York: Verso.

Cole, D. (2005). The new McCarthyism: Repeating history in the war on terrorism. 2In: A. Sarat (Ed.), *Dissent in dangerous times* (pp. 111–145). Ann Arbor: The University of Michigan Press.

Connerton, P. (1989). *How societies remember*. Cambridge: Cambridge University Press.

Constable, M. (2006). *Just silences: The limits and possibilities of modern law*. Princeton, Oxford: Princeton University Press.

Darian-Smith, Eve. (2004). Ethnographies of Law. In: Austin Sarat (Ed.), *Blackwell Companion to Law and Society* (pp. 545–568).

David, H. (1936). *The history of the Haymarket affair: A study in American social-revolutionary and labor movements*. New York: Russell & Russell.

Dawson, J. P. (1968). *The oracles of the law*. Ann Arbor, MI: University of Michigan Law School.

Foner, P. S. (Ed.) (1969). *Autobiographies of the Haymarket martyrs*. New York: Humanities Press.

Foner, P. S. (1986). *May Day: A short history of the international workers' holiday 1886–1986*. New York, NY: International Publishers.

Garth, B. G. (2006). Introduction: Taking new legal realism to transnational issues and institutions. *Law & Social Inquiry*, *31*(4), 939–946.

Green, J. (2006). *Death in the Haymarket: A story of Chicago, the first labor movement and the bombing that divided gilded age America*. New York, NY: Pantheon Books.

Halbwachs, M. (1980). *The collective memory*. New York, NY: Harper & Row Colophon Books.

Ignatiev, N. (1996). *How the Irish became white*. New York, London: Routledge.

Kennedy, D. M. (1980). *Over here: The First World War and American Society*. New York, NY: Oxford University Press.

Llewellyn, K. N. (1951). *The bramble bush*. Dobbs Ferry, New York: Oceana Press Publications.

López, I. F. H. (1996). *White by law: The legal construction of race*. New York, London: New York University Press.

Lowenthal, D. (1985). *The past is a foreign country*. Cambridge: Cambridge University Press.

MacCormick, D. N. (1997). Introduction. In: D. N. MacCormick & R. S. Summers (Eds), *Interpreting precedents: A comparative study* (pp. 1–16). Aldershot: Ashgate/Darmouth.

MacCormick, D. N., & Summers, R. S. (Eds). (1997). *Interpreting precedents: A comparative study*. Aldershot: Ashgate/Darmouth.

Nelson, B. C. (1988). *Beyond the martyrs: A social history of Chicago's anarchists, 1870–1900*. New Brunswick, NJ: Rutgers University Press.

Parsons, L. (1969). *Famous speeches of the eight Chicago anarchists*. New York: Arno Press & The New York Times.

Pedriana, N., & Stryker, R. (1997). Political culture wars 1960s style: Equal employment opportunity–affirmative action law, and the Philadelphia plan. *American Journal of Sociology*, *103*(3), 633–691.

Renan, E. (1882, 1999). What is a nation? In: H. K. Bhabha (Ed.), *Nation and narration* (pp. 8–22). London, New York: Routledge.

Roediger, D., & Rosemont, F. (Eds). (1986). *Haymarket scrapbook*. Chicago, IL: Charles H. Kerr Publishing Company.

Sarat, A., Douglas, L., & Umphrey, M. M. (Eds). (2005). The Limits of Law. *The Amherst Series in Law, Jurisprudence and Social Thought*. Stanford: Stanford University Press.

Sarat, A., Garth, B., & Kagan, R. A. (Eds). (2002). *Looking back at law's century*. Ithaca, London: Cornell University Press.

Sarat, A., & Kearns, T. (Eds). (1999). History, memory, and the law. *The Amherst Series in Law, Jurisprudence and Social Thought*. Ann Arbor: The University of Michigan Press.

Siltala, R. (2000). *A theory of precedent: From analytical positivism to a post-analytical philosophy of law*. Oxford, Portland Oregon: Hart.

Summers, R. S. (1997). Precedent in the United States (New York State). In: M. D. Neil & R. S. Summers (Eds), *Interpreting precedents: A comparative study* (pp. 355–406). Aldershot: Ashgate/Darmouth.

Tomlins, C. L. (1985). *The state and the unions: Labor relations, law and the organized labor movement in America, 1880–1960 (studies in economic history and policy: USA in the twentieth century)*. Cambridge: Cambridge University Press.

Tomlins, C. L. (1993). *Law, labor, and ideology in the early American republic*. Cambridge: Cambridge University Press.

DECONSTRUCTING LAW AND SOCIETY: A SOCIOLEGAL AESTHETICS

Jonathan Goldberg-Hiller

> "Deconstruction, as a form of politics, is ultimately disabling … . The grand theories of the Left have collapsed. The humane side of the Enlightenment is under attack. However, I question the value of postmodernism as transformative politics."
>
> –Joel Handler (1992a, p. 698)

Joel Handler's presidential address to the Law and Society Association in 1992 was heard as a challenge to the enterprise of sociolegal studies delivered by one of its founding and revered intellectuals. In his disquiet over the emergent philosophies of postmodernism – particularly the method of deconstruction and the ontology of anti-foundationalism – and the nihilistic and contingent jurisprudence and political theory that it had spawned in the Anglo-American academy, Handler drew a line (an old-style, structuralist, and foundationalist line) against scholarship that would weaken the critical commitments that founded and continued to inspire law and society. Handler's address, its later publication with extended commentary in the *Law and Society Review*, and its subsequent life as the most-cited LSA presidential address have made it a seismic event in the scholarly politics of the legal academy, another rumbling of the realist fault-line running between the courtroom and the classroom. As an event renewed by its periodic echoes and its parallel struggles (e.g., Farber & Sherry, 1997; Greer, 2001), it also marks one of the last significant expressions of

Special Issue: Law and Society Reconsidered
Studies in Law, Politics, and Society, Volume 41, 83–120

ISSN: 1059-4337/doi:10.1016/S1059-4337(07)00004-X

self-assessment, stock-taking, and state-of-the-discipline accounting in the last 15 years.

Handler's challenge and the responses it provoked within the sociolegal academy expose many contemporary layers of meaning about the enterprise of sociolegal studies. In this chapter, I use his address and the discourse – scholarly, mythological, and partisan – that has subsequently swirled around and invested in it in order to prod and interrogate this delamination. My goal is to reveal some aspects of the field in the 15 years since Handler's speech. As a scholar of social movements and the discourse of rights who has embraced various theories that were indicted in Handler's address, I nonetheless resist a defense of these methods, although I acknowledge at the outset that I rely upon some of them in order to gain insight into and definition of the academic spaces that we denote as our common field. Rather than grudgingly return to an old debate, or bring newly sharpened tools to the defense of an older threat, my goal is to see this event in a new light and offer a way of tracing, investigating, and questioning our common professional activities, values, and anxieties. I seek, in short, to find the points of rupture that Handler's speech initiated, and trace the contradictory intellectual efforts to produce knowledge and enforce silence that such a fissure lets loose.

My technique in this chapter is to look obliquely at the field that Handler jostled through an aesthetic lens. My reliance on aesthetics is not meant to ignore alternative concerns about power and law that largely motivate our shared understandings as well as our collegial disagreements. Instead, I hope to show that aesthetics – particularly a critical form of aesthetics – can shed light on the nature of the conflict provoked by Handler's address, the way that we remember and memorialize this conflict, and more generally, on the controversies that have surrounded the sociolegal field since, all while redirecting our attention to how we may renew our progressive commitments. Despite our own disagreements on whether law and society constitutes a discipline or whether we remain interdisciplinary in our approaches to law – questions that often devolve to whether there is a canon and a paradigm of sorts (Erlanger, 2005; Tomlins, 2000, 2004) – aesthetics may reveal the ways in which we have long been expressing our disciplinarity in other ways, such as in our social commitments and our common aspirations for the social purposes to which our research be put. Aesthetics, as I will argue below, may also allow us to gain a better understanding of our own social composition as scholars. It may usefully reveal our own decomposition as well; despite the broad commitment to the diversity of ways that law promotes and restrains social justice and social participation, the large meetings of the Law and Society Association seem to have slowly become less racially and ethnically diverse since Handler's address as alternative scholarly venues have emerged.[1] Finally, attention to the aesthetic may make a significant contribution to an understanding of the new conservative reaction to law that haunts and limits progressive politics and scholarship today. I aim, in short, to use aesthetics to think differently about the question of how sociolegal scholarship has changed and developed in the last few years, not just in the ways that we think about law and society, but how we see ourselves as thinkers.

AESTHETICS, DISCIPLINARITY, AND POLITICS

Handler's genealogy of postmodernism recounted in his address recognizes its origin in aesthetic disciplines and its somewhat viral transcription into social jurisprudence: "the postmodern concept of subversion developed first in language and literary theory, art, and architecture and then spread into politics and law" (1992a, p. 698). Although Handler's rejection of deconstruction stems from what he sees to be its political quiescence, its association with aesthetic critiques of modernism haunts his claims as one source of its essential conservatism. Aesthetic values, he implies, remain distant or distinct from pressing issues of political and social inequality.

Handler's indictment of aesthetics accords well with a dominant complaint about aesthetic knowledge based on an interpretation of Kant's *Critique of Judgment* (1952), while affirming a more Jeffersonian philosophical tradition that emphasizes the essential connection between democratic equality and the facticity of nature (Shapiro, 2006a; see also Shklar, 1990). As Michael Shapiro (2006b, p. 663) notes, Kant, writing contemporaneously with Jefferson, threatened the political assurance of nature with his aesthetics:

> Kant's critical treatment of aesthetic comprehension in his analytic of the sublime constitutes an annulment of the mind-nature marriage that Jefferson assumed. Moreover, the Kantian insight constitutes a pervasive discrediting of the Jeffersonian version of enlightenment, which prescribes "highly elaborated modes of attention, observation, and description, applied to natural objects," and gives too little heed to the productive imagination in which objects are presented. As Kant puts it, "true sublimity must be sought only in the mind of the [subject] judging, not in the natural object."

If nature can no longer be seen to press its truth into the mind, a philosophical presumption inherent in Kant's concept of the sublime, aesthetic knowledge, and its influence upon postmodern theory appears disconcertingly disconnected from politics and even self-conscious about its limitations. In Handler's charge, scholarship imbued with an aesthetic postmodernism emphasizes "smallish, localized narrative[s]" and "a justice of multiplicities" (Fraser & Nicholson, 1988; Lyotard, 1984 quoted in Handler, 1992a, p. 706) rather than vigorous social "meta-narrative" able to grasp genuinely troublesome social facts such as subordination.

I suggest we take Handler's genealogy seriously while stressing, contrarily, the value of the aesthetic for a critique of the alliance between knowledge and politics, an approach to aesthetics that relies upon a more post-Kantian turn. While a long modernist tradition building on Kant stressed a romantic, autonomous realization of the nation (consider Schiller and Hegel), and many contemporary aestheticians have followed a more critical pathway in which the Kantian sublime has been the basis for a critical discourse of mourning and melancholia, or a Benjaminian notion of an aestheticized politics specific to a mass age, aesthetics does not necessarily do the bidding of the political. Nonetheless, the alternative need not be a return to a Kantian ideal of aesthetic knowledge as an absolutely neutral realm, one ethically or instrumentally divorced from what Robert Cover (1986) has argued to be the central organizing fact of law, that it is written in "a field of pain and death." Although the stakes of professional academic life are mercifully less, aesthetic knowledge may help us understand law and politics in this very register by revealing the ways in which both law and politics are about more than state violence and our values towards it (as Handler suggests), but fundamentally include a disagreement about the political and aesthetic worlds themselves. Paradoxically, this may bring the violence of law back into focus at the same time that it reorients us toward our own and others' ideas of social justice, with important implications for our own associational life.

Rancière and the Aesthetics of Dissensus

Jacques Rancière's (2003, p. 5) work on political aesthetics deploys this paradox as its philosophical inception.[2] "The political and … aesthetical are strongly interconnected" he argues, because politics should not be seen "as a specific single world but as a conflictive world: not a world of competing interests or values but a world of competing worlds." Aesthetic knowledge forms a broad horizon, including "the forms, images, tropes, perceptions, and sensibilities that help shape the creation, apprehension, and even identity of human endeavors, including … law" (Schlag, 2002, p. 1050), what Rancière has called "the distribution of the sensible":

> It is a delimitation of spaces and time, of the visible and the invisible, of speech and noise, that simultaneously determines the place and the stakes of politics as a form of experience. Politics revolves around what is seen and what can be said about it, around who has the ability to see and the talent to speak, around the properties of spaces and the possibilities of time. (Rancière, 2004b, p. 13)

One implication is that the distribution of the sensible encompasses numerous debates and petty disagreements that fail to rise to a level of significance challenging what can be seen and said. The aesthetic, for Rancière, takes us to a distance beyond these conflicts, into another framework from which we can see something new. The aesthetic "is not political owing to the messages and feelings that it conveys on the state of social and political issues. Nor is it political owing to the way it represents social structures, conflicts or identities. It is political by virtue of the very distance that it takes with respect to those functions" (Rancière, 2004a). More than a pragmatic search for tactical novelty or a salvific ideal of communicative action, the political for Rancière attends to the inclusiveness of debates as well as the subjectivity associated with tactical repertoires, imaginations of what is possible in other social worlds.

This aesthetic distance may produce a radical idea of what counts as politics, with important implications for the law. In an effort to unsettle common assumptions, Rancière writes that "[p]olitics is not the exercise of power" (2001, Thesis 1). Nor does the study of power exhaust the political. "If there is something proper to politics, it consists entirely in this relationship which is not a relationship between subjects, but one between two contradictory terms through which a subject is defined" (Rancière, 2001). Knowing who counts and how to count them is foundational to politics and, Rancière suggests, democracy is its grammar. This idea escapes most political and jurisprudential thought conflating power and state with the function of politics; for Rancière, there is a necessary ontological division between politics and philosophy (Deranty, 2003) that is dependent upon contradiction and dissensus over fundamental ways of seeing.

In order to capture the valence of aesthetic dissensus, Rancière differentiates *police* from what he calls *politics.* Police is established through practices of representation that politics tries to subvert. Police is an aesthetic problem for it uses what is visible or invisible to establish a share of what is in common, as well as a piece of what is shared out (from the two possible meanings in French of the term *partage du sensible*, or distribution of the sensible):

> The police is, essentially, the law, generally implicit, that defines a party's share or lack of it. But to define this, you first must define the configuration of the perceptible in which one or the other is inscribed. The police is thus first an order of bodies that defines the allocation of ways of doing, ways of being, and ways of saying, and sees that those bodies are assigned by name to a particular place and task. (Rancière, 1999, p. 29)

Disagreement is not eliminated by police regulation, but neither does it rise to the fundamental challenge of democratic limits that is politics. Handler's complaint that postmodernism celebrates dissensus thereby subverting progressive ends, becomes an empirical question in Rancière's distinction.

Rancière's reference to the law in his definition of police can be taken somewhat literally, but it is more extensive than our criminological notions of the functions of contemporary policing. The law governs the distribution of the sensible through the regulation of bodies, dividing those who participate from those excluded, establishing a regime of groups, social positions, and functions: the police powers of the sovereign thought broadly. Legality is, therefore, a matrix of institutions, identities, and consciousness not unlike that studied by law and society types: it patterns social interaction in ways and places more extensive than a formal state apparatus. Indeed, academic projects, as I discuss more below, can contribute to policing.

The matrix of formal and informal institutions is vulnerable to the interruptions that emerge from within this extensive social field since "words and discourses ... freely circulate ... divert[ing] bodies from their destinations, engaging them in movements in the neighborhood of certain words: people, liberty, equality, etc." (Rancière, 2006, p. 9). Because these terms are empty and ambivalent signifiers, emergent political discourses relying upon them can shift identities in a qualitative way, articulating what Rancière calls a political surplus capable of challenging police regimes through novel demands for inclusion:

> Political subjects are surplus subjects. They inscribe the count of the uncounted as a supplement. Politics does not separate a specific sphere of political life from the other spheres. It separates the whole of the community from itself. It opposes two counts of counting it. You can count the community as the sum of its parts – of its groups and of the qualifications that each of them bears. I call this way of counting police. You can count a supplement to the sum, a part of those who have no part, which separates the community from its parts, places, functions, and qualifications. This is politics, which is not a sphere but a process. (Rancière, 2004c, p. 305)

Politics as process is, in short, more than a system for allocating values or a scheme of governance, and it is more than can be contained within the sociological idea of structure or the political analysis of power. Rather, it remains a "specific rupture in the logic ... of the 'normal' distribution of positions" (Rancière, 2001, Thesis 3), a "break ... with the tangible configuration whereby parties and parts or lack of them are defined" (Rancière, 1999, p. 29), "a dispute ... about the frame within which we see something as given" (Rancière, 2004c, p. 304). As an example, Rancière turns to labor which broke:

> the law of the police, where everybody is in his own place, with his own job and his own culture, her own body and her own forms of expression. [This] was an "aesthetic" revolution as I understand the term, an overturning of the partition of the sensuous which assigned to workers their place in (or outside of) the symbolic space of the community, in the "private" realm of production and reproduction ... . For [French workers of the nineteenth century, political] emancipation meant breaking the partition of the sensuous that determined the day as the time workers work, and night as the time they rest. The beginning of emancipation was the decision to make something more of their night: to write, read, think and discuss instead of sleeping. Emancipation first meant reframing their own existence, breaking with their workers' identity, their workers' culture, their worker's time and space ... . Emancipation ... first meant constituting themselves as aesthetic subjects, capable of this kind of "disinterested" gaze that Kant analyzes in the *Critique of Judgment*. (Rancière, 2005, p. 293)

When politics is considered a sphere of activity, as it was for Arendt, it is held "beyond any account in terms of conflict and repression, or law and violence" (Rancière, 2004c, p. 299). Yet when politics reveals a surplus by refiguring the distribution of the sensible and making aesthetic dissensus inescapable, this aesthetic distance brings law, power, and violence back into focus.

The Discipline: From Consensus to Dissensus

What type of knowledge is produced by an aesthetics that divides an immanent politics from the omnipresent police? How can Rancière's foregrounding of an aesthetic dissensus inform us about our own field, including the relationships among like-minded scholars and the relationships between scholars and the subjects of our studies? Aesthetic knowledge, for Rancière, seeks to uncover what lies unsaid within police regimes. "To speak of an aesthetic dimension of knowledge is to speak of a dimension of ignorance which divides the idea and the practice of knowledge themselves ... a pleasure disconnected from every science of ends" (Rancière, 2006, p. 1, 5).

Although this disinvestment in ends and in desires for an object can be found in reflections on art, that is not its only form. As adjective and not domain, the aesthetic emerges, as well, in reflections on society (Robson, 2006), but only where the policing power of the disciplines can be lessened by an assertion and expansion of the heresies of the unsaid.

Rancière's theory suggests a new form of gap study, one with radically different implications than those instrumentalist concerns that founded Law and Society (Macaulay, 1963; Sarat & Kearns, 1993a, 1993b), and have continued in new ways today (Marshall & Barclay, 2003). These familiar forms of gap study are projects of consensus that seek to collapse the distance between law and fact, to span, or plug gaps with disciplinary knowledge in an effort to perfect what Trubek (1990, p. 8) has called a "legally constructed domain." Closing gaps between the life of the law and the law on the books reflects an enduring scientific opposition to aesthetic dissensus; for Rancière, as for Trubek, it reenacts police even within our own scholarly projects. In an explicit argument with Pierre Bourdieu's sociological definition of a field, Rancière claims that sociology is itself a project to ensure consensus by filling gaps.

> Before being the "science of society," sociology was first historically the project of a reorganisation of society. It wanted to remake a body for this society supposedly divided by philosophical abstraction, protestant individualism and revolutionary formalism. It wanted to reconstitute the social fabric such that individuals and groups at a given place would have the *ethos*, the ways of feeling and thinking, which corresponded at once to their place and to a collective harmony. Sociology today has certainly distanced itself from this organicist vision of society. But it continues, for the benefit of science, to want what science wants for the good of society, to understand [*savoir*] the rule of correspondence between social conditions and the attitudes and judgments of those who belong to it. The scientific war against the allodoxy of judgments continues the political war against "anomie" of behavior, the war against the aesthetic and democratic unrest of the division of the body politic within itself. (Rancière, 2006, p. 7)

Rancière's point is that the normative hopes of Handler and other sociolegal scholars for a "transformative politics" depends upon closing gaps between what is known by those actors who are the object of our study, and what is known by those who study them, a closure whose costs involve a struggle against the possibility of an imaginative distance across which democratic unrest can expand. Rancière asks us to question this assumption of what constitutes an adequate politics as well as an adequate academic knowledge of the social. In effect, Rancière asks for a double gap in the possibility that everyone – scholar and subject alike – makes work a means of creating the world through a distancing, an aesthetic project that retains the gaps as a vital source of meaning.

The permanence of gaps and their impermeability to scrutiny changes the dynamics of the academic field. For Bourdieu (1987) and others influenced by him, sociolegal studies addresses the circulation of power within society by fixing people to their places and their habitus through their knowledge of the law. For Rancière, this is "the demonstration of a certain idea of knowledge – in other words, a certain idea of the rapport between knowledge and a distribution of [social] positions" (Rancière, 2006, p. 6). For Rancière, disciplines don't organize knowledge about power as much as they wage war, "a war against the claim that there is another knowledge and another ignorance than that which belongs to their condition. In other words, they must engage in a war against the war that the worker is himself fighting" (Rancière, 2006, p. 9). Rather than disciplinary knowledge, the goal for Rancière is "in-disciplinary thought" that reinstantiates the ignorance at the heart of knowledge.

Attention to aesthetic dissensus suggests several further questions for analysis of Handler's address and its subsequent treatment within the academic community. To what extent does Handler's challenge and the scholarly responses it has subsequently generated constitute a significant dissensus, dividing political projects and sociolegal scholars in commensurate ways to the politics/police distinction? How does the controversy depict and expand the gaps between ourselves as scholars and our social subjects, and in what ways does it reach for closure and a police regime? What are the implications for understanding or at least not overlooking emerging forms of politics?

Before using these questions to analyse Handler's controversy, I want to summarize four concepts from Rancière's aesthetic theory that reveal new ways of looking at academic disciplines and their relationship to social conflicts: Distance, Doubling, Mastery, and Indisciplinarity. Rancière suggests that aesthetic distance from practical concerns is not simply a pretense that symbolic violence does not exist for the sake of the sublime. Rather, aesthetic distance has the potential to reveal the kind of commitments that lay submerged within the meanings of everyday activities and their reform by hierarchies of knowledge. Ironically, it is this aesthetic distance that allows us to see that "in the aesthetic regime … art endures as art insofar as it remains fundamentally implicated in non-art, or *life*" (Hallward, 2006, p. 36). Temporally, this distancing may also be seen in the desequencing of social transformation, an emphasis on "a break in the present rather than an ideal put in the future" (Rancière, 2005, p. 292).

Doubling is a consequence of this distancing: it is the logic of dissensus mapped onto the social, the belief, against critical sociology, that the gap between a popular ignorance and elite insight (Hallward, 2006, p. 31) collapses in the recognition that all who work have the ability and practice to think creatively and constructively in opposition to social orders.

> The artist's emancipatory lesson, opposed on every count to the professor's stultifying lesson, is this: each one of us is an artist to the extent that he carries out a double process; he is not content with being a mere journeyman but wants to make all work a means of expression, and he is not content to feel something but tries to impart it to others. The artist needs equality as the explicator needs inequality. (Rancière quoted in Robson, 2006, p. 85)

To master a topic is to explicate it, to regulate dissensus by imposing inequality as the sole form of order. One form that this regulation takes is the discipline that seeks a form of consensus over knowledge. Despite an acknowledgment of pluralism, this consensus concerns a stability of places and social roles that can take an anxious form in the limitation of the political dissensus. As Žižek (2005, p. 120) has captured this, "Liberal attitudes towards the other are characterized both by respect for otherness, openness to it, and an obsessive fear of harassment. In short, the other is welcomed insofar as its presence is not intrusive, insofar as it is not really the other." Crossing this psychological limit permits the celebration of in-disciplinary thought, a challenge to all academic programs.

In the section that follows, I analyse Handler's address and its aftermath. I choose a close reading of his temporal supporters and critics, as well as the constructed meaning of his address that lives on in numerous scholarly footnotes. My argument is that Handler's challenge was muted by him and moderated by his interlocutors in such a way that a consensus about what can be experienced has come to dominate law and society and its scholarly projects. Inasmuch as this consensus over the limits of the non-scholarly imagination defines a discipline for Rancière, we should perhaps be unsurprised. How well this consensus is inclusive of the diversity of scholars, and how well it permits us to understand political movements increasingly motivated by aesthetic dissensus are two significant questions motivating the next two sections of this chapter.

Handler and the Regulation of Dissensus

> I think Joel Handler asked the right question. It is important for our scholarly research to be guided by a commitment to social justice. But I think he looked too narrowly for ways that law contributes to social justice and transformative politics … . The study of

> resistance within, by means of, and through law is of consequence for emancipatory projects. (Merry, 1995, pp. 14–23)

Sally Merry's presidential address delivered two years after Handler's own challenge sought to find room for theorists working with a constitutive notion of law that upheld "the importance of research on the cultural meanings produced by law in the habitual, possibly resistant, practices of everyday life as well as through major social movements" (1995, p. 25). Not all forms of resistance were "constructive," she cautioned, nor were all "subordinated individuals able to critique the conditions of their subordination" (1995, p. 24), lessons that she drew from analyses of recent research conducted on ethnic, gender, and indigenous identity groups. Despite the erosion of law's "heroic role as the scaffold for social justice" (1995, p. 13) in both the popular and scholarly imaginations, her talk sought to map a more hospitable territory in which cultural theory, deeply inflected by deconstructionist methods and postmodernist anti-universalism, could be subsumed within the normative commitments that Handler had espoused.

Merry's address was delivered to defuse some of the tension that emerged around Handler's piece, in part by offering a set of affirmations. Rather than acknowledge a dissensus over scholarly commitments, Merry affirmed Handler's reading of core values as social justice. She also affirmed the value of research into social struggles that was culturally inflected, subject-sceptical, and new-social-movement inspired, applying a complex and cautionary evaluation to tease out the meaningful forms of resistance from those less constructive types. By including research into emergent political areas of indigenous and ethnic identities along with the case of gender politics that had exercised Handler two years before, she also suggested that evolving groups held knowledge for all sociolegal scholars; that they could, in short, benefit from and actively advance the scholarly agenda. In bringing these groups in, some postmodern and deconstructive theory was also saved from banishment. At the same time, the discipline – understood in Rancière's terms as a project of enlightening objects of study to their subjective ends – was left snugly in place.

Some of Handler's more trenchant criticisms were left unchallenged, however. Two areas of his critique seem to evade Merry's reparation. First, Handler worried about the persistence of grand narratives among some social movements at a time when postmodern scholars were rejecting these discursive forms.

> When we look around, everyone else is operating *as if* there were Grand Narratives. In the West, we see the ideological and political sweep of liberal capitalism. Much of the

> world adheres to religious fundamentalism. Major economic powers are communal, authoritarian societies. We see the rise of ethnic nationalism. (Handler, 1992a, p. 726)

> I hear the solid, massed marching bands of capitalism, religious fundamentalism and ethnic nationalism rather than the cacophony of deconstructive reflexivity. (Handler, 1992b, p. 823)

Handler's implication in these statements was that divergent logics of action and different theories of democratic order would exacerbate the structural economic and racial inequality that threatened to undermine a progressive agenda unless some scholarly set of methodological instruments were available to harmonize these voices. These tools should be derived from something other than a tired liberalism and an obsolete Marxism, he argued. While epistemological diversity was a social fact, it need not become detrimental to the scholarly field as long as there remained a commitment to developing "an alternative vision, a vision of the economy and of the polity that will complement its vision of community" (Handler, 1992a, p. 727). If this vision had any epistemological anchoring it was "key elements of pragmatism" (Handler, 1992b, p. 820); if it had an ontological grounding, it could be located in "core concepts of human nature or human capacities that we believe in" (Handler, 1992b, p. 822).

From Rancière's perspective, Handler could be seen to champion a war on two levels that could be seen to define the discipline: first, a war against the ignorance rooted in the false and ineffective deconstruction of the world oblivious to a dimension of structural inequality and violence – a struggle that Merry contrarily believed to be advanced by some postmodernist theory; second, a war against those political forces that would exploit this imaginative vacuum in order to assert convenient and reprehensible narratives that competed against those that a critical social science of law could provide. Merry's resolution never went so far. Her address is less exercised over the structural conditions that could permit the growth of anti-progressive narratives, and more confident that study of culturally defined social movements provided the progressive impetus that was needed. Where Handler's war required a common set of methodological commitments by sociolegal scholars, Merry seems less concerned over establishing an internal police regime, but neither does she acknowledge an aesthetic dissensus that might obstruct or inhibit sociolegal theory formation.

There is a second criticism that Merry didn't address. Handler worried about a methodological fragmentation that could split social movements with significant implications for the study of and progressive responsiveness to these activists. For example, feminism was threatened by theories that questioned the possibility of generalizing about the sexes. Handler's interest was not to essentialize gender, but rather to rely on feminist scholarship to show that women's subordination revealed structural inequalities worth addressing:

> The postmodern conception of feminism argues that there is no such thing as a generic "woman" … . Such talk masks the heterogeneity of women and perpetuates the privileged position and domination of white middle-class feminists. There is a difference between sex and gender, and it is an error to focus on gender in isolation from identity. Identity is constructed by race, ethnicity, class, community, nation; it is both multiple and unstable. (Handler, 1992a, p. 706)

Similarly with legal scholarship about race that was rapidly recovering from the "trashing" of rights language advocated by Critical Legal Studies (CLS) since the mid 1980s (e.g., Dalton, 1985; Kelman, 1984; Tushnet, 1984, 1989). Handler praised the founders of Critical Race Theory (CRT), especially Patricia Williams and Harlon Dalton, who argued that African Americans were consistently positioned within structures of race relations:

> In the postmodern tradition, Williams acknowledges the richness of ethnic and political diversity; nevertheless, [she writes,] "I do believe … that the simple matter of the color of one's skin so profoundly affects the way one is treated, so radically shapes what one is allowed to think and feel about this society, that the decision to generalize from this division is valid." (Williams quoted in Handler, 1992a, p. 708)

While the experiences of African Americans were distinctive and could require and explain an anti-trashing regard for rights language, the structural reality of racism provided a common bridge to the relevance of law and society scholarship. As Regina Austin argued in defense of Handler's position, "blacks have to be suspicious of any narrative that denies the existence of 'Grand Narratives,' given that white supremacy still constrains the lives of most of us" (1992 , p. 752). For Handler, there was no epistemological barrier installed by CRT despite the culturally unique circumstances that informed its critique.

Handler's position was ambivalent from the perspective of Rancière's advocacy of doubling. Social movements such as those for racial justice and women's equality could produce distinctive knowledges about the world, but they nonetheless shared a common knowledge of structural inequality able to uphold the value of rights and cohere the normative and epistemological commitments of sociolegal studies to advance social movement research. In other words, while the knowledge produced by academics associated with social movements threatened aesthetic dissensus, their discovery of common structural inequalities reaffirmed an academic consensus for Handler. And this consensus was, in part, realized in the perspectives developed about law. Where CLS dove too far into the realist and deconstructive scepticism about rights, valued forms of feminism and CRT, for Handler, placed law in the context of "full dimensions of ... subordination[;] full historical, ubiquitous, structural manifestations" (Handler, 1992a, pp. 707, 709–710). By resuscitating law as one dimension of the common critical enterprise, this affirmed law as a marker of a police regime at the same time as it rejected the implications of an equality that sought "not so much to unify as to declassify, to undo the supposed naturalness of order and replace it with controversial figures of division" (Rancière, 1995, pp. 32–33).

Merry's address never seemed as motivated by Handler's anxiety over division and separatism, but both missed what was soon apparent: that the Law and Society Association had already reached a high point of participatory pluralism. Although the first Critical Race conference was held in 1989, it wasn't long before critical race scholars began to drift away from or cease participating in Law and Society Association conferences much as CLS had done in the 1980s. And these divisions rapidly multiplied. The LatCrit conference was initiated in 1996 and the Critical Race Feminism conferences began in the mid 1990s following the embryonic meeting of the Women of Color in the Law in 1988. Soon AsianCrit (Chang, 1999), QueerCrit, and Critical White Studies added more scholars organized around the production of "outsider jurisprudence" (Matsuda, 1989) or "out-crit" (Valdes, 1999). These academic venues were peopled mostly by minority scholars and their founding histories reveal the importance of breaking the silence they experienced as academics in predominantly white institutions and the internalized oppression they faced (Hutchinson, 2004; Padilla, 2001, p. 101 and ff.; Smith, 2000, p. 1128 and ff.).[3] These histories also reveal the silence of white radicals within the academy (commonly understood to be CLS advocates) who avoided "the role of deep-seated racism in American life" (West, 1995, p. xi) and ignored other forms of subordination. Their theories "presented a conception of law different from any other – a conception so complete and unique that it comprised a new jurisprudence" (Matsuda, 1996, p. 48). This uniqueness was often reproduced through autobiographical method (Lawrence, 1987; Montoya, 1994; Schur, 2002) that sharply distinguished the social contexts of its practitioners, and perpetuated by separate meetings, distinctive languages, and forms of exchange that constituted distinct "counterpublics" (Warner, 2002). In short, progressive scholarly exchange was fragmenting not only at the level of theory, but also among and between distinctive scholarly communities.

Handler's address was commented upon extensively in the pages of the LSR, and most of his published respondents resisted the threat of distinctive counterpublics oriented in opposition to sociolegal scholars by rebuilding consensus. For Kitty Calavita and Carroll Seron (1992, p. 769), Handler was a siren against the postmodern loss of "sight of the polity and economy, macro-forces that inexorably both shape the parameters within which our lives are lived and trigger or limit social change." This loss of sight – a reminder of what is visible within the distribution of the sensible – was also a vital loss of the sociological imagination itself, as their published title suggested, an explicit reference to C. Wright Mills' (1959) concept of a difficult and rare linkage of lived lives to what he called "the larger historical scene." Many later citations to Handler's address narrow to just this warning: that postmodern theory is incompatible with macro-sociological change by underestimating social structures (Buchanan, 1996, p. 73; Burns, 2005, p. 284; Buss, 1999, p. 966; Carle, 2005, p. 342), ignoring social institutions (Stark, 2001, p. 51), dissolving a moral grounding for transformative action (Winter, 1994, p. 3), or dismissing coherent sociological visions (Southworth, 1999, p. 247). In these dominant readings, Handler is a romantic with a "nostalgic call for renewed optimism in instrumental approaches and large-scale social transformation" (Buchanan, 1996, p. 1005; see also McCann, 1992, p. 740). Romanticism's genealogy in nineteenth century rejections of the atomization observed in modernity was reproduced by Handler's implied advocacy of a progressive separation from anomic and melancholic movements.

Other commentators interpreted Handler's position in more subtle terms. Patty Ewick (1992) argued that Handler had ignored the possibility that postmodern theory signalled a change in the material condition of social life at the same time that he projected the immaterial possibility of a strategic choice to reject its limitations, a melancholic moment of his own. This was, if inadvertently, an aesthetic moment: an identification of the poetic possibilities of knowledge, the projection of Handler as a Kantian. Nonetheless, the window closed in the reduction of the poetic to power capable of closing this gap. If postmodern theory were epiphenomenal to economic relations, it could promote social understanding between theorist and agent, culminating in new approaches to Handler's own interests in "challenging and unsettling power" (p. 762; see also Gilliom, 2001, p. 163).

In like ways, Michael McCann charged Handler with having avoided the epistemological challenges brought by "the fundamental reorientation to power that has influenced so much contemporary political analysis" (1992, p. 734). Far from an epistemological break threatening the association of theorists, McCann stressed that new elements of power relations retained an evolutionary continuity to previous relations revealed by empirical studies of social movements. Old and new-social movements were not as disaggregated as Handler feared [and as others have subsequently interpreted Handler's address to substantiate (e.g., Cummings & Eagly, 2001, p. 486; Harris, 1994, p. 79)] since differences in form could be attributed to variation among long-term institutions (McCann, p. 739) and a national political culture that always valued "locally oriented, voluntaristic, pluralistic, pragmatic, issue-oriented reform politics lacking in radical visionary design, lacking in class (or other broad group) orientation, and lacking faith in a centralized state – all of which are the target of Handler's rebuke" (p. 735). McCann agreed with Handler, however, that scholarly theorizing of contemporary politics emerging from social movements was weak, inattentive to class and race, and ultimately uninspiring. His solution differed from Handler's call to the faithful: "our intellectual praxis must be informed by our own practical experience as well as by the experiences of subjugated others who are subjects in our research … . Here I think new scholarship about everyday struggles is on the right path" (p. 747).

McCann has since become one of the most significant social movement scholars in sociolegal studies, his book, *Rights at work* (1994), elevated to a modern classic within the field. Central to McCann's argument in that book as well as in his response to Handler is the idea that the empirical study of legal consciousness reveals both an aspirational and tactical politics that compounds institutionally into valuable forms of resistance. Although I will have more to say about legal consciousness studies later, what is valuable now is to acknowledge the way that McCann's position resolves Handler's concern about political disengagement by revealing the common institutional and legal threads suturing social movement activism to scholarly invention. McCann both underscores the potential for aesthetic dissensus and immediately resolves it through a constitutive theory of law privileging academic accessibility and responsibility, e.g., "recent micro-studies of resistance hold the potential of contributing new insights regarding how, when and where progressive politics might flourish in contemporary society" (McCann, 1992, p. 743). From Rancière's point of view, McCann's role within the law and society association, and the flourishing of a legal consciousness literature since (Engel & Munger, 2003; Ewick & Silbey, 1998) might be seen as the linchpin securing a discipline devoted to enforcing consensus.

One manner of waging consensus that Rancière has noted is through the deployment of temporalizing narratives. He writes, "The idea of modernity would like there to be only one meaning and direction in history, whereas the temporality specific to the aesthetic regime … is a co-presence of heterogeneous temporalities" (Rancière, 2004b, p. 26). Allan Hutchinson's criticism of Handler's address follows this notion, focusing on Handler's commitment to the *longue durée* that he saw paralleling Fukuyama's (1992) reactionary, Hegelian, end-of-history thesis. Both were "members of the same philosophical family" (Hutchinson, 1992, p. 776) because they adhered to some idea of history as grand narrative. And, more like siblings than distant cousins, they also shared a commitment to a temporality expressed at the micro-level: "When people take to the streets of Johannesburg, Prague, Beijing, Moscow, Timisoara, Frankfurt, or Los Angelus, they are rarely motivated by any particular or perfected plans for social renovation" (Hutchinson, 1992, p. 777). In a similar vein, Ewick challenged the rationalistic theoretical assumptions ascribed to Handler and other sociologists of social movements such as Gusfield and Tilly that "consist[] of determining the presence or absence of this thing called consciousness and systematically identifying the mechanisms that lead to its 'awakening'" (1992, p. 760). Both Ewick and McCann defended some aspects of the "stories of subversion" that Handler had derided as so much flatulence (Handler, 1992a, p. 727). Nonetheless, McCann, Ewick, and Hutchinson all return to the value of small-scale protest – and with it, the postmodern theoretical alternatives – expressed in the "generat[ion of] collective engagement" (Hutchinson, 1992, p. 779), a redemption of a linearity appealing to critically self-identified scholars.

Steven Winter's critique of Handler was, perhaps, the most willing to refuse these redemptive measures, suggesting that the postmodern critique raised significant doubts about the stability of the subject and the reinscription of "a rationalist distinction between discourse and action" (Winter, 1992, p. 800). He understood the implications of this insight to go far beyond the empirical study of social movements by moving inwards and revealing the contingent and performative dimensions of academic life (p. 797) that constrain the production of knowledge:

> The problem with Handler and others of his ilk is that they invariably situate themselves outside (if not, indeed, above) the social field that postmodernism seeks to interrogate. Thus, they never once pause to consider that what postmodernism has to say about prefiguration, the decentering of the subject, or the privileging of one's normative commitments might conceivably apply to them. Not surprisingly, this makes meaningful dialogue virtually impossible. (Winter, 1992, p. 801)

If postmodern thought offers a new way to see one's own aesthetic commitments from a new vantage point as Winter suggests, it threatens a much more significant breach in academic discourse.

Handler's *Reply* does shirk the value of dialogue ("postmodern politics … I believe is going nowhere," he declares (1992b, p. 823)) but also subtly acquiesces to the performative analysis of scholarly life, a significant aesthetic distancing about which little notice is taken by his subsequent champions or detractors. Handler argues,

> I don't think I disagree with Ewick or McCann's analysis of the dialectic between individual acts and collective behavior. It is a tricky question as to when people come to believe that they can fight city hall. It is also a very open question as to when social movements take hold, when certain ideas seize the historical moment. But I am talking about the *scholars* of resistance – what choices *they* are making … . My point … is not to debate the ontology of human agency. My point is that we must begin. (821, 3 additional emphasis mine)

If this imperative of scholarly choice can be read as the existential fate of a critical scholar-subject – one aware of, though unwilling to interrogate, the performative dimensions of one's own profession: "Well, what are we here for?" as Stewart Macaulay (1992, p. 829) colloquially verbalized it in his postscript – it can just as easily be read as a form of empirical detachment. Although movements "out there" may create new aesthetic forms in which to conceive the political and, so, interrupt police regimes, Handler seems to suggest that it is the critical will to build narratives attentive to progress and concerned with social structure that will restore an academic consensus. The imperative *to begin* transcends doubt and difference; politics – even academic politics – is reduced to the grand narrative even when history reveals nothing so certain than dissensus.

Regina Austin's short response to Handler is the best amplification of his position (one that lives on in citational memory (Harris, 1994, p. 23; Padilla, 2001, p. 79; Valdes, 1996, p. 24)). Postmodernism offers a significant cultural set of idioms, she suggests, but the overriding concern for African Americans is the construction of viable communities that condition its limits, ruling out the free flow of multiple subjectivities, or the suspicion of grand narratives. Blacks, she argues, embrace essentialism strategically, but the black public sphere eschews "one overriding credo" (1992, p. 752). This political pragmatism opens public culture to academic influence, and some of the blame for failures of community development

> can be laid at the feet of academics who have given themselves over to the immaterial disabling reflectivity Handler identifies with postmodernism. First and foremost, there is no economic game plan for poor black communities. Both the antiwhite vitriolics of the strident Afrocentrists and the equal-share begging to the integrationists are beside the point. We particularly need a plan because the absence of material hope has produced a social and moral vacuum that is swallowing up our young. At the same time, however,

> too many black elites are solidifying their own positions by decrying the moral degeneracy of the black urban poor without painting a fair and realistic picture of their suffocating life chances. (Austin, 1992, pp. 752–753)

Austin's argument that too many African Americans have been abandoned by both local elites and academic theory suggested a trajectory for critical academics: "they need to go 'home' every once in awhile" (p. 754) in order to revitalize institutions, alleviate material suffering, revivify black activism, and seed economic development. Handler, too, wants academics to understand and respond to this compulsion of home as an ethical lever and a professional guide, a home revealed in and anchored to progressive stories of collective action (Handler, 1992a, p. 717 and ff.). Rancière suggests that "before recalling law, morality or value, *ethos* indicates the abode. Further, it indicates the way of being which corresponds to this abode, the way of feeling and thinking which belongs to whoever occupies any given place" (2006, p. 5). Figuratively, these homes are doubled, as much the homes of our subjects as they are the home of progressive scholars attentive to these other quarters. Such a home may be Madison, the progressive, intellectual, and the real – if fading – home to the Law and Society Association, a home immortalized in collective memories of The Ice Cream Social (Trubek, 1990, p. 1) and the individual memories of the still-productive founders and the many diasporic scholars who once studied there. In anchoring scholar and subject to a place, the lure of home that Handler, Austin, and other critics compel is the end of aesthetics.

Scholars and Subjects

Handler's rejection of postmodernism appears aesthetically as an effort to retain a scholarly community involved in championing and developing progressive scholarly narratives, a liaison maintained in the effort to create "a reliable guide for transformative politics" (Handler, 1992a, p. 723). Many of his commentators as well as subsequent citations to his address interpret his provocation in this fashion. Even those who argue that postmodern theory can offer this guidance agree that this activist goal is what our scholarship ultimately should be about. For Rancière, this shared normative expectation is sufficient to call ourselves a discipline, especially because it rests upon a commitment to resist and reject a politics about the given place in which non-academic actors find themselves, to insist as a form of regulating the distribution of the sensible that it is the scholars of resistance who must be called home, if only to help call home those who seek a political transformation.

The assurance of a linkage between scholar and subject has been, as Rancière argues, a necessary part of the academic enterprise, and the aesthetic critique designed to make these connections stand out in stark relief. These bridges between scholar and subject have been made most explicit during public occasions for law and society stock-taking (e.g., Engel, 1999; Merry, 1995; Seron, 2002). Although there has been a long and diverse history of the law and society movement, these liaisons have often been seen as strongest when the association

> has identified with the dispossessed and the marginal in American life. It has recognized that America harbors racism, sexism, and elitism. It has favored civil rights, supported efforts to eradicate poverty, and challenged patriarchal relationships. It has tried, at times, to speak for those marginal groups and interests in our society who lack a voice in the "higher" culture of law and social science. (Trubek, 1990, p. 54)

Speaking for the socially marginal has been a conceptual project that has defined and refined scholarly tools that *police* this task. Where gap studies once promised both an empirical, objective knowledge about law as well as an implicit call for progressive reform based on the appropriate narrowing of the gap, the linkage between intellectual and society was modulated by the centripetal pull of policy makers and bureaucrats and their own forms of statist rationality that did not always deliver the goods (Sarat & Silbey, 1988). Handler reaffirmed the criticism of both empiricism and policy studies that had been steadily growing from within the law and society mainstream (Macaulay, 1984; Silbey & Sarat, 1988) and he challenged the centrifugal implications of CLS and postmodern theory in order to preserve a progressive meaning to the study of law in the interests of the dispossessed.

Handler asked for a methodological consensus in order to preserve a progressive political tradition, and as I have suggested, even those most immediately involved in the disputes over his address often provided it. Today, several influential projects within sociolegal studies continue to reproduce it (while reducing the threat posed by the continuing development of postmodern legal studies). I see these as central progressive projects as they are used to absorb and train many politically progressive sociolegal scholars and because they modulate the threat of aesthetic dissensus inherent within what Scheingold (2004, p. xxii) has recently called "radical decentering" approaches to law and society. This radical reformulation replaces sociolegal models that stress a symmetry of state/society from which to imagine bottom-up or top-down inquiries into legal meanings, with an asymmetric, constitutive model marked by the "interpenetration of multiple levels of legality" as well as the "imbrication" of law into social practices and consciousness (Scheingold, 2004 citing Sarat, 1993). In the study of social movements, radical decentering may become radical detachment, loosened from the policing character of the law. As Silverstein (1996, p. 8) suggests, "people do not simply absorb legal meaning into their consciousness. Incorporating legal meaning into thought and action involves reconstruction of legal meaning." It is this "imagination and recreation" of legal meaning that has sometimes even dissolved some aspects of a progressive legal imagination for sexual minorities (Bower, 1994; Butler, 1993; Stychin, 1998; Warner, 1999) or for indigenous people (Milner & Goldberg-Hiller, 2008) and others (Cooper, 1998). Against this dissolution – Handler's threat of postmodernism, Rancière's championing of aesthetic dissensus – these projects stabilize the possibility of progressive knowledge for the academy.

I turn to a very brief discussion of these projects before addressing one of the more challenging dimensions of the field – the conservative and other types of countermobilization of the past decade, and our sociolegal attention to it. My goal is not to be detailed in the short space I have, but rather synoptic, examining the ways in which these projects manage dissensus. I ask what these projects do for the society of legal researchers and for what their relationship to non-academic actors is imagined to be. The case of countermobilization raises anew the importance of dissensus, and I ask in conclusion what we may have to gain were we to fear this less. Handler's insistence that it is *scholars* we should worry about is my minder.

Method and Mind

The study of legal consciousness and legal mobilization may be seen as separate projects, but they both share an interest in the ways that practices – including such purely conceptual practices such as autobiography (Engel & Munger, 2003) – create and incorporate legal meanings and they both inform the other about social conflict. Both types of studies also stress the significance of pulling order from the fragmentary jumble of common sense, what Gramsci called the "chaotic aggregate of disparate conceptions [in which] one can find … anything that one likes" (Gramsci, 1971, p. 422). Where legal mobilization studies now focus more on collective action than on the individual mobilization of law for political (Zemans, 1983) or for disputing (Bumiller, 1988) reasons, many studies of legal consciousness also privilege collective understandings such as the construction of social and political identities. And both operate against a backdrop of more conservative and radical theories arguing that legal institutions (Klare, 1978; Rosenberg, 1991) and rights consciousness (Feinman & Gabel, 1990; Glendon, 1991) are impotent or retard effective social institutions, or, alternatively, are mere byproducts of more significant political dynamics (Dudziak, 2000; Johnson, 2003).

Recent studies of legal mobilization critically examine the reproduction and successes of rights advocacy with the understanding that "legal norms and discourses derive their meaning primarily through the practical forms of activity in which they are developed and expressed" (McCann, 1994, pp. 261–262). This meaning is seen to be conducive to social alliance, and therefore facilitative of group conflict (Milner, 1986; Scheingold, 2004; Silverstein, 1996; Stychin, 1998). Legal meaning is therefore not precise and definitive in these studies, but rather contingently mapped onto wider social textures and dependent on divergent experiences with and beliefs about rights as well as the "inclinations, tactical skills, and resources of the contending parties who mobilize judicial endowments" (McCann, 1994, p. 170). Legal consciousness emerges in this theory as "variable, volatile, complex and contradictory" (McCann, 1994, p. 8). Nonetheless, it is disciplined by collective dimensions of political struggle and rendered pliable by emerging forms of social relations (Milner & Goldberg-Hiller, 2002) as well as recognition by formal legal institutions (Goldberg-Hiller, 2002; McCann, 1994).

Legal mobilization studies are said to contribute to a progressive agenda by assessing the potentialities for collective action produced by litigation and within legal culture. Influential scholars such as McCann and Charles Epp (1998) rely upon resource mobilization theory (Zald & McCarthy, 1979) that links these potentialities to such concerns as favourable rules, the availability of lawyers, money and community ideologies, bringing the study of collective action into explicit alignment with the study of social and political structures of opportunity. Law is understood as both resource and constraint, operating constitutively in both direct ways (legal rulings) as well as indirect and pluralistic pathways of inspiration, public support, and tactical multiplication. Resource mobilization theory supplants older conceptions of protest actions as deviant and marginal in part by stressing an autonomous rationality that "only appears unstructured when set against the dominant norms of the social order and against the interests which that order wishes to maintain" (Melucci, 1996, p. 18).

The study of legal mobilization accomplishes several aesthetic tasks for the progressive scholar. It polices aesthetic dissensus by projecting a field of rationality that suppresses the significance of ideologies that might defeat comparative analysis. The most sophisticated of these works also pay particular attention to the developmental lifecycle of movements whose regularized patterns – from movement building to engagement with policy, etc. – stage the analysis of legal impact while forging a consistency to legal consciousness over which the scholar gains a sophistication and mastery. This progressive chronology works as a "delimitation of spaces and time" (Rancière, 2004b, p. 13), privileging order against spontaneity in "the place and the stakes of politics as a form of experience" (*ibid.*). Perhaps the most significant regulation of aesthetic dissensus in the name of progressive ends has been the decision to study groups already understood to be progressive, generalizing an implicit model developed from the civil rights movement. These patterns of inquiry allow us to avoid asking ourselves whether the production of new ideas takes incongruous pathways, and they may hide from us how disparate movements may borrow ideas from each other [such as exchanges between the Christian right and queer activists (Patton, 1997)]. We also avoid asking questions that do not diverge from this policing logic, questions that might be designed "to unsettle prevailing logics, to 'unthink' the law, and to ask the unaskable, which is why … do we strive to maintain law as we know it at all?" (Darian-Smith, 1998, p. 117). My point is not to argue that these are the central questions that must be pursued, but instead to merely point out some of the ways that we have accommodated ourselves to inquiries over which we maintain some conceptual control, a mastery that composes part of our commitments to being progressive scholars.

Consciousness studies that don't foreground the study of collective action also structure inquiry to minimize the possibility of dissensus. Collected narratives about legal disputes or more-diffuse legal encounters reveal an ambivalence about law and a distance of law from everyday events. From this perspective, law seems an "emergent feature of social relations" (Ewick & Silbey, 1998, p. 17) leaving "us all legal agents insofar as we actively make law, even when no formal legal agent is involved" (p. 20). As agents think and act, law is understood as necessarily pluralistic. These literatures manage this pluralism in several ways. Ewick and Silbey analyse various narrative styles that position law as exterior to everyday life, as a tactical terrain on which strategic choices can be wagered, and as an arbitrary enemy that people oppose, trick, and mimic. These schemas are shown to be mutually interdependent, ideal, and practical, constitutive aspects that lead to law's hegemonic power. Power and resistance become their major focus, but so are the dignity and integrity of those people who tell these stories, as well as the social structures that archetypically exemplify these narrative forms (p. 248). The effort to dignify our subjects and place them within meaningful relationships to power is an important progressive ethic (Herzog, 2002; Lévinas, 1999). Nonetheless it also risks normalization by reconstituting subjects who are "home" within police regimes (Mufti, 2003) or whose dignity is understood to be expressed within small subversive acts rather than the more transformative events comprising aesthetic politics.

Studies of cause lawyering – a third consensus-building project – rarely transcend the limits of social movement or consciousness studies. The framework of cause lawyer studies explores the boundary between professional knowledge of law and political action (McCann, 1994; Sarat & Scheingold, 1997, 2005, 2006; Scheingold & Sarat, 2004). Originating from efforts to study the public interest of the bar that transcends its duties to a frequently elite clientele (Sarat & Scheingold, 1998, p. 4), and inspired by the historical successes of the Legal Defense Fund of the NAACP that demonstrated the role of lawyers in progressive social change, the study of cause lawyering has explored the ways that legal professionals create contexts for legal consciousness and legal action (McCann & Silverstein, 1998; Milner, 1986). Studies of cause lawyering extend the resource mobilization framework by foregrounding lawyers as a critical resource, and further legal consciousness research by examining the strategic choices made by clients as well as lawyers to rely upon legal action.

Although the study of cause lawyers reveal the oftentimes ambivalent professional and personal ideologies in which lawyers work, including the precarious public image of the profession that has provoked some pro bono and activist practice, the study of aesthetic dissensus is deemphasized through several techniques. Borrowing from sophisticated legal mobilization studies, empirical regularities and patterns are found in the stages of social movement development to which cause lawyers contribute (Sarat & Scheingold, 2006, Section 1). Despite critical, poststructural, conceptions of cause lawyering in which lawyers and clients learn from one another and "conspire together" (López, 1992 quoted in Sarat & Scheingold, 1998, p. 9), studies of cause lawyering remain predominantly top–down in their attention to professional actors (Krishnan, 2006), one way in which consensus is retained. Where studies have expanded to include conservative cause lawyers (Den Dulk, 2006; Heinz, Paik, & Southworth, 2003; Southworth, 2005), patterns of persuasion, despite the greater proximity of elite interests to supportive doctrine and antipathy between evangelical and economic constituencies nonetheless reveal little that is unique: "conservative counter-mobilization, although politically at odds with egalitarian evocations of the politics of rights, seems analytically indistinguishable from them" (Sarat & Scheingold, 2006, p. 8).

Countermobilization

Handler's motivation for progressive sociolegal scholarship cited concerns for an emerging fundamentalism that he saw on the political horizon in 1992, and expressed an anxiety over the destruction of the rule of law that such politics would bring. I, too, began to react to this mobilization and to study it as it emerged in Hawai'i and internationally over the issue of same-sex marriage. In this section, I draw on a more personal account of this research in order to highlight the significance of a greater appreciation of aesthetic dissensus. In the conclusion, I draw these implications out more generally for the discipline.

The emergence of a series of anti-gay constitutional amendments in Oregon at the time of Handler's address (Tedesco, 2002), Colorado's Amendment 2 preventing local anti-discrimination ordinances from redressing gay and lesbian complaints (Goldberg, 1994), and the political eruption over the Hawai'i high court's ruling for same-sex plaintiffs seeking marriage licenses in 1993 highlighted the rhetorical power of the accusation of special rights (Benjamin, 1996; Schacter, 1994). As the common organizing slogan for conservative opponents of gay rights, "equal rights, not special rights" appeared to transform the political imagination in some complicated ways and with it the sociolegal dynamics that I had learned and taught. For one, it was apparent that there were emergent social movements whose public rhetoric was opposed to progressive ideals of rights, even though they were clearly mobilizing rights to their political end. These groups could not easily be seen to seek to "fulfill basic needs and interests of disadvantaged citizen groups" (McCann, 1994, p. 93) as had other groups in the civil rights tradition studied by sociolegal scholars. While the use of special rights could potentially be illuminated with resource mobilization theory chosen to emphasize and assess law as tactic, the mobilization *against* rights seemed in many ways to be incompatible with the aspirational ideals of rights, as well as the resources and constraints about their mobilization that such theory considered significant.

Second, it appeared that the ultimate value of mobilizing rights language to these groups stemmed from the ways in which legal discourse could transform the playing field for others, raising the political costs of blaming, claiming, and litigating. Rights were not totally external to these organizations; although rights rhetoric could provide a coordinating resource for these organizations, many of the activists relied upon more religious ideologies in their internal communication, revealing the tactical quality of rights languages. The juxtaposition of equal rights with special rights did something else, however. Special rights language seemed to imagine and project an alternative, non-legal set of social positions and institutions in order to reassert social hierarchies: sometimes religious, often times familial and national. Thus, where special rights denigrated some legal arguments, the express contrast with equal rights valorized a "space" that was remarkably dissimilar to that projected by progressive social movements (Goldberg-Hiller & Milner, 2003). In the name of equal rights, these groups opposed the power of courts, attacked judicial activism, and denigrated progressive rights mobilization, incongruously imagining themselves as victims who were the authentic inheritors of an equality discourse, the new model for civil rights subjects. The rhetoric of equal rights buttressed the political value of rights, to be sure, but it did so on the condition that sexual minorities be seen to already have sufficient rights. As gay rights were seen to be excessive in this accounting, rights were materialized and the cost of inclusion as a legal subject seen to be more a zero-sum matter than a matter for political recognition.

As the resonance of this discourse expanded to produce some of the largest electoral majorities this country has recently seen, leading to constitutional changes in dozens of states, it became clear that the political imagination expressed in the public claims of these opponents was unusually productive. Other scholars pointed out that post-civil-rights countermobilization was expanding to include indigenous rights, environmental politics, affirmative action, and immigration rights, as well as a resurgent anti-abortion politics (Balkin, 2004; Dudas, 2004). Perhaps this conservative alternative has always been lurking within and besides more progressive traditions of legal mobilizations (Smith, 1997), linked to republican ideals of "restrained citizenship" (Kann, 1991) or communitarian norms (Engel, 1994). But if it is immanent, how might we account for it, and how assure ourselves as scholars that the knowledge we pursue of conservative forms of legal mobilization may be assimilable to Handler's progressive ends? Scheingold has recently argued that despite its contrary political valence, the conservative countermobilization of rights is "analytically indistinguishable" (2004, p. xxxiv) from the politics of rights, that the two forms are "dialectically entangled" (p. xxxv), implying that this is a new set of movements with similar possibilities for knowledge as the old.

In some ways, Scheingold is right. The dialectical entanglement is revealed in the ways that some conservatives today understand themselves to be victims and hence legitimate subjects of civil rights protection. Their deployment of rights discourse can be seen to position subjects, give them a home, and fix them a place located by the scholarly and judicial imaginations. But, in other ways, Scheingold's language may not sufficiently acknowledge the ways in which a different imagination about the rule of law and its limits has taken hold. The newer forms of conservative countermobilizations oppose "activist judges" and "legal excess," emphasizing the limited capacities of states, political economies, and societal institutions to continue the pluralist division of space on the basis of legal right (Currah, 1997; Herman, 1994, p. 112 and ff., 1997, pp. 28–59; Patton, 1995, 1997). The concomitant rejection of a temporal progress within the law and a reformulation of the spaces that rights occupy effectively draws a social and political enclosure with rights languages. This field is reinforced through many rhetorical mechanisms, including an emphasis on authenticity that militates against conceptual novelties (e.g., it helps distinguish "real marriage" from the ersatz) while disturbing the basis for analogical reasoning intrinsic to civil rights talk (Richards, 1999). It can also be seen in the reactions against and fear of international precedent and human rights discourse cited in several recent high-profile court cases[4] that simultaneously expand the ambit of national concern and dissolve the centrality of the nation for legal authority.

The conservative imagination invents new ideas of citizenship within the political and sovereign enclosures that it frames distinguishing a proper forum for political speech. At the same time, it also expresses the value of silence by carving exceptions to the use of political institutions such as courts that can compel the unpracticed defense of social privilege. In this regard, these countermobilizations are brought into alignment with increasingly visible exceptions to the law exemplified by executive determination of the legal status of detainees and other political phenomena (Agamben, 2005; Butler, 2004; Feldman, 2004; Hussain & Sarat, 2006; Sarat, Douglas, & Umphrey, 2005b). The Schmittian perspectives that animate these studies often tend to erase and efface politics in their theoretical attention to sovereign and biopolitical needs, once again leaving us unattentive to dissensus.

Rancière does offer an alternative. His emphasis on aesthetic dissensus suggests that we might usefully exploit the ways that rights always have an undecided character about them, able to reinstitute new limits to space and time, visibility and invisibility, speech and noise that constitutes the distribution of the sensible:

> Rights are not a kind of absolute … They are inscriptions of the *demos*, an inscription of the part of those who have no part. As such, they are always litigious, oriented toward staging conflict in the process of verification. There is a basic uncertainty about what and whom rights include. The act of political subjects is to build such or such case for the verification of their extension and their comprehension … As I view it, the gap between

> "man" and "citizen" is not the mark of illusion. It is an interval where political subjects can act and put rights to the test. (2005, pp. 288–289)

When the struggle for "verification" uses rights, it aims for the "empty names of subjects" (p. 289), signalling a dissensus over who should be counted. In special rights discourse, this is illustrated by the busy investment in "equal rights" that is designed to unsettle previous conceptions, to disturb taken-for-granted lines separating public and private, to renegotiate them. It is a "disidentifying moment that shifts from an identity or an entity as a worker, as a woman, as a black, to a space of subjectification of the uncounted that is open to anyone" (p. 290).

Rancière's concept of aesthetic dissensus that opens into this undecided and democratic moment has not yet been applied by him to conservative movements; the manner in which equality stages a universalizing politics in the gap between man and citizen may pose some of the most acute problems for his own political leanings. But his aesthetics makes a point for progressive sociolegal scholars: until we can account for these divergent aesthetic worlds and recognize the powerful forms of aesthetic dissensus caught up in the volatility of equality, we may never be able to understand the forms of resistance around us or recognize their full potentials.

CONCLUSION

My suspicion is that we progressive scholars have more to gain by assuming a larger degree of aesthetic dissensus rather than trying to methodologically control or eliminate its vestiges. That gain, as Handler reminds us, really ought to be directed at ourselves as scholars as much as it may renew a place for aesthetics in our understanding of the interactions of law and society. There are at least three ways in which we might go about this in order to enrich our conceptions of our scholarly object as well as regain a firmer understanding of our own commitments to progressive ends as scholars.

First, we can embrace new methods that allow us to explore the territory of aesthetic dissensus. Cultural studies is one way that we can embrace the aesthetic dimension of legality, and we have significant works with which to begin to understand Western cultural production as well as its postcolonial variants (Merry, 2000; Sarat, Douglas, & Umphrey, 2005a; Sarat & Simon, 2003). Judging from the ways that scholars have come to see the compounding effects of resistance through some of these studies – e.g., the impact that native Hawaiian postcolonial reconstructions of rights have had in Hawai'i (Merry & Brenneis, 2004; Milner & Goldberg-Hiller, 2008) – Handler's fears of depoliticization by aesthetic postmodernism seem to have decreasing resonance. Nor do all studies of aesthetic dissensus demand postmodern genealogies. Engel and Munger's (2003) participatory methodological interest in letting their subjects react to their scholarly interpretations about legal consciousness borrows ideas from feminism, ethnomethodology, and some native studies in an effort to highlight and revivify the positions and connections between scholar and subject. More than just a sensitivity to power, this co-production of knowledge assumes the divergent worlds in which each operate and strives for an ambivalent resolution. Heyer's (forthcoming) review of Engel and Munger's book goes even further, suggesting a new avenue for sociolegal scholarship of social movements. In an implicit recognition of the significance of aesthetic dissensus, she reads their work on legal consciousness from the perspective of disability studies, examining the divergent ways that each field distinctively constructs issues of identity, ontology, and political action. This conversation offers insights of relevance to disability activists and people with disabilities, as much as it forces self-reflection for law and society scholars, transcending disciplinary boundaries. She argues that

> life stories of experiences with disability, rights, and identity also point to ways that thinking about disability rights can have transformative potential beyond disciplinary boundaries. Thinking about disability discrimination at the workplace, for example, illuminates taken for granted assumptions about workplace norms, such as working hours, qualifications, and spaces. What elements in a job description, for example, are truly the "essential functions" of a job, and which ones arise from tradition, habit, and comfort of the known? ... Thinking about disability rights and the ADA can inspire both sociolegal and disability scholarship to ponder larger assumptions about how we work, how we teach and learn, and the role of rights in both.

Second, as Heyer suggests, divergent understandings of the life of the law have important implications for our own identities as scholars, forcing us to question where it is that we are at home, and what this locus of enunciation requires of us as well as how it limits our rationality. In this very sense, Handler's challenge to progressive law and society scholars echoes as an important reminder of our ethical duties. Handler was, I think, too quick in his rejection of postmodern methods, and the rise of conservative counter-mobilization, indigenous rights activism, disability activism, and other new forms in which rights are imagined and put to work suggests that perhaps the gauntlet against new methods should not be thrown so hastily. Nonetheless, it should be thrown now and then. One is hard pressed to find post-Handler pieces examining the state of the sociolegal field (but see

Macaulay, 2005; Sarat, 1998). If disciplinary knowledge aims, as Rancière suggests, to wage a war of sorts on the imaginations of our subjects, we must certainly be better off aware and self-conscious of our impulses. If we are to seek progressive ends – to wage a war *with* those we study against their subordination – then we had better seek, now and then, a knowledge of limits within our own scholarship on the way to an expanded imagination about our role in the world.

Finally, we must heed the ways that our own scholarship has narrowed itself in ways that separate those progressive scholars who should be seen as fellow travellers. Žižek's earlier-recounted fear that an openness to the other nonetheless risks anxiety over their new-found proximity must be a goad to reconnect with those no longer sensing a welcome at the Law and Society Association meetings. LatCrit, e.g., quickly embraced aesthetic dissensus in its recognition of divergent ways of interpreting legal meaning. Borrowing from Latina/o experience in the southwest United States where lives were defined by the interwoven spaces of the border, the community of LatCrit scholars embraced the importance of the borderlands (Ansley, 2001; Anzaldua, 1999; Broad, 2001) and of the religious imagination (Montoya, 1998) in an effort to avoid essentialist accounts of Latina/o experience. For LatCrit theorists, the mutual implications of language, religion, family life and sexuality, internationalism, race, poverty, and the like have all become important interrelated yet hierarchically unprivileged points of analysis in an effort to produce critical knowledge, advance social transformation, expand and connect anti-subordination struggles, and cultivate progressive coalitions (Gomez, 1998; Iglesias & Valdes, 1998; Montoya, 1998; Valdes, 1997). LatCrit scholars have been a part of the mainstream sociolegal community, but often as tokens and not as regular interlocutors despite broadly compatible anti-subordination objectives. An openness to the imaginative worlds of our subjects may lead to a renewed embrace of our progressive colleagues.

Fifteen years ago, Handler sought progressive ends for sociolegal scholars by challenging methods that he believed cut us off from transformation in society and from our professional potentials. His alarm against postmodernism is not well-heeded today. Our projects are open to postmodern and other new methods, but they have also served to cover up Handler's important challenge to consensus, securing the idea of a congealing discipline. Our own desire for an academic home need not be built on these foundations. Rancière suggests to us that the more we cling to an academic home, the more we fix our subjects to their own. Finding new ways to imagine our field can lead to progressive politics disrupting our own contributions to the prevailing distribution of the sensible.

NOTES

1. Although empirical evidence for this claim is more anecdotal and informal than systematic, some progressive scholars of color have publicly voiced this claim. As Emily M.S. Houh has written (Houh, 2006, p. 481), "[e]ven those who do not identify as 'race crits' or 'fem race crits' – as I do – are likely aware that law and society is known in certain academic circles for being overwhelmingly liberal (and, therefore, *not* critical) and overwhelmingly white." See also Osagie Obosagie (2005) who notes the lack of race-focused articles in the *Law and Society Review* and describes race-focused studies as theoretically limited.

2. As Rancière is not well-known in the Anglo-American world, and since his thought has yet to be applied to law in any sustained way, I present a brief synopsis of his ideas here. I then explain his redirection of inquiry.

3. For example, Pamela Smith (2000, pp. 1128–1129) writes, "But to break the silence and the fear of silence, we must speak and affirm the value of resisting the tyrannies of silence. We must ask ourselves: "What are the words we do not yet have? What do we need to say? What are the tyrannies we swallow day by day and attempt to make our own, until we will sicken and die of them, still in silence?" Many of us are dying inside because of the silence. Each day, we swallow racial and gendered micro-aggressions but are afraid to speak out because of our tenure vulnerability. Sometimes we are so afraid and have been so silenced that we need the help of others to remember that we are entitled to speak. Some times we need a little help from our friends in legal academia to overcome the fear."

4. E.g., *Lawrence v. Texas* 123 S. Ct. 2472 at 2483 (2003) that struck down the constitutionality of sodomy statutes: "Other nations, too, have taken action consistent with an affirmation of the protected right of homosexual adults to engage in intimate, consensual conduct .... The right the petitioners seek in this case has been accepted as an integral part of human freedom in many other countries" (J. Kennedy); *Goodridge v. Massachusetts* 440 Mass. 309 at 313 n.3 (2003) that upheld a right to same-sex marriage in Massachusetts citing *Halpern v. Toronto* (City), 172 O.A.C. 276 (2003); *Egale Canada, Inc. v. Canada* (Attorney Gen.), 13 B.C.L.R. (4th) 1 (2003); *Roper v. Simmons* 543 U.S. 551 at 578 (2005) that ruled unconstitutional the death penalty for juvenile murderers: "It does not lessen our fidelity to the Constitution or our pride in its origins to acknowledge that the express affirmation of certain fundamental rights by other nations and peoples simply underscores the centrality of those same rights within our own heritage of freedom (J. Kennedy). All of these cases provoked strong dissents and congressional attempts to overturn their reliance on international precedent. See Goldberg-Hiller (2004–2005).

REFERENCES

Agamben, G. (2005). *State of exception*. Chicago: University of Chicago Press.

Ansley, F. (2001). Borders. *Denver University Law Review*, *78*, p. 965.

Anzaldua, G. (1999). *Borderlands=La frontera* (2nd ed.). San Francisco, CA: Aunt Lute Books.

Austin, R. (1992). Left at the post: One take on blacks and postmodernism. *Law & Society Review*, *26*, 751–754.

Balkin, J. M. (2004). What *Brown* teaches us about constitutional theory. *Virginia Law Review*, *90*, p. 1537.

Benjamin, S. M. (1996). Equal protection and the special relationship: The case of native Hawaiians. *Yale Law Journal*, *106*(3), p. 537.

Bourdieu, P. (1987). The force of law. *Hastings Law Journal*, *38*, p. 201.

Bower, L. (1994). Queer acts and the politics of "direct access": Rethinking law, culture, and community. *Law & Society Review*, *28*(5), p. 1009.

Broad, K. L. (2001). Critical borderlands and interdisciplinary, intersectional coalitions. *Denver University Law Review*, *78*, p. 1141.

Buchanan, R. M. (1996). Context, continuity, and difference in poverty law scholarship. *University of Miami Law Review*, *48*, p. 999.

Bumiller, K. (1988). *The civil rights society*. Baltimore, MD: Johns Hopkins University Press.

Burns, G. (2005). *The moral veto: Framing contraception, abortion, and cultural pluralism in the United States*. Cambridge, England; New York: Cambridge University Press.

Buss, E. (1999). Confronting developmental barriers to the empowerment of child clients. *Cornell Law Review*, *84*, p. 895.

Butler, J. (1993). *Bodies that matter*. New York: Routledge.

Butler, J. (2004). *Precarious life: The powers of mourning and violence*. London: Verso.

Calavita, K., & Seron, C. (1992). Postmodernism and protest: Recovering the sociological imagination. *Law & Society Review*, *26*, 765–772.

Carle, S. D. (2005). Theorizing agency. *American University Law Review*, *55*, p. 307.

Chang, R. S. (1999). *Disoriented: Asian Americans, law, and the nation-state*. New York: New York University Press.

Cooper, D. (1998). *Governing out of order: Space, law, and the politics of belonging*. London; New York: Rivers Oram Press; Distributed in the USA by New York University Press.

Cover, R. (1986). Violence and the word. *Yale Law Journal*, *95*, p. 1601.

Cummings, S. L., & Eagly, I. V. (2001). A critical reflection on law and organizing. *UCLA Law Review*, *48*, p. 443.

Currah, P. (1997). Politics, practices, publics: Identity and queer rights. In: S. Phelan (Ed.), *Playing with fire: Queer politics, queer theories*. New York: Routledge.

Dalton, C. (1985). An essay in the deconstruction of contract doctrine. *Yale Law Journal*, *94*, 997–1114.

Darian-Smith, E. (1998). Power in paradise: The political implications of Santos's utopia. *Law & Social Inquiry*, *23*, p. 81.

Deranty, J.-P. (2003). Rancière and contemporary political ontology. *Theory and Event*, *6*(4).

Dudas, J. (2004). In the name of equal rights: "Special" rights and the politics of resentment in post-civil rights America. *Law & Society Review*, *39*, p. 723.

Dudziak, M. L. (2000). *Cold War civil rights: Race and the image of American democracy*. Princeton, NJ: Princeton University Press.

Dulk, K. D. (2006). In legal culture, but not of it: The role of cause lawyers in evangelical legal mobilization. In: A. Sarat & S. Scheingold (Eds), *Cause lawyers and social movements*. Stanford, CA: Stanford University Press.

Engel, D. (1999). Making connections: Law and society researchers and their subjects. *Law & Society Review*, *33*, p. 3.

Engel, D. M. (1994). The oven bird's song: Insiders, outsiders, and personal injuries in an American community. In: C. J. Greeenhouse, B. Yngvesson & D. M. Engel (Eds), *Law and community in three American towns*. Ithaca, NY: Cornell University Press.

Engel, D. M., & Munger, F. W. (2003). *Rights of inclusion: Law and identity in the life stories of Americans with disabilities*. Chicago: University of Chicago Press.

Epp, C. R. (1998). *The rights revolution: Lawyers, activists, and supreme courts in comparative perspective*. Chicago: University of Chicago Press.

Erlanger, H. (2005). Organizations, institutions, and the story of Shmuel: Reflections on the 40th Anniversary of the Law and Society Association. *Law & Society Review*, *39*, p. 1.

Ewick, P. (1992). Postmodern melancholia. *Law & Society Review*, *26*, p. 755.

Ewick, P., & Silbey, S. (1998). *The common place of law: Stories from everyday life*. Chicago: University of Chicago Press.

Farber, D. A., & Sherry, S. (1997). *Beyond all reason: The radical assault on truth in American law*. New York: Oxford University Press.

Feinman, J., & Gabel, P. (1990). Contract law as ideology. In: D. Kairys (Ed.), *The politics of law: A progressive critique*. New York: Pantheon Books.

Feldman, L. C. (2004). *Citizens without shelter: Homelessness, democracy, and political exclusion*. Ithaca, NY: Cornell University Press.

Fraser, N., & Nicholson, L. (1988). Social criticism without philosophy: An encounter between feminism and postmodernism. In: A. Ross (Ed.), *Universal abandon? The politics of postmodernism*. Minneapolis, MN: University of Minnesota Press.

Fukuyama, F. (1992). *The end of history and the last man*. New York: Free Press.

Gilliom, J. (2001). *Overseers of the poor: Surveillance, resistance, and the limits of privacy*. Chicago: University of Chicago Press.

Glendon, M. A. (1991). *Rights talk: The impoverishment of political discourse*. New York: Free Press.

Goldberg, S. (1994). Gay rights through the looking glass: Politics, morality and the trial of Colorado's Amendment 2. *Fordham Urban Law Journal*, *XXI*, p. 1057.

Goldberg-Hiller, J. (2002). *The limits to union: Same-sex marriage and the politics of civil rights*. Ann Arbor, MI: University of Michigan Press.

Goldberg-Hiller, J. (2004–2005). Canada is a blue state: Global jurisprudence and domestic consciousness in American gay rights discourse. *Journal of International Law and International Relations*, *I*(1), 261–277.

Goldberg-Hiller, J., & Milner, N. (2003). Rights as excess: Understanding the politics of special rights. *Law & Social Inquiry*, *28*, 1075–1118.

Gomez, L. (1998). Constructing Latina/o identities. *Chicano-Latino Law Review*, *19*, p. 187.

Gramsci, A. (1971). *Selections from the prison notebooks of Antonio Gramsci*. New York: International Publishers.

Greer, E. (2001). Beyond whose reason? Of blacks, jews, and the quest for truth n1beyond all reason: The radical assault on truth in American law. By Daniel A. Farber n2 and Suzanna Sherry. *Texas Hispanic Journal of Law and Policy*, *5*, p. 59.

Hallward, P. (Ed.) (2006). The subversion of mastery. In: M. Robson (Ed.). Edinburgh: University of Edinburgh Press.

Handler, J. (1992a). Postmodernism, protest, and the new social movements. *Law & Society Review*, *26*(4), 697–732.

Handler, J. (1992b). A reply. *Law & Society Review*, *26*, 819–824.

Harris, A. (1994). The jurisprudence of reconstruction. *California Law Review*, *82*, p. 741.

Heinz, J., Paik, A., & Southworth, A. (2003). Lawyers for conservative causes: Clients, ideology, and social distance. *Law & Society Review*, *37*, p. 5.

Herman, D. (1994). *Rights of passage*. Toronto, Ont: University of Toronto Press.

Herman, D. (1997). *The antigay agenda: Orthodox vision and the Christian right*. Chicago: University of Chicago Press.

Herzog, A. (2002). Is liberalism "All we need"? Levinas's politics of surplus. *Political Theory*, *30*(2), 204–227.

Heyer, K. (forthcoming). A disability lens on sociolegal research: Reading rights of inclusion from a disability studies perspective. *Law & Society Review*.

Houh, E. M. S. (2006). Still, at the Margins: Austin Sarat, ed., The Social Organization of Law: Introductory Readings. *Law & Society Review*, *40*, p. 481.

Hussain, N., & Sarat, A. (2006). *Forgiveness, mercy, and clemency*. Stanford, CA: Stanford University Press.

Hutchinson, A. C. (1992). Doing the right thing? Toward a postmodern politics. *Law & Society Review*, *26*, p. 773.

Hutchinson, D. L. (2004). Critical race histories: In and out. *American University Law Review*, *53*, p. 1187.

Iglesias, E., & Valdes, F. (1998). Afterward: Religion, gender, sexuality, race and class in coalitional theory: A critical and self-critical analysis of Latcrit social justice agendas. *Chicano-Latino Law Review*, *19*, 503–588.

Johnson, D. K. (2003). *The lavender scare: The cold war persecution of gays and lesbians in the federal government*. Chicago: University of Chicago Press.

Kann, M. E. (1991). *On the man question: Gender and civic virtue in America*. Philadelphia, PA: Temple University Press.

Kant, I. (1952). *The critique of judgement*. Oxford: Oxford University Press <imprint: Clarendon>.

Kelman, M. (1984). Trashing. *Stanford Law Review*, *36*, p. 293.

Klare, K. (1978). Judicial deradicalization of the Wagner Act and the origins of modern legal consciousness. *Minnesota Law Review*, *62*, p. 265.

Krishnan, J. K. (2006). Lawyering for a cause and experiences from abroad. *California Law Review*, *94*, p. 575.

Lawrence, C., III. (1987). The Id, the ego, and equal protection: Reckoning with unconscious racism. *Stanford Law Review*, *39*, p. 317.

Lévinas, E. (1999). *Alterity and transcendence*. New York: Columbia University Press.

López, G. P. (1992). *Rebellious lawyering: One Chicano's vision of progressive law practice*. Boulder, CO: Westview Press.

Lyotard, J.-F. (1984). *The postmodern condition: A report on knowledge. Theory and history of literature* (Vol. 10). Minneapolis, MN: University of Minnesota Press.

Macaulay, S. (1963). Non-contractual relations in business: A preliminary study. *American Sociological Review*, *28*, p. 55.

Macaulay, S. (1984). Law and the behavioral sciences: Is there any there there? *Law and Policy Quarterly*, *6*, p. 149.

Macaulay, S. (1992). On rattling cages: Joel Handler goes to Philadelphia and gives a presidential address. *Law & Society Review*, *26*, p. 825.

Macaulay, S. (2005). The new versus the old legal realism: "Things ain't what they used to be". *Wisconsin Law Review*, *2005*, p. 365.

Marshall, A.-M., & Barclay, S. (2003). Introduction: In their own words: How ordinary people construct the legal world. *Law & Social Inquiry*, *28*, 617–628.

Matsuda, M. (1989). Legal storytelling: Public response to racist speech: Considering the victim's story. *Michigan Law Review*, *87*, p. 2320.

Matsuda, M. J. (1996). *Where is your body? And other essays on race, gender, and the law*. Boston, MA: Beacon Press.

McCann, M. (1992). Resistance, reconstruction, and romance in legal scholarship. *Law & Society Review*, *26*(4), p. 733.

McCann, M. (1994). *Rights at work: Pay equity reform and the politics of legal mobilization*. Chicago: University of Chicago Press.

McCann, M., & Silverstein, H. (1998). Rethinking law's "Allurement": A relational analysis of social movement lawyers in the United States. In: A. Sarat & S. Scheingold (Eds), *Cause lawyering: Political commitments and professional responsibilities*. New York: Oxford.

Melucci, A. (1996). *Challenging codes: Collective action in the information age*. Cambridge, England; New York: Cambridge University Press.

Merry, S. (1995). Resistance and the cultural power of law. *Law & Society Review*, *29*(1), 11–26.

Merry, S. E. (2000). *Colonizing Hawai'i: The cultural power of law*. Princeton, NJ: Princeton University Press.

Merry, S. E., & Brenneis, D. L. (2004). *Law and empire in the Pacific: Fiji and Hawai'i* (1st ed.). Santa Fe, NM: School of American Research Press.

Mills, C. W. (1959). *The sociological imagination*. New York: Oxford University Press.

Milner, N. (1986). The dilemmas of legal mobilization: Ideologies and strategies of mental patient liberation. *Law & Policy*, *8*, 105–129.

Milner, N., & Goldberg-Hiller, J. (2002). Reimagining rights: Tunnels, nations, spaces. *Law & Social Inquiry*, *27*, 339–368.

Milner, N., & Goldberg-Hiller, J. (2008). "Feeble echoes of the heart": A postcolonial legal struggle in Hawai'i. *Law, Culture and Humanities*.

Montoya, M. (1994). Mascaras, Trenzas y grenas: Un/masking the self while un/braiding Latina stories and legal discourse. *Harvard Women's Law Journal*, *17*, p. 185.

Montoya, M. (1998). Religious rituals and Latcrit theorizing. *Chicano-Latino Law Review*, *19*, p. 417.

Mufti, A. R. (2003). Reading Jacques Rancière's "ten theses on politics": After September 11th. *Theory and Event*, *6*(4).

Obosagie, O. K. (2005). *Race in law and society*. Unpublished paper presented at the Annual Meeting of the Law and Society Association. Las Vegas, NV.

Padilla, L. (2001). "But you're not a dirty Mexican": Internalized oppression, latinos and law. *Texas Hispanic Journal of Law and Policy*, *7*, p. 59.

Patton, C. (1995). Refiguring social space. In: L. Nicholson & S. Seidman (Eds), *Social postmodernism: Beyond identity politics*. Cambridge: Cambridge University Press.

Patton, C. (1997). Queer space/God's space: Counting down to the apocalypse. *Rethinking Marxism*, *9*(2), 1–23.

Rancière, J. (1995). *On the shores of politics*. London; New York: Verso.

Rancière, J. (1999). *Disagreement: Politics and philosophy*. Minneapolis, MN: University of Minnesota Press.

Rancière, J. (2001). Ten theses on politics. *Theory and Event*, *5*(3).

Rancière, J. (2003). The thinking of dissensus: Politics and aesthetics. Paper presented at the conference Fidelity to the Disagreement: Jacques Rancière and the Political organized by the Post-Structuralism and Radical Politics and Marxism specialist groups of the Political Studies Association of the UK in Goldsmiths College, London, 16-17 September.

Rancière, J. (2004a). In: B. Cvejic (Trans.), *The politics of aesthetics*. Originally published in http://theater.kein.org. Retrieved from http://www.metamute.org/en/node/8441/print on 15 August 2007.

Rancière, J. (2004b). In: G. Rockhill (Trans.), *The politics of aesthetics: The distribution of the sensible*. London: Continuum.

Rancière, J. (2004c). Who is the subject of the rights of man. *The South Atlantic Quarterly*, *103*, 297–310.

Rancière, J. (2005). Democracy, dissensus and the aesthetics of class struggle: An exchange with jacques rancière. *Historical materialism: Research in critical Marxist theory*, *13*(4), 285–301.

Rancière, J. (2006). Thinking between disciplines: An aesthetics of knowledge. *Parrhesia*, *1*(1), 1–12.

Richards, D. (1999). *Identity and the case for gay rights: Race, gender, religion as analogies*. Chicago: University of Chicago Press.

Robson, M. (2006). Jacques Rancière's aesthetic communities. In: M. Robson (Ed.), *Paragraph*. Edinburgh: Edinburgh University Press.

Rosenberg, G. N. (1991). *The hollow hope: Can courts bring about social change?* Chicago: University of Chicago.

Sarat, A. (1998). *Crossing boundaries: Traditions and transformations in law and society research*. American Bar Foundation: Evanston, Ill.

Sarat, A., & Kearns, T. R. (1993b). *Law in everyday life*. Ann Arbor, MI: University of Michigan Press.

Sarat, A., Douglas, L., & Umphrey, M. M. (2005a). *Law on the screen*. Stanford, CA: Stanford University Press.

Sarat, A., Douglas, L., & Umphrey, M. M. (2005b). *The limits of law*. Stanford, CA: Stanford University Press.

Sarat, A., & Kearns, T. (1993a). Beyond the great divide: Forms of legal scholarship and everyday life. In: A. Sarat & T. Kearns (Eds), *Law in everyday life*. Ann Arbor, MI: University of Michigan Press.

Sarat, A., & Scheingold, S. A. (Eds). (1997). *Cause lawyering*. New York: Oxford University Press.

Sarat, A., & Scheingold, S. A. (1998). *Cause lawyering: Political commitments and professional responsibilities*. New York: Oxford University Press.

Sarat, A., & Scheingold, S. A. (2005). *The worlds cause lawyers make: Structure and agency in legal practice*. Stanford, CA: Stanford Law and Politics.

Sarat, A., & Scheingold, S. A. (2006). *Cause lawyers and social movements*. Stanford, CA: Stanford Law and Politics.

Sarat, A., & Silbey, S. (1988). The pull of the policy audience. *Law and Policy*, *10*, p. 97.

Sarat, A., & Simon, J. (2003). *Cultural analysis, cultural studies, and the law: Moving beyond legal realism*. Durham, NC: Duke University Press.

Schacter, J. (1994). The gay civil rights debate in the states: Decoding the discourse of equivalents. *Harvard Civil Rights–Civil Liberties Law Review*, *29*, p. 283.

Scheingold, S. A. (2004). *The politics of rights: Lawyers, public policy, and political change* (2nd ed.). Ann Arbor, MI: University of Michigan Press.

Scheingold, S. A., & Sarat, A. (2004). *Something to believe in: Politics, professionalism, and cause lawyering*. Stanford, CA: Stanford Law and Politics.

Schlag, P. (2002). The aesthetics of American law. *Harvard Law Review, 115*, 1047–1118.

Schur, R. (2002). Critical race theory and the limits of auto/biography: Reading patricia Williams' *the alchemy of race and rights* through/against postcolonial theory. *Biography: An Interdisciplinary Quarterly, 25*(3), 445–477.

Seron, C. (2002). The teacher–scholar. *Law & Society Review, 36*, p. 21.

Shapiro, M. J. (2006a). *Deforming American political thought: Ethnicity, facticity, and genre*. Lexington: University Press of Kentucky.

Shapiro, M. J. (2006b). The sublime today: Re-partitioning the global sensible. *Millenium: Journal of International Studies, 34*, 657–681.

Shklar, J. (1990). Redeeming American political theory. *American Political Science Review, 85*, 3–15.

Silbey, S., & Sarat, A. (1988). Critical traditions in law and society research. *Law & Society Review, 21*, p. 165.

Silverstein, H. (1996). *Unleashing rights: Law, meaning, and the animal rights movement*. Ann Arbor, MI: University of Michigan Press.

Smith, P. J. (2000). The tyrannies of silence of the untenured professors of color. *UC Davis Law Review, 33*, p. 1105.

Smith, R. M. (1997). *Civic ideals: Conflicting visions of citizenship in US history*. New Haven, CT: Yale University Press.

Southworth, A. (1999). Lawyers and the "Myth of Rights" in civil rights and poverty practice. *Boston University Public Interest Law Journal, 8*, p. 469.

Southworth, A. (2005). Professional identity and political commitment among lawyers for conservative causes. In: A. Sarat & S. Scheingold (Eds), *The worlds cause lawyers make: Structure and agency in legal practice*. Stanford, CA: Stanford University Press.

Stark, B. (2001). Marriage proposals: From one-size-fits-all to postmodern marriage law. *California Law Review, 89*, p. 1479.

Stychin, C. F. (1998). *A nation by rights: National cultures, sexual identity politics, and the discourse of rights*. Philadelphia, PA: Temple University Press.

Tedesco, E. (2002). "Humanity on the ballot": The citizen initiative and Oregon's war over gay civil rights. *Boston College Third World Law Journal, 22*, p. 163.

Tomlins, C. (2000). Framing the field of Law's disciplinary encounters: A historical narrative. *Law & Society Review, 34*, p. 911.

Tomlins, C. (2004). History in the American juridical field: Narrative, justification, and explanation. *Yale Journal of Law and the Humanities, 16*, p. 323.

Trubek, D. (1990). Back to the future: The short, happy life of the law and society movement. *Florida State University Law Review, 18*, p. 4.

Tushnet, M. (1984). An essay on rights. *University of Texas Law Review, 32*, p. 1363.

Tushnet, M (1989). Rights: An essay in informal political theory. *Politics & Society, 17*, p. 403.

Valdes, F. (1996). Latina/o ethnicities, critical race theory, and post-identity politics in postmodern Legal culture: From practices to possibilities. *La Raza Law Journal, 9*, p. 1.

Valdes, F. (1997). Under construction: LatCrit consciousness, community and theory. *California Law Review, 85*, 1087–1142.

Valdes, F. (1999). Theorizing "OutCrit" theories: coalitional method and comparative jurisprudential experience – RaceCrits, QueerCrits and LatCrits. *University of Miami Law Review, 53*, p. 1265.

Warner, M. (1999). *The trouble with normal: Sex, politics and the ethics of queer life*. New York: Free Press.

Warner, M. (2002). *Publics and counterpublics*. New York; Cambridge, MA: Zone Books, Distributed by MIT Press.

West, C. (1995). Foreward. In: K. Crenshaw, N. Gotanda, G. Peller & K. Thomas (Eds), *Critical Race theory: The Key writings that formed the movement*. New York: The New Press.

Winter, S. L. (1992). For what it's worth. *Law & Society Review*, *26*(789), 789–818.

Winter, S. L. (1994). Cusing the darkness. *University of Miami Law Review*, *48*, p. 1115.

Zald, M. N., & McCarthy, J. D. (1979). *The dynamics of social movements: Resource mobilization, social control, and tactics*. Cambridge, MA: Winthrop Publishers.

Zemans, F. (1983). Legal mobilization: The neglected role of the law in the political system. *American Political Science Review*, *77*, 690–703.

Žižek, S. (2005). Against human rights. *New Left Review*, *34*, 115–131.

WOULD YOU LIKE THEORY WITH THAT? BRIDGING THE DIVIDE BETWEEN POLICY-ORIENTED EMPIRICAL LEGAL RESEARCH, CRITICAL THEORY AND POLITICS

Rosemary Hunter

ABSTRACT

In response to the divides identified by some UK writers between critical legal scholarship, left political agendas, and empirical, policy-driven, socio-legal research, and indications of similar divides in the US, this essay seeks to demonstrate the possibilities for work that negotiates between progressive political commitments, social and political theory, policy concerns, and social scientific approaches to the interface between law and society. It does so by reference to three case studies of critical, feminist socio-legal scholarship, which address policy issues in the areas of family law, the legal profession, and access to justice.

Special Issue: Law and Society Reconsidered
Studies in Law, Politics, and Society, Volume 41, 121–148

ISSN: 1059-4337/doi:10.1016/S1059-4337(07)00005-1

1. INTRODUCTION

In the opening chapter of their edited collection, *Theory and method in socio-legal research*, Reza Banakar and Max Travers (2005) observe that:

> In … recent times, the [socio-legal] field [in the UK] has become divided between policy researchers who have a positivist understanding of method, and critical scholars who have little interest in doing empirical research. (p. 4)

The first part of this observation, at least, seems to be borne out in the recent report of the Nuffield Inquiry on Empirical Research in Law, which investigated the current and future 'capacity for empirical legal research among lawyers and social scientists' in the UK (Genn, Partington, & Wheeler, 2006, p. 2). Empirical legal research is discussed within the report primarily as a tool for policy makers, and almost entirely in positivist terms, without reference to other 'uses' of and frameworks for thinking about such research, and without any consideration of the relationship between empirical research and critical scholarship.

In the US, law and society scholarship has rarely been atheoretical, but it has also rarely engaged with critical theory or progressive politics. Law and society scholarship has typically involved the gathering and analysis of empirical data in order to generate or develop mid-range theories about the nature of legal and socio-legal phenomena. Classic examples include 'Naming, blaming and claiming' (Felstiner, Abel, & Sarat, 1981), 'Why the "haves" come out ahead' (Galanter, 1974),[1] 'Bargaining in the shadow of the law', (Mnookin & Kornhauser, 1979), and the importance of procedural justice (e.g., Lind & Tyler, 1988; Conley & O'Barr, 1990). More recently, the law and society field has become much more heterogeneous and fractured. The post-modern turn has generated suspicion of empirical data and returned some scholars to the interpretation of legal and cultural texts, a move which has seen the creation of the Association for the Study of Law, Culture and the Humanities at one end of the law and society spectrum. At the other end, the establishment of the SSRN list and subsequent inaugural conference on Empirical Legal Studies signals a turn away from free-range theorising towards a focus on the contribution of empirical research to the neo-liberal project of legal efficiency.

The potentially vanishing middle of the US law and society spectrum appears now to have been occupied by the 'new legal realism'. This project aims to translate between law and the social sciences, so that each discipline properly understands and therefore is properly able to deploy and operate within the other's methods, assumptions and paradigms.

This will enable the production of better empirical research for the purposes of providing a more reliable foundation for policy formation.[2] The project thus is clearly positivist but non-normative (except in methodological terms). It believes that empirical research can produce important and valuable truths as a means to policy ends, whatever those ends might be, and in this respect it appears to have much in common with the UK Nuffield Inquiry noted above. Further, although the new legal realist 'manifesto' talks about bringing together empirical research and legal theory, the legal theory referred to is not critical or metaphysical, but mid-range theories about law such as 'contract theory' and 'property theory' (Erlanger et al., 2005, p. 337). In this model, theories are used to generate assumptions and predictions, which are then tested 'on the ground' by means of rigorous empirical research, to discover what is 'really happening'. This discovery feeds into both the refinement of the theories and the development of sound policy proposals. Once those policies are implemented, their 'success' in practice should then be monitored and tested by means of further empirical research (Erlanger et al., 2005, p. 343).

The internally focused nature of new legal realism and its eschewal of normative agendas are explicitly acknowledged in the association of the project with pragmatist philosophy (Erlanger et al., 2005, p. 358). According to the authors of the new legal realist manifesto, pragmatism requires looking at law not from a distance but from within, and determining what relationships drive its dynamics. The new legal realist practitioner should not ask whether law succeeds or fails against some externally imposed normative goal, but rather should suspend judgement and examine how legal rules are transformed and reconfigured in the process of implementation, in order to understand how institutions translate and create law, and what law means and does in practice (Erlanger et al., 2005, p. 358). It is not obvious, however, why it is imperative to erect a boundary between empirical research on the one hand and normative goals on the other. In the US context, this could be seen as a reaction to the dominance of law and economics scholarship and associated neo-liberal agendas. But while the assertion that new legal realist scholarship should be used exclusively for policy purposes might effectively preserve a liberal approach against more conservative incursions, it also excludes the possibility of an alliance between empirical research and critical theoretical or more progressive political agendas.

By contrast, other interventions into debates about the role and scope of socio-legal scholarship have espoused different ideals about the relationships between progressive politics, critical theory, empirical research and state policy agendas. In an early essay on the subject, US law and society scholars Austin Sarat and Susan Silbey (1988) pointed to what they viewed as an undesirable 'alliance between socio-legal scholarship and policy elites of the liberal state' (p. 113), arguing that this alliance had the effect of limiting the critical potential of socio-legal scholarship (p. 122). The desire to be useful had the effect of constraining the kinds of arguments and perspectives offered by socio-legal researchers, resulting in a focus on whether chosen legal means were appropriate to pre-given ends, rather than any questioning of those ends, or of other effects of the chosen means, or of the power relations involved (p. 102). They argued that '[s]ocio-legal scholarship can, and should, be politically engaged without adopting the agenda of those who currently make or administer policy' (p. 99), and called for socio-legal scholars to distance themselves from policy elites in order to achieve this goal.

Similarly, in the UK, Paddy Hillyard (2002) has called for an alliance between left politics (which he refers to as 'a vision of a just society which is informed by moral indignation' (p. 656)) and empirical legal research. His target, however, is not the cosy relationship between empirical researchers and policy elites, but the perceived capture of critical legal scholarship by 'theory', particularly in its post-modern and post-structuralist forms. According to Hillyard, socio-legal studies needs to engage less in theoretical debates and invest more energy in research on 'the material realities of modern life' (p. 646). Rather than ignoring growing global inequalities of wealth and resources, socio-legal studies should explore the role of law and legal institutions in creating and maintaining inequalities, via empirical research (pp. 653–654).

By contrast to Hillyard, UK legal scholar Nicola Lacey (1996) has suggested that the forging of a desirable linkage between critical legal agendas and empirical socio-legal research precisely requires the introduction of 'theory' into the equation – specifically, sociology of law and social theory more broadly. Like Sarat and Silbey, Lacey expresses concern about the 'technocratic instrumentalism of "policy-oriented" studies' which are little theorized and not explicit about their political or ethical values (p. 132). In her account, the lack of productive dialogue between critical and empirical legal scholarship is attributable to the fact that the latter 'takes up a quasi-scientific stance which distances evaluative or political questions' and 'fails to take a sophisticated approach to the complexity of interactions between legal and extra-legal practices' (p. 138). Thus, it tends to be written off by critical legal theorists as theoretically and politically naïve (p. 138), with the result that there continues to be:

> a seemingly unbridgeable gap between critiques and Utopianism on the one hand, and reformism on the other (p. 143),

with reformist empirical research losing the opportunity to generate insights for critical theory as to how legal practices might be reconstructed (p. 138).

Lacey (1996) argues that in order to be successful, both legal reformist, policy-oriented projects and critical legal and Utopian political projects need to raise their eyes above the immediate horizon and understand how law and other social institutions interact with each other (pp. 141–143). Thus, for example, one problem with narrowly focused reformism is that the institutions which reformists seek to change are themselves interrelated with other institutions in a complex network. Consequently, an intervention in one location may have unseen, adverse consequences elsewhere, while attempts to redress power imbalances in one location are unlikely to succeed if the same configurations of power pervade all social institutions (Lacey, 1996, p. 141). An adequate sociology of law, understood as a 'systematic attempt to explicate the nature of law within specific social formations, as part of the social framework', would benefit both reformism, and the critical project of critiquing existing legal and social arrangements and imagining better ones (Lacey, 1996, pp. 132, 143). The sociology of law could thus provide a meeting point for the two approaches, and in particular enable critical approaches to draw upon and learn from 'a more theoretically self-reflective socio-legal studies' (Lacey, 1996, p. 133).

Of course, it must be acknowledged that the technocratic instrumentalism of many policy-oriented, empirical socio-legal studies, particularly in countries like the UK and Australia, is not simply a product of researchers eschewing theory and politics, and avoiding conversations with their critical colleagues in favour of the more seductive 'pull of the policy audience' (Sarat & Silbey, 1988). Rather, socio-legal researchers have also been pushed into the arms of the policy audience by institutional demands for research income in the form of grants and consultancies, and valuations of research in terms of its 'impact', 'national benefit', worth to (non-academic) 'end users' and so on (see, e.g., Collier, 2004).[3] Minimally theorized, reformist, policy-oriented empirical research may thus be seen as instrumental not just in terms of the requirements of the policy audience, but also in terms of the authors' own institutional survival. Indeed, engaging in this kind of work may create space for the production of more theoretically informed, critical academic publications, in which data collected for a policy-oriented project is 'retrofitted' with a theoretical and/or political analysis.

Yet these institutional tendencies towards the production of uncritical policy research are not (or have not yet become) totalizing. Critical, theoretical and non-empirical scholarship in law, for example, continues to thrive in the UK. Moreover, as Lacey (1996) has also noted:

> feminist scholarship has generally been characterized by a less radical divide between theoretical and socio-legal concerns than has non-feminist legal theory. (p. 134)

It is this last insight that I wish to take up in this chapter, in showing how my own and other feminist socio-legal scholarship has combined empirically based, often policy-driven research with critical theoretical analysis and (often) a progressive political agenda. Although not all of the examples discussed below conform to Lacey's prescription for uniting reformism and critique via social theory or the sociology of law, they do show that it is possible to move beyond policy/politics and empirical/critical dichotomies, and to 'quadrangulate' critical theoretical, progressive political, policy-oriented and empirical approaches to law.

The fact that my work and the other examples provided proceed from a feminist theoretical and political framework means that they engage with debates within feminist legal scholarship as well as articulating policy positions within the substantive field of inquiry (family law, women in the legal profession and access to justice). In feminist scholarship more broadly, it is more accurate to speak of feminisms rather than a unitary feminism, and feminist legal scholarship has reflected this trend. Thus, feminist legal scholarship includes strands of liberal feminism, socialist or materialist feminism, radical feminism, cultural feminism and post-structuralist feminism. Radical feminism is now a more prominent strand in US feminist legal scholarship than in other national contexts, while materialist feminism is more prominent in the UK. I would argue that a progressive politics might be based on any form of feminism, however, not all forms of feminism engage with critical (social) theories, with liberal and cultural feminisms less likely to do so than materialist and post-structuralist feminisms.

I do not intend to suggest in this essay that work that takes a critical theoretical, progressive political, policy-oriented and empirical approach to law has not been and cannot be done in a non-feminist frame. A range of other left, critical and ethical stances also incorporate both theoretical understandings of the world and progressive normative visions of a better one, to which empirical legal studies might be harnessed. There is also a sense in which right-wing or conservative approaches such as those informed by neo-liberal economics may be theoretical and political as well as empirical. But to the extent that they are unreflective about their political stance, or purport to be neutral, apolitical, or to propound objective truths (see also Sarat & Silbey, 1988, p. 98), I do not include them in my category of analysis.

2. FEMINISM, CHILD WELFARE, NARRATIVITY AND FAMILY LAW

UK socio-legal scholarship includes several writers who combine empirical research, policy analysis and feminist theory. Perhaps the most well-known of these internationally is Carol Smart, who is the author of major texts of feminist legal theory (Smart, 1989) and feminist criminology (Smart, 1995), and has also, over many years, investigated empirically and analysed insightfully the meanings and impacts of shifting policy debates and reform processes in family law (e.g., Smart, 1984; Smart & Neale, 1999; Smart, Neale, & Wade, 2001, inter alia). In this chapter, however, I want to focus on the work of two other feminist empirical researchers in the field of family law in the UK, Felicity Kaganas and Shelley Day Sclater (Day Sclater & Kaganas, 2003; Kaganas & Day Sclater, 2004).

In 1999–2000, Kaganas and Day Sclater undertook an empirical research project with parents who had been involved in protracted disputes (lasting at least a year) over the amount of contact (if any) their children should have with their non-resident parent (Day Sclater & Kaganas, 2003, p. 158). The aim of the research was to:

> discover why some parents become involved in protracted litigation over post-separation arrangements for their children, to examine how parents make sense of their experiences, and to understand what those disputes mean for parents themselves. (Kaganas & Day Sclater, 2004, p. 2)

Their focus in the project was on:

> the ways in which individuals themselves make sense of their lives, drawing on the range of biographical experiences and cultural resources that are available to them. … We were particularly interested in the ways in which disputing parents framed their thoughts, feelings and actions, with particular reference to the welfare discourse in family law. (Kaganas & Day Sclater, 2004, p. 2, note 4)

To this end, they adopted a narrative approach, inviting parents to talk freely about their dispute with the other party, the reasons why they were pursuing it, and their experiences of the court system, and then undertaking a content analysis of the resulting narrative texts. This methodology might be described as post-structuralist. It is premised not on the assumed existence of an objective, singular reality that can be observed, measured and revealed by the researcher, nor on the view that people's consciousness and behaviour are determined by their position in the social and economic order, but rather on the belief that individuals 'conceived of as active human agents' (Day Sclater & Kaganas, 2003, p. 158), construct different realities based on their own particular social locations, experiences, interactions with others, and the languages and concepts provided by social discourses. Such research embraces 'issues of diversity, complexity and contradiction', and confronts 'problems of language, meaning and context' (Day Sclater & Kaganas, 2003, p. 158). As such, the methodology is influenced by theorists such as Foucault (understandings of discourse, power and the regulation of the self), Gramsci (notions of hegemony and resistance) and Barthes (the technique of close reading of texts to reveal multiple meanings) and is far from the positivist/empiricist approach taken by many policy-focused socio-legal researchers and objected to by critical theorists like Lacey.

The welfare discourse in family law is the dominant set of ideas around divorce and separation, deriving from the field of child welfare but also reflected in law and government policy, that prescribe what constitutes a 'good' divorce and 'good' post-separation parenting, from the perspective of maximizing child welfare and minimizing the risk of harm to children arising from the divorce (Kaganas & Day Sclater, 2004, p. 3). Central to this discourse within UK law is the notion that children's well-being is best assured by means of regular contact with the non-resident parent and an ongoing, cooperative relationship between their parents (Kaganas & Day Sclater, 2004, p. 3). Parents are expected to manage their divorce and post-separation relationship in a way that conforms to these prescriptions. By definition, parents who engage in litigation over post-separation arrangements for their children do not conform to the norms of 'good' post-separation parenting, and must be educated, persuaded, and if necessary ordered to do so. Kaganas and Day Sclater's research, therefore, sought to investigate the extent to which this dominant welfare discourse shaped the way parents understood their disputes or, alternatively, the extent to which their narratives challenged the dominant discourse and asserted different norms or values.

Although this research was not initiated with a specific policy agenda in view, the fact that it addressed a 'live' policy issue around the ways in which the developing welfare discourse was or ought to be promoted through the family law system meant that it had a high degree of policy relevance. And indeed, shortly after the research interviews were completed, the Children Act Sub-Committee of the Lord Chancellor's Advisory Board on Family Law published a consultation paper and subsequent report on the facilitation of contact between children and their non-residential parents, and the enforcement of contact orders (Lord Chancellor's Advisory Board, 2001, 2002). In a 2004 article, Kaganas and Day Sclater discuss and critique that report, *Making contact work*, by reference to a critical feminist analysis of the welfare discourse and potential competing (parental) rights discourse, the way these discourses are implemented in law through 'a process of reconstruction and simplification' and the production of regimes of 'truth' (Kaganas & Day Sclater, 2004, pp. 3, 12), and their empirical research data.

The narratives of disputing parents gathered by Kaganas and Day Sclater indicated that parents had both absorbed and internalized the dominant welfare discourse, but also sought to resist and reinterpret that discourse in a variety of ways:

> the welfare discourse commonly provides a basic framework for parents' talk. But the law's prescriptions for parenting and assumptions about what is best for children are not passively accepted. They are matters for ongoing negotiation, with mothers and fathers interpreting and reframing notions of children's best interests according to their own criteria. ... A verbal performance of the dominant discourse is often in evidence, but it is undermined by the simultaneous expression of more critical discourses. (Kaganas & Day Sclater, 2004, p. 6)

Thus, for example, mothers opposing contact between their children and their former partners tended to accept that contact was generally desirable, but to create an exception in their own case. Nevertheless, they were concerned to construct themselves as 'good' mothers, by arguing that it was in the best interests of their children not to have contact with their incompetent or abusive fathers. Fathers, on the other hand, also constructed themselves as 'good' parents by denying or minimizing their violence, constructing their former partners as 'bad' mothers, and vigorously supporting the view that contact was in children's best interests. When judicial decisions went against them, aggrieved mothers and fathers both accused the courts of gender bias, rejecting the legal construct of the gender-neutral 'good' parent. In these situations, parents also contested the ideal of conflict-free post-separation parenting by arguing that continuing to battle in court to gain or prevent contact was necessary to protect their children from (further) harm. The litigation over contact was presented as being vitally important to their children's best interests, and the only option available to them as 'good' parents putting their children's needs ahead of their own (Kaganas & Day Sclater, 2004, pp. 16–22; Day Sclater & Kaganas, 2003, pp. 159–166).

These readings of disputing parents' narratives suggest that disputes over contact will not readily be eliminated, despite the political desire for that outcome. On the proposals in *Making contact work* for the promotion of contact and cooperative post-separation relationships through further education and persuasion of parents, Kaganas and Day Sclater comment that:

> Our research suggests that the roots of protracted contact disputes do not lie in parents' ignorance or rejection of the dominant discourse. (p. 24)

They predict, therefore, that the proposals will have little impact in practice, partly because they are not aimed at the root of the problem (the law's insistence on a set of norms for a 'good' divorce that these parents do not accept as applying to their situation), and partly because the desired educative effect is unlikely to be realized. Research elsewhere indicates that information campaigns in this area may do little to change parenting behaviour, because the other parent is seen to be the one at fault (Kaganas & Day Sclater, 2004, p. 24). Thus:

> It seems quite possible that, in the same way as parents currently reframe the dominant discourse … they will reframe the information and education imparted to them under the proposed scheme. We should not underestimate the capacity of parents to reinterpret their own conduct and the best interests of their children in ways that induce a sense of grievance and that impels them to continue to fight the 'good' fight. (Kaganas & Day Sclater, 2004, pp. 24–25)

This example illustrates the capacity for theoretically informed, critical and post-structuralist empirical research to make a useful intervention into policy debates. Interestingly, prior to the publication of Kaganas and Day Sclater's research, Carol Smart and her research team were funded by the Lord Chancellor's Department (now the Ministry of Justice) to undertake a study of court files in residence and contact cases to shed light on the questions of why the issue of post-separation contact is so difficult for parents and the legal system, and why disputes over contact seem so hard to resolve, and have not diminished, despite the aim of the Children Act 1989 to reduce post-separation parental conflict (see Smart, May, Wade, & Furniss, 2003; Smart & May, 2004a, 2004b; May & Smart, 2004; Smart, May, Furniss, Sharma, & Strelitz, 2005). Because this study drew its data from court files rather than parental narratives, it necessarily observed versions of the disputes that had been shaped by legal advisers to 'fit with the legal framework and to address the issues that were relevant in the eyes of the law' – i.e. primarily issues of children's welfare (Smart & May, 2004b, p. 349). Nonetheless, this did not stop parents from introducing 'illegitimate arguments' that they appeared to view as extremely important to put before the court to explain their position. Consequently, it became evident that underlying many residence and contact disputes were legally irrelevant but subjectively motivating disputes over property, child support, the reasons for the breakdown of the parties' relationship, the new relationship of one or other of the parties, and normative expectations about family life (Smart & May, 2004b, pp. 350–357).

Like Kaganas and Day Sclater, Smart and May emphasized the complexity of these disputes, and argued that the current legal approach focused closely on a particular version of children's welfare was not likely to reduce or resolve disputes over contact. Similarly to Kaganas and Day Sclater, they observed that such disputes:

> encompass a variety of quite thorny ethical issues. Issues of proper parenting, appropriate financial support, fairness, responsibility and the welfare of children are stubbornly interwoven rather than forming discrete matters that can be conveniently shelved or deflected. (Smart & May, 2004b, p. 358)

They concluded that:

> it is important for policy to grasp that divorce is a more traumatic and complex process than current practices often allow. (Smart & May, 2004b, p. 358)

And, referring to the current political context in which debates over the norms to be embodied in family law are located, they expressed the hope that:

> the Government gives due attention to the complexity of these disputes rather than reacting to a powerful fathers' lobby whose arguments tend to hide how difficult and multi-faceted these conflicts can be. (Smart & May, 2004b, p. 359)

Finally, using a similar rhetorical strategy to that employed by the parents interviewed by Kaganas and Day Sclater, they produced their own reinterpretation of dominant welfare discourse to justify their position:

> Acknowledging and dealing with the ethical and emotional conflicts between parents, rather than insisting that they are ignored for the sake of the children, might actually produce a system that will be more attentive to the long-term welfare of children. (Smart & May, 2004b, p. 358)

Clear-eyed critical research, however, even when it is policy oriented and based on empirical evidence, is not always greeted warmly. While successive studies of the 'problem' of contact disputes have demonstrated the mismatch between welfare discourse in relation to 'good' post-separation parenting and disputing parents' understandings and motivations, the recent Children and Adoption Act 2006 treads a familiar path in relation to 'making contact work'. It provides a more elaborate regulatory pyramid for the facilitation and enforcement of contact (beginning with information, programs, classes, counselling and guidance for parents, and ending with punitive enforcement orders, and orders for compensation where breach of a contact order has caused the other party financial loss), but does not depart from the dominant welfare discourse. Regrettably, the argument made by Kaganas and Day Sclater, and reinforced by Smart and May, that the current approach is futile and the law needs to comprehend the complexity of disputing parents' positions, remains to be taken up by policy makers, thereby demonstrating the non-neutral, ideological nature of policy agendas in this area.

3. FEMINISM, CRITICAL SOCIOLOGY AND WOMEN SOLICITORS

Hilary Sommerlad and Peter Sanderson's (1998) book *Gender, choice and commitment: Women solicitors in England and Wales and the struggle for equal status* is a tour de force of empirically based, policy-oriented, theoretically sophisticated and politically aware research and analysis. The book began life as a research project commissioned by the Law Society of England and Wales and a local Training and Enterprise Council into the kind of training necessary to support the re-entry of women solicitors into the profession, a matter of interest to the Law Society due to the threatened shortage of solicitors in the late 1980s resulting from a commercial property boom (Sommerlad & Sanderson, 1998, p. 8). However, it became:

> clear to the principal researcher [Sommerlad] that before the efficacy of returner training could be evaluated, there were general issues relating to the profession's attitudes and practices in respect of women employees which needed to be addressed, and the focus was shifted slightly … . (p. 8)

Rather than accepting the Law Society's:

> assumption that women solicitors were, and were regarded as, a valuable human resource which employers would want to attract back into the profession, and that the main problem was how to ease their re-entry (p. 8),

the project was turned around to question this very assumption, and to determine how women solicitors were in fact regarded, and how they experienced their professional lives. Ultimately, the empirical data collected in order to address these questions included postal surveys of, and face-to-face interviews with, both male and female solicitors, and both employee solicitors and law firm partners and managers, over a period of several years (pp. 8–10).

In analysing their data, Sommerlad and Sanderson (1998) draw upon – and integrate in novel ways – a wide range of theoretical perspectives, in order to develop their own, mid-range 'theory of women solicitors' articulation into the professional labour market' (p. 15).[4] But their major theoretical sources are feminism and Bourdieu. In relation to feminist theory generally, they note the overwhelming evidence that women lawyers both face and internalize gendered and sexualized expectations about their work performance (p. 3). While acknowledging that women occupy different positions within the profession and have somewhat different experiences of professional life according to a range of other factors and characteristics, they conclude that gender itself clearly remains both a salient and a dominant category of experience and hence of analysis, constituting 'a principal determinant in the career trajectories of women solicitors', and of the shape of legal practice (p. 4).

More specifically, they draw upon Carole Pateman's (1998) conception of the sexual contract, which:

> challenges the common assumption of many labour market theories that practices in the public world of work ... are entirely independent of the private world of work in the home and family. (Sommerlad & Sanderson, 1998, p. 15)

Instead, the labour market and the private sphere are interrelated in a way that enables the reproduction of masculine power. For example, the work commitments required to build professional careers are dependent upon 'domestic servicing', and the qualities ascribed to women associated with their role in the private sphere are viewed as inappropriate for high status, high paid professional roles in the public sphere (Sommerlad & Sanderson, 1998, pp. 15–16).

In Bourdieusian terms, the legal profession constitutes a particular social 'field'. The 'field' determines the positions of individuals within it through a set of objective power relations imposed on all entrants, which are not reducible to the intentions of individual agents or even to direct interactions between agents. Consequently, individuals have a limited capacity to challenge uncongenial environments, and may find the only opportunity for change is to exit the field (Sommerlad & Sanderson, 1998, p. 33). All fields are characterized by hierarchies of difference (Sommerlad & Sanderson, 1998, p. 34), which in the case of the legal profession includes gender difference. Within the field, individuals exercise power or are subordinated by reason of the social, cultural and symbolic capital they are able to deploy, or that is ascribed to them (Sommerlad & Sanderson, 1998, pp. 17, 32). Social capital is seen, for example, in the way in which the sexual contract 'enables men to gain systematic labour market advantages' (Sanderson & Sommerlad, 1998, p. 11). Cultural capital is often non-technical and informal, and includes a person's 'habitus' (sets of dispositions acquired through education and socialization, and conferring the ability to function in particular milieux) (Sommerlad & Sanderson, 1998, p. 33), and socially validated or devalued (gendered) attributes (Sommerlad & Sanderson, 1998, p. 6), such as those associated with activity in the public or private spheres.

Sommerlad and Sanderson also draw upon elements of organizational and Weberian theories to construct their model of women solicitors' articulation into the professional labour market. Prompted by the initial impetus of the research, they observe that women solicitors tend to have flatter career trajectories than their male colleagues, and to leave the profession mid-career. Given the relatively stable nature of this phenomenon, why is it tolerated rather than being perceived by law firms as 'a wasteful disaster' (Sommerlad & Sanderson, 1998, p. 18)? The reason they identify is that changes in the nature of legal work and the structure of law firms have created a need for 'a stratum of workers who will never achieve the professional dream of partnership' (Sommerlad & Sanderson, 1998, p. 18), and women fit perfectly into this niche. This then creates a self-perpetuating cycle: women's 'choices' about their careers are shaped by their coming to understand that they have only limited scope for advancement within the law firm context. Consequently, they downgrade their ambitions, take career breaks, go part-time, move to the public sector or leave the profession altogether. And because of the relatively low level at which they have been working, when they leave, they do not generally take clients with them, thus minimizing the cost to the firm of their departure (Sommerlad & Sanderson, 1998, pp. 18, 28, 44). The overall result is a segmented legal labour market with women occupying a subsidiary or secondary position, akin to a 'reserve army' of legal labour (Sommerlad & Sanderson, 1998, pp. 18–19).

Finally, Sommerlad and Sanderson use the Weberian idea of 'social closure' to examine the ways in which the exclusion of women/the feminine has been integral to 'the legal professional project' in the UK over time (Sommerlad & Sanderson, 1998, p. 7). For most of its history, women were kept out of the profession by being denied access to the qualifications needed to gain entry. Then, when women did gain access to the necessary academic qualifications, they were often excluded at the vocational stage required for induction into the profession. Now, when women have gained relatively free access to vocational training, the notion of 'commitment' functions as an exclusionary device, ascribing to women a lack of seriousness about their careers, channelling them into work that has limited career prospects, and resulting in the cycle of reduced expectations and departure outlined above (Sommerlad & Sanderson, 1998, pp. 39–40). In this context, while individual women may attempt to assimilate as closely as possible to the male norm in order to demonstrate their professional 'commitment' and get to the top, this can only work for women as individuals, not as a group. Moreover, the process of social closure is an institutional and cultural phenomenon. Individual men are socialized in this culture and participate in the marginalization and exclusion of women, but exclusion is not simply the product of the actions of a few individuals (Sommerlad & Sanderson, 1998, p. 19).

It follows from this model of women's participation that Sommerlad and Sanderson (1998) reject liberal constructs such as voluntarism and human capital theories of labour market attachment and behaviour (p. 6). These theories, premised on formal equality, are blind to underlying structures of domination, ignoring both the 'materiality of power' and historical processes of gender differentiation such as those outlined above (p. 29). Human capital theorists cannot account for the less favourable outcomes for women solicitors despite their identical investment in training and so forth, other than by ascribing them to women's 'choices' to specialize elsewhere. This fails to recognize the structures and processes within the professional field that constrain those choices, and also fails to recognize the operation of less measurable, cultural capital in terms of the ascription of 'feminine' attributes to women. Thus, it does not matter whether women are in fact the same as or different from men, what is important is 'the power of the profession to construct them as different, and then to both exploit and devalue that difference' (Sommerlad & Sanderson, 1998, pp. 28–29).

A notable feature of Sommerlad and Sanderson's work is the dynamic, iterative relationship between theory and empirical data. They begin with an initial theoretical frame of inquiry, which suggests the gathering of particular kinds of data. The theory is then tested against the empirical evidence, which may illustrate, refute, or complicate the theory, and result in a corresponding strengthening, adjustment or expansion of the theoretical frame. Further data may then be sought, and so on. Their theoretical frame also attempts to account for the complexity of the phenomenon being observed, rather than being either theoretically or empirically reductionist. They neither adopted the strategy identified earlier of collecting empirical data and then 'retrofitting' it with a theoretical analysis, nor did they allow a chosen, one-dimensional theoretical frame to drive the data gathering process to such an extent that only material that confirmed the original theory was able to emerge.

Sommerlad and Sanderson's careful analysis finally leads to a very clear policy conclusion. The 'problem' of a shortage of solicitors, and the major barrier to women returning to the profession after taking time out to have children, does not reside in the availability or nature of retraining. Rather, the issues are much more fundamental. Consequently, change in the entrenched patterns of women's participation/marginalization/exclusion can only occur through cultural transformation – transformation of what it means to be a lawyer for both men and women, and an accompanying transformation of gendered responsibilities in the private sphere (Sommerlad & Sanderson, 1998, p. 20). This is a much longer-term and far more uncomfortable project for professional bodies to face up to, and again, one that is yet to be fully acknowledged by policy makers.

4. FEMINISM, STATE WELFARE POLICIES, PUBLIC SECTOR MANAGEMENT AND WOMEN'S ACCESS TO JUSTICE

As an Australian academic subject to the kinds of institutional pressures identified above, I have, at various times, engaged in reformist, policy-oriented research and analysis, and then 'retrofitted' theory to my empirical research data for the purposes of an academic as opposed to a policy audience (see, e.g., Hunter & McKelvie, 1998; Hunter & McKelvie, 1999; Melville & Hunter, 2001; Hunter, 2002a; Hunter, 2002b; Hunter, 2003; Hunter, 2005). The project I wish to describe here, however, was one which, like Sommerlad and Sanderson's, began with both a policy imperative and a theoretical framework, followed by the collection of empirical data, which resulted in both adjustment of the theoretical frame, and policy recommendations. This was a study of women's access to legal aid in Australia, undertaken in conjunction with one of the State legal aid funding bodies, Legal Aid Queensland (LAQ). Two managers of specialist units within LAQ initially approached me with concerns about women's access to legal aid funding for family and civil law matters, and particularly the position of women living in regional and rural areas. Together we devised a research proposal and made funding applications. The project was ultimately funded jointly by the Australian Research Council (ARC) and LAQ.[5]

The research proposal drew upon both earlier feminist critiques of legal aid provision for women in Australia – centred around liberal theories of equality and citizenship (e.g., Australian Law Reform Commission, 1994; Office of Legal Aid and Family Services, 1994; Graycar & Morgan, 1995) – and the concept of 'intersectionality', derived from critical race feminism (e.g., Crenshaw, 1992; Spelman, 1988; Harris, 1990; Grillo, 1995; Hunter, 1996). The notion of 'intersectionality' suggests that 'women' should not be regarded theoretically as an undifferentiated whole defined solely by their gender, but rather should be recognized as occupying differing positions and therefore having different life experiences according to the intersection of their gender with other characteristics such as race, ethnicity, class, sexuality, dis/ability, geographical location and so forth. Applying this concept to our legal aid research meant that rather than examining 'women's access to legal aid, as had been the case in the previous Australian studies, we should determine whether differently situated women encountered particular barriers to access. This was both a theoretically more nuanced and inclusive approach that had been taken by earlier feminist critiques, and one that was more realistic in policy and political terms. Given long-term restrictions on the availability of legal aid funding and the practical unlikelihood of either federal or State governments providing sufficient funding fully to satisfy the demand from women for family law and civil legal aid,[6] it made more sense to investigate whether scarce legal aid funding was actually reaching the women who might need it most. This approach also meant that our research focused exclusively on women, and on potential differences between women, rather than undertaking a liberal gender analysis, which would require comparisons between the positions of 'women' and 'men' as a whole, or a radical gender analysis, which would focus on women for the purpose of identifying women's common experiences of patriarchal oppression (see, e.g., Reinharz, 1992). As well as representing a departure from earlier feminist approaches, this strategy was also, initially, somewhat controversial at the policy level. Our intention not to include men among our research subjects met with some objections, but we persisted, and the LAQ Board ultimately approved the proposal in its original terms.

The groups of women targeted for the project were Indigenous women, women from non-English speaking backgrounds (NESB), women with disabilities, women living in rural and regional areas, older women (aged 60+) and younger women (aged 18–20). The research involved the gathering and analysis of LAQ statistics on application and refusal rates over an eight-year period for women in these groups compared to overall patterns (and this element of the study did include comparisons with men in the relevant groups); statistical analysis of files of women refused legal aid over a two-year period, comparing women from the target groups with women who did not fall within one of these groups; interviews with a sample of the women whose files were analysed; interviews with lawyers, legal services, LAQ specialist staff, women's organizations and community organizations dealing with women in the target groups, and with LAQ grants officers; and interviews with women representing themselves in court in family law and domestic violence proceedings. The objective was to determine whether refusals of women's applications for legal aid had any adverse impact by reference to age, Aboriginality, ethnicity, disability or regional location; whether any groups of women with legal needs disproportionately failed to apply for legal aid; and what happened to women with legal needs, from the target groups or otherwise, who were refused or failed to apply for legal aid. The areas of law that formed the focus for the study were family law, domestic violence restraining orders and anti-discrimination complaints. We also focused on applications made to the main capital city (Brisbane) office of LAQ, together with four regional offices where preliminary statistical analysis suggested high rates of refusal of women's applications for legal aid in these areas of law. Because some of the target groups formed a numerically small proportion of the population (Aboriginal women, women with a disability), and/or tended to make few legal aid applications (younger and older women), it was necessary to be group-conscious not only into the analysis of our data, but also in the way the data was collected. For example, we overrepresented the target groups in the sample of refusal files, in order to gain sufficient numbers of files and interviewees from each target group. And the recruitment of service providers to be interviewed also focused on organizations having particular contact with women in the various target groups.

As data gathering proceeded and I became more familiar with the internal operations of LAQ and the grants decision-making process, it became clear that we needed to expand and adjust our theoretical frame in a variety of ways, in order to fully understand the phenomena we were observing. Just as Kaganas and Day Sclater found a split in the family law field between the ideology of welfare discourse and the complex reality of parental conflict, and Sommerlad and Sanderson found a split in the legal professional field between the ideology of women's equality and the reality of processes excluding women from the profession and its highest rewards, so too did we discover a split in the legal aid field between the welfare state ideology of access to justice and the reality of legal aid processes that operated to exclude from assistance and to create further disadvantage.

While purporting to espouse values of procedural fairness, effective resolution of clients' problems and the promotion of social justice, LAQ in fact operated very clearly within a New Public Management (NPM), paradigm, which appeared incompatible with those values (see, e.g., Sinclair, 1989; Halligan, 1993; Sommerlad, 1999, 2004; Freiberg, 2005). An understanding of NPM and its critiques thus became essential for comprehending the grants decision-making process. We traced in some detail the parameters of NPM in LAQ, with its emphasis on cost containment, standardization of services and processes, and quantitative performance indicators. This accounted for the fact that grant applications were decided by non-legally qualified officers whose performance was measured in terms of processing time, approval targets, overturn rates on appeal and compliance with periodic directives to free up or tighten spending according to the local and Statewide budget position. At the same time, our study was able to contribute empirical evidence to the literature on the effects of NPM. These included severely limited access to lawyers for women in rural areas due to LAQ's rationalization of its dealings with private law firms via the introduction of a 'preferred supplier' scheme; perceptions of poor service from preferred suppliers for clients who needed extra assistance; differential treatment of applications for legal aid made through lawyers and those made directly by applicants themselves, with the latter having much lower chances of success; grants officers refusing (direct) applications containing insufficient information rather than seeking further details, in order to comply with performance indicators for processing times; significant inconsistencies of decision making between offices and over time due to frequently changing budget directives; and funding guidelines having systematically adverse impacts on particular (gendered) categories of cases and legal problems.

In addition, the quantitative data from our refusal files threw up an unexpected and striking finding about the history of dealings with LAQ by the applicants who were refused legal aid in these cases. Almost all of the women refused legal aid during the two-year period examined (87%) had prior or subsequent dealings with LAQ, in the form of seeking free legal advice (one of the services provided by the organization) or making another application for legal aid funding, or both. Moreover, these were not occasional encounters; rather, the women whose files were examined had an average of six dealings with LAQ prior or subsequent to the relevant refused application. In almost all cases, too, prior and subsequent dealings with LAQ involved family law problems (93%), and a significant number of cases involved domestic violence problems (47%), although a very wide range of other civil matters were also mentioned. Older women and women living in rural areas were least likely to have a history of dealings with LAQ, but all of the NESB women in the file sample had a history of dealings with LAQ in relation to family law, and 92% of them also had a history in relation to domestic violence.

In order to make sense of these patterns, we drew upon a series of 'legal needs' studies undertaken in the UK in the last 10 years (Genn, 1999; Genn & Paterson, 2001; Pleasence et al., 2004; Pleasence, Balmer, & Buck, 2006). Rather than being legal aid 'impact' studies as ours was, these 'legal needs' studies have attempted to quantify demand for legal aid by undertaking large-scale population surveys asking about the incidence of 'justiciable problems' in the community, and what people tend to do when faced with such problems. Among other things, they have found that 'the experience of problems [is] far from randomly distributed across the … population' (Pleasence et al., 2004, p. 44), and that 'socially excluded groups' are especially vulnerable to experiencing multiple legal problems (Pleasence et al., 2004, p. 45). Moreover, people tend to experience clusters of legal problems (Genn, 1999, pp. 31–36), with particular groups being more vulnerable to particular clusters of problems than others. An identifiable 'family cluster' of problems comprises problems with domestic violence, divorce and problems related to relationship breakdown (Genn, 1999; Pleasence et al., 2004, pp. 37–40; Pleasence et al., 2006, pp. 66–70). Problems in this cluster tend to last longer than other problem types before being resolved (Pleasence et al., 2004, p. 98; Pleasence et al., 2006, p. 146), and in the UK, lone parents, people with a chronic illness or disability, and those living in rented housing have a high likelihood of experiencing multiple problems in this cluster (Pleasence et al., 2004, pp. 43–44; Pleasence et al., 2006, p. 73). On the basis of these findings, the legal needs studies have suggested a need for coordinated services so that problems are not dealt with in isolation and the likelihood of them leading to further problems can be minimized by means of early, preventative action (Pleasence et al., 2004, p. 105). They have also argued that given the association between socially excluded groups and the experience of multiple justiciable problems, promoting access to justice is an important means of tackling social exclusion (Pleasence et al., 2006, p. 155).

Our own findings from the refusal files similarly suggested a family law/domestic violence cluster of problems experienced by many of the female lone parents in our sample, and in particular by NESB women. Moreover, where those women had received grants of legal aid in the past, they had not been successful in resolving fully the problems the women experienced, but rather had led them into a recursive loop of unsatisfactory encounters with legal aid, lurching from crises over rejection to temporary fixes, while the underlying problems continued to escalate. Even within the objectives of NPM, it is hardly cost-effective for the organization to be repeatedly processing the same or related applications from the same applicants over and over. While the fact that socially disadvantaged groups tend to experience multiple legal problems, including a cluster of problems around family law and domestic violence, may seem to be stating the obvious, this has not been so obvious to date as to receive policy recognition in the design of legal aid systems. The Australia system rigidly separates constitutional responsibility – and hence legal aid funding responsibility – for family law (federal) and domestic violence (State) issues, and when grants officers make decisions on applications for legal aid in one of these areas, they pay no regard to previous applications or advice-seeking in the other area. Moreover, rather than any notion of dealing with people's legal (and social) problems holistically, the opposite occurs. Even in relation to single issues, grants are broken down into stages of proceedings in order to minimize expenditure on individual cases. Thus, a set of findings and recommendations that highlighted the experiences of applicants, and portrayed the application process from their rather than from the organization's perspective, was both novel and confronting.

Similarly, our research findings challenged feminist thinking on intersectionality. The study clearly demonstrated that the incidence of legal aid refusals was not randomly distributed across the applicant population, but it did not indicate that any particular identity category was universally or consistently disadvantaged. Rather, the picture was complex. Some aspects of the legal aid application and refusal process affected all women (and no doubt men as well). Other aspects did affect women in particular identity categories, especially NESB women trying to deal with combined family law and domestic violence problems in an alien legal system with few other sources of advice and support. Other aspects affected women living in parts of the State served by particular regional offices, or those living in areas where they did not have access to a lawyer to make a legal aid application. Finally, women with particular kinds of family law and domestic violence problems were disadvantaged by legal aid eligibility rules and guidelines. In other words, gender and other personal characteristics proved to be salient in the application and refusal process some but not all of the time. This suggests not only that a simple gender analysis (looking at differences between women as a group and men and as a group) may not always be helpful, but also that an intersectional analysis (looking at differences between women in different identity categories) may prove inadequate. Both approaches may fail to account for, or tend to reduce, the complexity of the situation. Rather, as a Foucauldian micro-politics might suggest, it is necessary to determine whether and how specific rules, policies and practices have the effect of highlighting particular identity categories (Grillo, 1995, p. 17) or producing other forms of disadvantage and exclusion. Arguably, the disparate groups of women identified above are those most in need of legal representation, both because they have difficult legal cases, and because they are obviously unable successfully to negotiate the legal aid application process without assistance. But this is as often the result of a combination of procedures and circumstances as it is of gender and other cultural categories.

This observation also has implications for the organizational structures of legal aid bodies like LAQ. The rationalizing impulse of NPM suggests that rather than having specialist units dealing with particular categories of clients (such as women, youth, rural and regional clients, and Indigenous clients), responsibility for the issues faced by these clients should be 'mainstreamed' throughout the organization (on 'gender mainstreaming', see, e.g., Moser & Moser, 2005, p. 12). But spreading responsibility in this way tends to result in crudely reductionist understandings both of the groups to be considered as the subjects of policy analysis (the 'mainstream' in mainstreaming), and of the issues involved for those groups. As Sylvia Walby has noted in relation to gender mainstreaming:

> Gender mainstreaming is always situated in the context of other diverse and intersecting inequalities. The practical recognition of such intersectionality is a current major concern. (Walby, 2005, p. 461)

It is highly unlikely, for example, that any Legal Aid officer would be able to identify the kind of complex impacts uncovered by our research. Indeed, the elimination of specialist units would be most likely to create further disadvantages and exclusions. But at the same time, there is a need for specialist units to consult and collaborate with each other on a regular basis, since the boundaries between them do not necessarily reflect the realities of clients' experiences of the system.

While some of the recommendations we made to the LAQ Board in the final report of the study (Hunter, De Simone, Whitaker, Bathgate, & Svensson 2006) were reformist in nature (suggesting adjustments to application, refusal and review processes and to legal aid eligibility criteria), the report also fully canvassed the theoretical issues around the identification of disadvantage in terms of gender and other identity categories, differential legal (aid) needs, and the effects of NPM on various applicant groups, and recommended a more far-reaching reconsideration of the institutional balance between the conception of legal aid as an instrument of social justice, and the implementation of NPM, with its tendency to subsume other values and concerns. While we did not expect LAQ to take all of these recommendations on board (and the organizational response to the report is still being developed at the time of writing), we hope at least to have sown some seeds of reflection that would not otherwise have been planted, and that may some day, in some (probably unexpected) way, bear fruit.

5. CONCLUSION

In response to the divides identified by some UK writers between critical legal scholarship, left political agendas, and empirical, policy-driven, socio-legal research, and indications of similar divides in the US, this essay has sought to demonstrate the possibilities for work that negotiates between progressive political commitments, social and political theory, policy concerns, and social scientific approaches to the interface between law and society, by reference to three exemplary case studies. These case studies were all produced in an academic climate that has been argued to discourage this kind of scholarship, and to emphasize instead the production of technocratic solutions to policy problems, discarding theoretical and political concerns that are of no interest to policy audiences. The fact that the case studies are three examples of feminist scholarship does not indicate a necessary feature of such work, but neither is it a coincidence. By its nature, feminism offers not just a set of analytical tools, but also a set of normative concerns that intersect with many contemporary policy issues. The addition of empirical research methodologies to this mix is less common, but potentially very fruitful, both for policy makers and for other feminist legal scholars.

The case studies discussed here employed a diverse array of empirical research methodologies, ranging from statistical analysis of quantitative data (our analysis of legal aid refusal files), to the 'reading' of personal narratives (Kaganas and Day Sclater's study of disputing parents). But they also reveal some commonalities between socio-legal work that falls within this genre. First, such work looks beyond the immediate operation of legal rules and institutions to connect law and the legal system with other systems, fields and discourses. Secondly, it seeks to represent, account for, and address complexity rather than producing simplified and bounded responses to often oversimplified or ideologically driven policy questions. Thirdly, no doubt as a result of going beyond specific policy questions to place them in a broader context and highlight the complexity of the situation, research that takes this approach may often be received with caution, if not coldly. It may be unlikely to provide a basis for ongoing consultancy relationships with policy makers, or to generate significant further funding opportunities. But since its value exceeds rather than being exhausted by the immediate policy context, it may continue to have a theoretical and/or policy life as part of broader, critical conversations about the legal system as it currently operates, and as we might imagine it becoming.

NOTES

1. Notably, Galanter's famous article did take a progressive (left) political stance.
2. See the New Legal Realism Home Page at http://www.newlegalrealism.org/
3. In the Australian higher education system, measurements such as 'research income' from grants and consultancies have formed a central element of federal government research funding formulae for universities for several years, with the 'impact' of research and value to 'end users' being more recent additions to the funding formula. In turn, 'national benefit' is one of the criteria used to assess applications for research funding to the major non-medical research funding body, the ARC.
4. Of course, similar research and theorizing has been undertaken in the US, Canada and Australia, with some similar results (see, e.g., Hagan, Zatz, Arnold, & Kay, 1991; Kay & Hagan, 1994; Kay & Hagan, 2003; Reichman & Sterling, 2001–2002; Reichman & Sterling, 2004–2005; Thornton, 1996), although not all of these studies shared the specific policy impetus of being commissioned by a legal professional body. Sommerlad and Sanderson refer to and draw upon previously published material by Thornton, and Hagan and Kay (and many other writers on women in the legal profession). In the description that follows, however, I am focusing on the specific approach taken by Sommerlad and Sanderson, and hence all references are to their book.

5. The research was funded under the ARC's 'Linkage' grant scheme, which involves joint funding by the ARC and one or more 'Industry Partners'. In this case, LAQ became the Industry Partner, and contributed well over half of the funding for the project, by a combination of cash and 'in-kind' contributions. The 'in-kind' contributions consisted primarily of the time of the two LAQ managers, who participated actively as part of the research team throughout the project. They were Tracey De Simone, then Coordinator of Women's Legal Aid, and Louise Whitaker, then Coordinator of Regional Access Strategies.

6. The Australian legal aid system is funded by both federal and State governments, with a broad division of responsibilities based on constitutional competence. Thus, family law legal aid is largely funded by the federal government, while legal aid for civil and criminal law is largely funded by the State governments. In 1995, the then federal Labor government announced a significant increase in legal aid funding in order, among other things, to redress identified shortfalls in women's access to legal aid. Before this funding program could be fully implemented, however, the government was voted out of office, and the newly elected federal conservative government made deep budget cuts to many federal funding programs, including legal aid, from July 1997. While additional funding has been made available for legal aid since 2001, previous levels have not been restored.

REFERENCES

Australian Law Reform Commission. (1994). *Report no.69, Part I – Equality before the law: Justice for women*. Sydney: Australian Law Reform Commission.

Banakar, R., & Travers, M. (2005). Law, sociology and method. In: R. Banakar & M. Travers (Eds), *Theory and method in socio-legal research* (pp. 1–25). Oxford: Hart Publishing.

Collier, R. (2004). 'We're all socio-legal now?' Legal education, scholarship and the 'global knowledge economy': Reflections on the UK experience. *Sydney Law Review, 26*, 503–536.

Conley, J. M., & O'Barr, W. M. (1990). *Rules versus relationships: The ethnography of legal discourse*. Chicago, IL: University of Chicago Press.

Crenshaw, K. (1992). A Black feminist critique of anti-discrimination law and politics. In: D. Kairys (Ed.), *The politics of law* (2nd ed., pp. 195–202). New York: Pantheon Books.

Day Sclater, S., & Kaganas, F. (2003). Contact: Mothers, welfare and rights. In: A. Bainham, B. Lindley, M. Richards & L. Trinder (Eds), *Children and their families: Contact, rights and welfare* (pp. 155–170). Oxford: Hart Publishing.

Erlanger, H., Garth, B., Larson, J., Mertz, E., Nourse, V., & Wilkins, D. (2005). Foreword: Is it time for a new legal realism? *Wisconsin Law Review, 2005*, 335–364.

Felstiner, W. L. F., Abel, R. L., & Sarat, A. (1981). The emergence and transformation of disputes: Naming, blaming, claiming … . *Law and Society Review, 15*, 631–654.

Freiberg, A. (2005). Managerialism in Australian justice: RIP for KPIs? *Monash University Law Review, 31*, 12–36.

Galanter, M. (1974). Why the 'haves' come out ahead: Speculations on the limits of legal change. *Law and Society Review, 9*, 95–160.

Genn, H. (1999). *Paths to justice: What people do and think about going to law*. Oxford: Hart Publishing.

Genn, H., Partington, M., & Wheeler, S. (2006). *Law in the real world: Improving our understanding of how law works – final report and recommendations*. London: The Nuffield Foundation.

Genn, H., & Paterson, A. (2001). *Paths to justice Scotland: What people in Scotland think and do about going to law*. Oxford: Hart Publishing.

Graycar, R., & Morgan, J. (1995). Disabling citizenship: Civil death of women in the 1990s. *Adelaide Law Review*, *17*, 49–76.

Grillo, T. (1995). Anti-essentialism and intersectionality: Tools to dismantle the master's house. *Berkeley Women's Law Journal*, *10*, 16–30.

Hagan, J., Zatz, M., Arnold, B., & Kay, F. (1991). Cultural capital, gender and the structural transformation of legal practice. *Law and Society Review*, *25*, 249–262.

Halligan, J. (1993). Defining a new public sector management: Australia and the international context. In: J. Guthrie (Ed.), *The Australian public sector: Pathways to change in the 1990s* (p. 22). North Sydney: IIR Conferences.

Harris, A. (1990). Race and essentialism in feminist legal theory. *Stanford Law Review*, *42*, 581–616.

Hillyard, P. (2002). Invoking indignation: Reflections on future directions of socio-legal studies. *Journal of Law and Society*, *29*, 645–656.

Hunter, R. (1996). Deconstructing the subjects of feminism: The essentialism debate in feminist theory and practice. *Australian Feminist Law Journal*, *6*, 135–162.

Hunter, R. (2002a). The mirage of justice: Women and the shrinking state. *Australian Feminist Law Journal*, *16*, 53–74.

Hunter, R. (2002b). Talking up equality: Women barristers and the denial of discrimination. *Feminist Legal Studies*, *10*, 113–130.

Hunter, R. (2003). Women barristers and gender difference in Australia. In: U. Schultz & G. Shaw (Eds), *Women in the world's legal professions* (pp. 103–121). Oxford: Hart Publishing.

Hunter, R. (2005). Discrimination against women barristers: Evidence from a study of court appearances and briefing practices. *International Journal of the Legal Profession*, *12*, 3–49.

Hunter, R., De Simone, T., Whitaker, L., Bathgate, J., & Svensson, A. (2006). *Women and legal aid: Identifying disadvantage – final report*. Brisbane: Griffith University and Legal Aid Queensland (available at http://www.griffith.edu.au/centre/slrc/).

Hunter, R., & McKelvie, H. (1998). *Equality of opportunity for women at the Victorian Bar*. Melbourne: Victorian Bar Council.

Hunter, R., & McKelvie, H. (1999). Balancing work and family responsibilities at the bar. *Australian Journal of Labour Law*, *12*, 167–192.

Kaganas, F., & Day Sclater, S. (2004). Contact disputes: Narrative constructions of 'good' parents. *Feminist Legal Studies*, *12*, 1–27.

Kay, F., & Hagan, J. (1994). Changing opportunities for partnership for men and women lawyers during the transformation of the modern law firm. *Osgoode Hall Law Journal*, *32*, 413–456.

Kay, F. M., & Hagan, J. (2003). Building trust: Social capital, distributive justice and loyalty to the firm. *Law and Social Inquiry*, *28*, 483–519.

Lacey, N. (1996). Normative reconstruction in socio-legal theory. *Social and Legal Studies*, *5*, 131–157.

Lind, E. A., & Tyler, T. R. (1988). *The social psychology of procedural justice*. New York: Plenum Press.

Lord Chancellor's Advisory Board on Family Law, Children Act Sub-Committee. (2001). *Consultation paper on making contact work: The facilitation of arrangements for contact between children and their non-residential parents and the enforcement of court orders for contact*. London: The Stationery Office.

Lord Chancellor's Advisory Board on Family Law, Children Act Sub-Committee. (2002). *Making contact work: A report to the Lord Chancellor on the facilitation of arrangements for contact between children and their non-residential parents and the enforcement of court orders for contact*. London: The Stationery Office.

May, V., & Smart, C. (2004). Silence in court? Hearing children in residence and contact disputes. *Child and Family Law Quarterly*, *16*, 305–316.

Melville, A., & Hunter, R. (2001). 'As everybody knows': Countering myths of gender bias in family law. *Griffith Law Review*, *10*, 124–138.

Mnookin, R. F., & Kornhauser, L. (1979). Bargaining in the shadow of the law: The case of divorce. *Yale Law Journal*, *88*, 950–997.

Moser, C., & Moser, A. (2005). Gender mainstreaming since Beijing: A review of success and limitations in international institutions. *Gender and Development*, *13*(2), 11–22.

Office of Legal Aid and Family Services. (1994). *Gender bias in litigation legal aid*. Canberra: Commonwealth Attorney-General's Department.

Pateman, C. (1988). *The sexual contract*. Oxford: Polity Press.

Pleasence, P., Balmer, N., & Buck, A. (2006). *Causes of action: Civil law and social justice* (2nd ed.). London: Legal Services Research Centre.

Pleasence, P., Buck, A., Balmer, N., O'Grady, A., Genn, H., & Smith, M. (2004). *Causes of action: Civil law and social justice*. London: Legal Services Research Centre.

Reichman, N. J., & Sterling, J. S. (2001–2002). Recasting the brass ring: Deconstructing and reconstructing workplace opportunities for women lawyers. *Capital University Law Review*, *29*, 923–977.

Reichman, N. J., & Sterling, J. S. (2004–2005). Sticky floors, broken steps, and concrete ceilings in legal careers. *Texas Journal of Women and the Law*, *14*, 27–76.

Reinharz, S. (1992). *Feminist methods in social research*. New York: Oxford University Press.

Sarat, A., & Silbey, S. (1988). The pull of the policy audience. *Law and Policy*, *10*, 98–166.

Sinclair, A. (1989). Public sector: Managerialism or multiculturalism? *Australian Journal of Public Administration*, *48*, 382.

Smart, C. (1984). *The ties that bind: Law, marriage and the reproduction of patriarchal relations*. London: Routledge & Kegan Paul.

Smart, C. (1989). *Feminism and the power of law*. London: Routledge.

Smart, C. (1995). *Law, crime and sexuality: Essays in feminism*. London: Sage.

Smart, C., & May, V. (2004a). Residence and contact disputes in court. *Family Law*, *34*, 36–42.

Smart, C., & May, V. (2004b). Why can't they agree? The underlying complexity of contact and residence disputes. *Journal of Social Welfare and Family Law*, *26*, 347–360.

Smart, C., May, V., Furniss, C., Sharma, K., & Strelitz, J. (2005). *Residence and contact disputes in court* (Vol. 2). London: Department for Constitutional Affairs.

Smart, C., May, V., Wade, A., & Furniss, C. (2003). *Residence and contact disputes in court* (Vol. 1). London: Department for Constitutional Affairs.

Smart, C., & Neale, B. (1999). *Family fragments?* Cambridge: Polity Press.

Smart, C., Neale, B., & Wade, A. (2001). *The changing experience of childhood: Families and divorce*. Cambridge: Polity Press.

Sommerlad, H. (1999). The implementation of quality initiatives and the new public management in the legal aid sector in England and Wales: Bureaucratisation, stratification and surveillance. *International Journal of the Legal Profession*, *6*, 311–341.

Sommerlad, H. (2004). Some reflections on the relationship between citizenship, access to justice and the reform of legal aid. *Journal of Law and Society*, *31*, 345–368.

Sommerlad, H., & Sanderson, P. (1998). *Gender, choice and commitment: Women solicitors in England and Wales and the struggle for equal status*. Aldershot: Ashgate.

Spelman, E. V. (1988). *Inessential woman: Problems of exclusion in feminist thought*. Boston, MA: Beacon Press.

Thornton, M. (1996). *Dissonance and distrust: Women in the legal profession*. Melbourne: Oxford University Press.

Walby, S. (2005). Comparative gender mainstreaming in a global era. *International Feminist Journal of Politics*, *7*, 453–470.

INTERNATIONAL LAW AND SOCIOLEGAL SCHOLARSHIP: TOWARD A SPATIAL GLOBAL LEGAL PLURALISM

Sally Engle Merry

At a recent conference on international law at UConn law school, I was intrigued by a talk on the bottom-up production of international law. Janet Koven Levit (2005), whose article is published in the *Yale Journal of International Law*, argued that she was describing a process quite different from that normally told by international law scholars (p. 126). The common approach to understanding international law is to tell a top-down story of states' treaty-based commitments or an intergovernmental organization formed by treaty. Insofar as there is a discussion of process, it focuses on diplomats in luxurious sites fine-tuning the language of a treaty. Yet, there are also forms of international lawmaking happening as practitioners figure out how to handle problems on a day-to-day basis. As they do so, they create and interpret rules, producing their own informal rules and practices. These ultimately become as much law as those based on top-down treaties. Levit (2005) says that there are many situations in which practice-based ways of doing things gradually become law. In the terminology of international law, "soft law" becomes "hard law." Soft law refers to a wide range of international instruments, communications, informal agreements, memoranda of understanding, codes of conduct, or "gentlemen's

Special Issue: Law and Society Reconsidered
Studies in Law, Politics, and Society, Volume 41, 149–168

ISSN: 1059-4337/doi:10.1016/S1059-4337(07)00006-3

agreements," while hard law are international rules and norms that at least technically binding (p. 127).

Levit (2005) looks at three little-known institutions in the world of international trade finance, one of which is the International Union of Credit and Investment Insurers (Berne Union), a non-governmental organization that regulates export credit insurance policies for its members, both public and private export credit insurers. Some of the rules developed by this organization have been adopted by formal international lawmaking institutions, transforming them into hard law. Yet, she notes that these rules have never been written about because the Berne Union rules have been accessible only to members (p. 128). Indeed, she had a great deal of difficulty getting access to the organization herself, which resisted her inquiries. As the conference attendees discussed why there was compliance with the technical rules which this group developed, she noted that the members form a close-knit group that comes from the same social class although from several different nations and routinely plays golf and socializes together.

I found this a fascinating example of a process of lawmaking eminently suitable to sociolegal analysis. It sounded like a close-knit group using informal social control. Exclusion would be financially as well as socially costly. This demonstrated for me the value of sociolegal research on international law. The Berne Union seemed ripe for this kind of study. Here is law made by a transnational group of public and private actors that shape the way transnational finance takes place. Furthermore, the idea that small groups of practitioners develop ways of doing things to make the system work and that these rules and practices are then appropriated by more formal institutions describes a process well known to anthropologists who study village law and its relationship to state law.

International law offers contemporary sociolegal scholars an opportunity to provide a sociological and cultural analysis of how international law works. This is a moment, as Levit notes, for the study of international law to move beyond a defensive insistence that international law is real law, with clear codes and formal institutions. It is a time to recognize the multiplicity of sources of law and practices that constitute it. Sociolegal studies took this approach to analyzing state law, showing that understanding it required looking at social organization, cultural meanings, and context as well as rules and formal institutions. Law and society scholarship insisted that law is constituted in multiple ways and that the practices that shape the way law operates take place not only in courts but also in lawyer's offices, district court clerk's rooms, mediation centers, and government offices where regulations are negotiated.

Despite the excellent legal scholarship on international law processes, however, there has been relatively little sociolegal scholarship in this domain (but see Halliday & Osinsky, 2006; Kingsbury, 2003). One consequence of the absence of sociological focus on international law is a lack of attention to three critical domains of sociolegal analysis: the relations of power among legal actors and legal regimes, processes of meaning making and legal consciousness, and the impact of various structures of social relationships on informal social processes such as shaming and social pressure. There are some exceptions: for example, Paul Schiff Berman (2005b) recently showed how theoretical frameworks from sociolegal scholarship such as legal consciousness, the study of governments and NGOs, and legal pluralism can contribute to analyzing to a variety of issues in the study of international law.

Although the concept of global legal pluralism has been proposed as an analytic framework for international law, it has not always been used with the theoretical depth of sociologically informed legal pluralism. This means considering the power relations among legal spheres, the extent to which any legal sphere expresses local normative standards, and social interactions among spheres. The concept can be used in a simplistic way to argue that there are multiple forms of law that exist side by side without examining the differences among them in the ways they exercise power and authority, their links to each other, and the various levels of moral and social support that they enjoy. This chapter suggests a framework of spatial legal pluralism that incorporates dimensions of power, meaning, and social relationships into a legal pluralist framework along with an analysis of spatial relationships.

The sociolegal study of international law is important because international law is increasingly imbricated in domestic law – the law of the nation-state. International regulations, agreements, human rights conventions, and other forms of law are increasingly merging with domestic law. It is no longer possible to study domestic law in isolation from these influences. International legal regimes like human rights shape domestic law, as do international tribunals such as those in Bosnia and Rwanda. Foreign aid is increasingly linked to instituting rule of law programs (Carothers, 2006; Upham, 2006; Zumbansen, 2007).

A sociolegal approach to international law begins from a recognition of the plurality of law. As Roger Cotterrell (2006) observes, the law and society relationship requires a rethinking of society under postmodern conditions. Communities shape the law that governs them and gives the law its authority and legitimacy. When communities are fragmented, fluid, and changing, linked through networks rather than territories and subject to movement of people and ideas, the law that they produce and that governs them becomes more plural. Imagining a stable system of law connected to a nation-state is no longer adequate. This fluidity and plurality of law is particularly characteristic of international law, with its competing forms of ordering and grounding in a highly mobile and fragmented set of social relationships.

The study of international law requires following the people who move transnationally as well as tracking the movement of legal ideas and practices. Communities of expertise made up of lawyers, judges, and business elites as well as social scientists move along these circuits. These communities of expertise, which include social science approaches, travel from the metropole to former colonies and back. Concepts such as culture, race, gender, and legal pluralism move through these global and neocolonial circuits as well. Translators play critical intermediary roles in circulating ideas from metropoles to more remote regions (Merry, 2006b). Thus, research on international law demands attention to the spatial distribution of actors and institutions as well multi-sited ethnography (Marcus, 1998).

The pioneering research of Yves Dezalay and Bryant Garth (2002), which traces the global circulation of "notables" between educational institutions and law firms in North America and governments and international agencies in Latin America is one example of this approach to sociolegal research on international law. But it is only a beginning. Clearly more is needed, including work that is more attentive to the role of social movements and non-elite actors than their Bourdieuian approach tends to be. Rajagopal's (2003) study of international law shows how international legal institutions have long been shaped by protest movements from Third World countries. Santos and Rodriquez' work on the mobilization of law from below, which they refer to as "subaltern cosmopolitan legality" (Santos & Rodriquez-Garavito, 2005), emphasizes the importance of transnational law to grassroots social movements (see also Rodriquez-Garavito, 2005). Sidney Tarrow's (1998) analysis of social movements focuses less on the role of law but foregrounds the importance of the diffusion of cultural conceptions of rights and social justice, linking the analysis of social movements with changes in legal consciousness.

Research on international law also demands attention to the new legal institutions that have been formed. This includes tribunals that endeavor to provide justice by prosecuting criminally those who have violated major human rights principles. These institutions include the formal tribunals established at the end of the Rwanda and Yugoslavia conflict and the International Criminal Court as well as more informal village tribunals in

Rwanda. Although these are new institutions, each incorporates in complicated ways laws, procedures, and practices from various previously existing national and local systems of law. These institutions are contributing to the creation of a new legal order, but they are also deeply constrained in their authority and practice by the system of sovereignty that underlies all transnational endeavors. They act both to hold leaders accountable and to create histories of periods of conflict and violence (see Teitel, 2000; Wilson, 2000, 2001, 2005; Hagan & Levi, 2005).

APPROACHES TO INTERNATIONAL LAW

This essay will consider three theories developed by international law scholars to analyze the international legal terrain and the strengths of each as well as issues it fails to address sufficiently in the dimensions of power, meaning, and social relationships: bottom-up lawmaking; transnational legal processes; and global legal pluralism. The idea of bottom-up lawmaking, already discussed, has the strength of beginning from the everyday practices by which problems are solved that lead eventually to the creation of a body of law. However, the phrase bottom-up suggests that this is a grassroots movement, while it is typically cosmopolitan elites who generate the informal rules that become established over time. Explicit attention to the power relationships underlying this process would help to clarify what "bottom-up" means. As Judith Resnick points out, the terms "soft law" and "hard law" are themselves problematic, incorporating gender ideologies and suggesting that some international laws are enforced firmly, which is rarely the case in practice (personal communication).

The transnational legal process approach argues that compliance with international law depends on normative change produced by social interactions among international legal actors. It is closely related to the work on international advocacy networks and coalitions in international relations that argue that these activities produce normative change over time. Transnational legal process joins both international and domestic law, public and private actors, state and non-state actors, and the dynamic production of new rules through interaction, interpretation, and practice which then shape further interactions and induce state compliance (Koh, 1996, p. 184). Even if nations are simply pursuing their interests, they internalize shared norms through interaction. Inside countries, interaction and discussion further internalization of norms into domestic social and political processes (Koh, 1996, p. 204).

This model addresses the question of why nations obey international law. Abram and Antonia Chayes propose a "managerial model," arguing that nations obey international law because of management by national actors pursing a cooperative model of compliance through interactive processes of justification, discourse, and persuasion (Chayes & Chayes, 1998; see also Koh, 1999, 2003, 1997, pp. 2635–2637). States are motivated to comply not because of fear of sanction but fear of loss of reputation. Compliance occurs through an iterative process of discourse among the parties, the treaties, and the wider public. Harold Hongju Koh builds on both the Chayes's managerial model and Thomas Franck's fairness model as ways to explain compliance, but finds them lacking in that both claim that compliance depends on voluntary choice. Instead, he advocates the idea of "transnational legal process":

> the complex process of institutional interaction whereby global norms are not just debated and interpreted, but ultimately internalized by domestic legal systems. Both the managerial and the fairness accounts fail to describe the pathways whereby a "managerial" discourse or "fair" international rule penetrates into a domestic legal system, thus becoming part of that nation's internal value set. (Koh, 1997)

His primary concern is norm internalization, which he sees as key to compliance. Koh (1997) argues that there is an evolutionary process whereby repeated compliance gradually becomes habitual obedience, and that it is this process of interaction, interpretation, and internalization of international norms into domestic legal systems that explains why nations follow international law rather than only conforming when it is convenient (pp. 2602–2603). The practices and norms become internalized and therefore shape future behavior.

Anne-Marie Slaughter (2004) has similarly examined the processes by which international law operates in practice, focusing on the role of liberal states (see also Hathaway, 2002). All of these theories place norm change at the center, since compliance ultimately depends on commitment to norms, whether on the basis of perceived interest, voluntary choice, or internalization. Koh (1996) offers a case study of the 1985 effort by Reagan and others in the US government to redefine the anti-ballistic missile treaty to enable the Star Wars program to develop. He notes that a variety of committed actors, political leaders, and NGOs, mobilized against the change. In 1993, along with a shift in the presidency, came an end to this effort. He argues that this outcome was the product not only of rules and interests, but also of the ongoing interactions among actors over time along with their normative commitments.

Studies of transnational advocacy networks in international relations, particularly by Keck and Sikkink (1998) and Khagram, Riker, and Sikkink (2002), similarly emphasize the centrality of normative change to the spread and effects of human rights (see also Risse, Ropp, & Sikkink, 1999). Some versions postulate a "norm cascade" when the process of adopting new international norms such as human rights becomes widespread in a country.

However, this body of scholarship focuses on states, institutions, and social movements rather than on the legal consciousness of ordinary citizens. These scholars recognize that the power of human rights depends on extensive local normative change, but they do not explore how and when actors change their normative understandings and subjectivities to incorporate a notion of rights. Thus, while this approach incorporates a sophisticated analysis of social interactions, it pays relatively little attention to processes of meaning making and individual consciousness. Anthropological work on meaning and subjectivity and law and society research on legal consciousness both offer a deeper understanding of how, where, and under what conditions norm change takes place (see Merry, 1990; McCann, 1994; Ewick & Silbey, 1998; Goodale, 2002; Nielsen, 2006).

Nor does this work theorize the effects of inequalities in power on processes of norm change and compliance. For example, while shaming is a critical normative process that is central to the way international law operates, it is more effective against weaker countries than stronger ones. Moreover, it is more effective when supplemented by political and economic pressure. When a group of rebels pulled off a coup against the elected government of Fiji in 2000, for example, the country faced serious economic and political sanctions. They were suspended from the Commonwealth, Australian tourists canceled trips and then boycotted the islands, and Australian longshoremen's unions refused to unload ships from Fiji, among other consequences. For a small, economically dependent country like Fiji, these economic pressures were major concerns, in addition to the shaming. In 2006, the military executed another coup, throwing out the elected prime minister and driving out its Australian-born police chief. Australia again threatened to suspend its membership in the Commonwealth and to implement defense and travel bans against the Fijian military and any government it set up (www.abc.net.au/news/newsitems/200612/s1804858.htm, December 5, 2006). The international community also threatened to suspend financial and technical assistance (*Fiji Times*, December 5, 2006).

Clearly, large and powerful countries are less vulnerable to such economic pressures than small and economically dependent ones. For example, both China and the US have resisted human rights surveillance of their domestic activities, showing that more powerful countries are less vulnerable to social pressure. Thus, the way transnational legal processes operate depends greatly on inequalities in power among nation-states.

A third approach to international law developed by legal scholars is global legal pluralism. This model focuses on the multiplicity of international and national laws, legal institutions, and forms of dispute resolution and the interactions among them. While the transnational legal process approach tells a story of increasing coherence and interconnections among laws as a result of these interactions, global legal pluralism focuses on the diversity and incompatibility of the systems. For some, this plurality provides myriad opportunities for social movements that use some forms of law and resist others while for others, it represents chaos and a weak international judicial order. For example, in Rajagopal's (2005) study of the Narmada dam dispute in India, he describes how international actors and organizations, human rights laws, and the Indian Supreme Court were all involved in determining the outcome of the conflict over the building of a dam on the Narmada River. This multiplicity of actors and normative systems provided greater space for mobilization and legal resistance than would a more coherent and integrated system.

Global legal pluralism builds on sociolegal and legal anthropological studies of situations of multiple regimes of law and applies it to international law. The concept, as used within anthropological scholarship, is used to describe the multiple forms law takes in different communities and the nature of the interactions among them. Legally plural situations have differing but coexisting conceptions of permissible actions, valid transactions, and ideas and procedures for dealing with conflict in the same social field (F. von Benda-Beckmann, 2002, p. 38; K. von Benda-Beckmann, 2001). During the colonization process, colonial legal systems were layered over indigenous ones. On occasion, colonial law recognized earlier systems of law, such as the British colonial incorporation of Hindu, Muslim, and Christian personal law into the administration of the Indian empire. The systems often have incompatible standards and procedures, and it is not unusual for individuals to engage in forum shopping among them (K. von Benda-Beckmann, 1981, 1984).

While some of the first work on legal pluralism imagined that relatively separate legal systems coexist, as they did in the dual legal systems common to British colonialism, Sally Falk Moore's (1978) notion of the "semi-autonomous social field" argued that such legal subgroups existed in industrial societies as well. Rather than seeing plural legal systems as circumscribed and bounded, she argued that they are semi-autonomous, operating within other social fields but not entirely governed by them.

But what constitutes a legal field? This question has caused major debates about the status of informal, non-state forms of normative ordering. Should these be called law? While some legal pluralists argue that a series of legal fields coexist, ranging from the informal regulations of family and neighborhood life to forms of private governance in institutions such as universities and state law, others counter that not all these forms of ordering should be called law (see Chanock, 1985; Melissaris, 2004). Brian Tamanaha (1993, 2000) made this argument forcefully and has since moderated his position. There are certainly differences among forms of ordering, particularly between informal forms of social ordering and state law. Indeed, much of the history of the anthropology of law has focused on this problem: can informal social ordering practices such as reciprocity and other binding obligations be called law, as Malinowski (1926) argued, or should the term be reserved for forms of ordering that represent a socially legitimate exercise of force, as E. Adamson Hoebel (1954) argued. Although the question of defining what law is remains unsettled in anthropology, from a pragmatic perspective, using a very broad conception that includes all forms of ordering has proved unhelpful, since it fails to distinguish those forms of law which exercise state power from those that do not. Moreover, various forms of order operate with quite different forms of authority and legitimacy. Lumping them all together, whether or not they are referred to as law, blurs these important distinctions.

Paul Schiff Berman (2002, 2005a, 2005b, 2006) suggests that legal pluralism offers a valuable framework for conflict of laws scholars in arenas as diverse as religions practices and Internet jurisdiction (see also Perez, 2003; Santos, 1995). Thinking of such clashes as conflicts among various legal regimes has several benefits, he thinks. It leads scholars to trace the shape of communities that hold particular views, even when they cross national boundaries. It forces state-sanctioned courts to take account of non-state normative commitments and treat them as law. It encourages respect for foreign judgments and laws. He argues that this framework provides a way for state-sanctioned courts to recognize the multiple sources of law and claims to authority so characteristic of modern society, including that of states, international bodies, or non-state entities (p. 7). Finally, he advocates viewing these conflicts as a good thing, a way of celebrating difference, rather than as a step on the path to convergence and harmony among the world's legal regimes. Instead of focusing on the emergence of "world law" as nation-state legal regimes converge, he advocates conflicts as a way of emphasizing the important differences among people.

Where Rajagopal and Berman see possibilities of creativity and resistance in the plurality of international law, others see global legal pluralism as a problem: a source of chaos and an assault on legitimacy. For international lawyers committed to a vision of increasing global coherence and order, the inconsistencies in the rulings of different tribunals and fora, the lack of a clear hierarchy, and the ambiguity of authority pose a serious problem. The multiplicity of tribunals with varying mandates and decisions weaken the force of international law. Koskenniemi and Leino (2002) describe the dismay over the fragmentation of international law expressed by leaders of the International Court of Justice, distressed at the proliferation of special tribunals not under their authority. This fragmentation reflects the different interest groups engaged in constructing international law (pp. 553–578).

But as a scholar of global legal pluralism, Koskenniemi and Leino (2002) see this proliferation of tribunals with overlapping jurisdictions and differing normative orders as a product of political pressures, not technical errors in the edifice of international law (p. 561). For example, he argues that human rights and economic values represent two competing universal logics, conventionally seen as quite different. The WTO and World Bank are engaged in promoting a regime of free trade, while human rights bodies are seeking to develop universalistic standards with a political orientation. In some ways, these two orders are quite separate in terms of ideology and institutional grounding. Yet, Koskenniemi and Leino argue that they are coming together as human rights bodies increasingly focusing on economic rights and the World Bank and other economic actors appropriate the language of human rights to describe their projects. This enables the World Bank to define them in ways compatible with their own ideologies, and at the same time acquire their legitimacy. Thus, political pressures have driven them together. However, Koskenniemi and Leino (2002) note that the risk is that as human rights become broader, they move toward indeterminacy (pp. 569–70).

The global legal pluralist model attends to both social interactions and to differences in the power of various legal regimes. Although it does not address questions of meaning and consciousness, it assumes that each legal regime bears with it a set of ideas about justice, rights, and process. Where it is portrayed in a static framework without sufficient attention to the interactions among systems and the way they are arranged in terms of relative power, the model fails to describe the nature of international legal processes adequately. However, a sociologically and culturally sophisticated version of global legal pluralism promises an effective analytic framework for understanding international law. But it needs to incorporate spatial considerations as well.

SPATIAL LEGAL PLURALISM

These three models of international law – bottom-up lawmaking; horizontal interactions leading to norm internalization, and global legal pluralism – all describe some dimensions of the practice of international law. If we add questions of space to global legal pluralism, it produces an even more useful way to theorize this complex legal field. Thinking in terms of law's geography foregrounds connections through spatial arrangements and leaves open questions about the nature of the overlaps and boundaries among systems. Spatial legal pluralism provides a way to conceptualize the state, with its domestic law and preeminent concerns about borders, as embedded within a global regime of law stretching across national lines. It also makes possible the analysis of forms of law that are not geographically circumscribed but move in a transnational way, jumping across borders and taking root in several separate and physically unconnected spaces. The legal systems of Native American tribes in the US, for example, represent pockets within the state legal system (see Biolsi, 1995). It provides a way around the global/local model, with its hierarchies and verticality.

Recent scholarship on a critical geography of law examines the connections among law, space, and power, recognizing that law constitutes not only identities and groups but also spaces and boundaries (Blomley, Delaney, & Ford, 2001). As a project of critical analysis, this body of scholarship joins questions of meaning, discourse, and normativity with questions of power, but does so with a "spatial turn," examining how the social meanings of spaces are shaped by power relationships and materialize those relationships (Blomley et al., 2001, p. xvii). Within anthropology, there is also substantial work on space and place that emphasizes the way places take on social and cultural meanings and significance (see Low & Lawrence-Zuniga, 2003).

Social phenomenon usually has spatial dimensions, although these often escape theorization. For example, certain spaces may be defined as open only to particular races, excluding others. Here, race and its spatialization reinforce each other, as the meanings of race are defined by spatial exclusions (Blomley et al., 2001, p. xvi). Similarly, the distinctions made in some societies between male public space and female private space which lead to restrictions on women's movements expressed through purdah, the need for women to get male permission to leave the home and travel, and the importance of women who move into male space to cover themselves and dress modestly are all ways that unequal power relationships are expressed through the demarcations of space. Insofar as these demarcations have a legal basis, as they did under the Jim Crow system in the American South and they do in some conservative Islamic countries, there is an inextricable link between the way law regulates persons and the way it regulates space.

The spatialized dimensions of law's power are likely to become naturalized and rendered invisible both in everyday social life and in sociolegal analyses (Blomley et al., 2001, p. xvi). As they observe, "much of social space represents a materialization of power, and much of law consists in highly significant and specialized descriptions and prescriptions of this same power" (p. xix). Although much of legal regulation defines spaces, from zoning regulations to immigration laws, its spatial grounding tends to escape analytic attention. Greater attention to the spatial dimension of law reveals not only its pervasiveness but also the extent to which it is overlapping, multiple, and inconsistent even in the same place.

Not only is law's power expressed through its demarcation of spaces, but the social meanings of spaces are defined by law. Borders, sovereign nations, and local communities are all spatial entities constructed by law. Indeed, Blomley et al. ask if law and space are in some ways identical, as in the example of the state, which is both a territorial and a legal entity at the same time. Transnational spaces are particularly interesting since they are simultaneously defined as part of local communities, as the UN is part of New York City, but also are constructing legal regimes that are global in reach and significance. The sociolegal analysis of international law raises questions of space with particular urgency. Where does it exist, how does it regulate, and how does it regulate differently in different spaces? There are a few transnationally regulated spaces that are not also regulated by other systems of law at the same time, raising questions about the intersections among these multiple forms of law.

A spatial version of legal pluralism emphasizes how law is different in different kinds of spaces such as urban, rural, global cities, isolated places and that there are connections among and across these spatial fields. It offers a way to think about the connections of legal regimes by examining the places they overlap, the boundaries and arenas of conflict, and the holes where no law governs. Unlike managerial approaches that assume that norm consensus emerges over time, a spatial approach suggests that normative and institutional differences may persist in separate spaces. Or they may coexist in the same space, remaining distinct but influencing each other. Unlike global legal pluralism models that see this multiplicity of legal orders as a problem, this approach recognizes that such contestations are inevitable and possibly productive.

Thinking of these interactions through the metaphor of geography highlights the dynamics of borders and contiguity, places where there is intersection and movement across, engagement and redefinition at the edges, the possibility of negotiation and adaptation. It also suggests that there are spheres of closure and refusal, where barriers are erected and the influence of other legal orders and conceptions is resisted. It suggests a complicated set of relationships among legal regimes and actors, international, regional, and domestic. For example, Tobias Kelly's (2004) study of law in the West Bank shows how changes in the legal demarcation of space shifts the mobility of Palestinian residents as it redefines their identities. Although they stay in one place, the law that governs them changes.

Spatial relations are very important to the constitution of social groups. Isin (2002) notes that "as groups realize themselves in space, they engage in strategies by inventing various technologies that alter configurations and properties of space so as to fragment, weaken, destabilize, constrain, immobilize, segregate, incarcerate, or disperse other groups as much as possible while increasing their own solidarities" (p. 49). The Berne Union is, after all, in Berne, and it is here that the members meet and perhaps where they play golf together (although they do not want to say so). Clearly, place matters.

The well-worn global/local dichotomy does imply spatiality, but not with any specificity. The local is any small place, while the global is everywhere and therefore nowhere. Dezalay and Garth (2002) emphasize the circulation of elites from North American economics departments and law schools to top governmental positions in Latin America and international agencies. They rely on Bourdieu's concept of the law as a social field, but do not theorize the spatial dimensions of that field. As Isin notes, although Bourdieu uses a spatial metaphor to describe "a network, or a configuration, of objective relations between positions," he does not investigate fields spatially but instead assumes that social space can be mapped more or less well onto physical space. Isin (2002) counters that social and physical spaces are in fact quite distinct in their constitution of groups (p. 42). My study of human rights and gender violence traced the circulation of ideas that violence against women was a human rights violation, a process linked to periodic conferences and meetings and the movement of individuals and knowledge across space (Merry, 2006a).

This model opens up the analysis of holes or gaps in state law: regions where state law does not reach and other forms of ordering take precedence. The tribal regions of Pakistan have long held this status. Janet Roitman's (2005) analysis of the Chad Basin in West Africa, a region of border crossing, smuggling, and organized criminal activity, is also a hole in state law, a place where legal regulation is local but not national, defined by border crossings rather than by a single state law. Clearly, people who are legal in one place become illegal in another and subject to deportation if they move, so that who they are depends on where they are (see Coutin, 2000; Yngvesson & Coutin, 2006).

The spatial metaphor provides a way to focus on regional regimes of international governance. There are regional human rights conventions and courts in the Americas and in Europe and one that is developing in Africa, for example. Some regions are organized into dominant powers and weaker ones, with the stronger ones taking the lead in establishing contacts with global regimes and housing the major regional organizations and governance systems. India plays this role in South Asia and Fiji in the Pacific. To call international law "global" suggests that it envelops the world equally. However, its regional influence is quite varied, depending on the form of government of a country or the strength of regional institutions. It may be stronger in the richer states of the global North than the poorer states in the global South. On the other hand, states of the global South are less able to set the terms of debate and often less free to ignore it.

The legal situation of Hong Kong provides a useful example of spatial legal pluralism. Hong Kong is a place with a complex and layered system of law that connects it geographically with a variety of other places depending on which layer of law is considered. It is tied to the Commonwealth through British colonial law, to China through its customary law, to the global community of states that have ratified the International Covenant on Civil and Political Rights (ICCPR), the basis of its 1991 Basic Law. Each of these fields of law has its own geography, its own shape and reach and incorporates different sections of the world in legal similarity. Each draws different kinds of connections and boundaries. Chinese customary law links the New Territories with Han communities in China, British colonial law with the British empire, mercantile law with trading partners, Chinese law with the People's Republic of China, and the human rights law of ICCPR with approximately 150 other signatories including the US and Canada.

Urban Hong Kong was governed by British colonial law since the 19th century, creating linkages between it and other former British colonies. When the British took over the rural New Territories near Hong Kong from China in 1899, they agreed to maintain its system of Chinese customary law. As the city worried about the handover to China in 1997, it passed a Basic Law based on the ICCPR in 1991. Since 1997, Hong Kong has been a Semi-Autonomous Region within China, under the oversight of a Standing Committee of the National People's Congress of China. Finally, Hong Kong shares mercantile regulations and treaties with many other parts of the world and is a desirable trading location because of its reliance on British law.

In its 2005 report from Hong Kong to the Human Rights Committee, the monitoring body for the ICCPR, China's regulation of Hong Kong came under international scrutiny. The Human Rights Committee asked for information on the Standing Committee's reinterpretation of the Basic Law in terms of its impact on the principle of universal suffrage in the elections of the Chief Executive and Legislative Council in 2007 and 2008 (CCPR/C/HKG/Q/2, December 7, 2005). The committee asked how this interpretation is consistent with the Standing Committee's obligation to respect civil and political rights in the Hong Kong Semi-Autonomous Region (p. 1). When I observed this hearing in New York in early 2006, the committee was critical of the Standing Committee's failure to abide by the terms of the Basic Law and sought to protect Hong Kong's autonomy from China, as specified in this law. Its intervention was part of a process that links Hong Kong to other ratifying states.

A dramatic confrontation over rules for women to inherit property in the early 1990s vividly illustrated the importance of taking a spatial approach to legal pluralism (see Merry & Stern, 2005). Although urban Hong Kong women could inherit property, when they moved to the New Towns built in the formerly rural areas, they unknowingly fell into the space of Chinese customary law. The urban women moved, but their law did not. The architects of these towns failed to petition to change the law, so that suddenly a large number of urbanites living in high rises in the New Territories discovered, in the early 1990s, that they had moved into the territory of a different legal regime of inheritance. The protest movement demanded equal inheritance rights for rural women as well as urban ones, thus demanding a shift in the law regulating the territory as a whole and not just for the urbanites who had moved there. Just as immigrants discover that their legal status changes as they cross borders, so these urban women found out that being in a different place changed their rights and privileges. Thinking of legal pluralism in terms of space thus opens up the analysis of movement and location in understanding how legal regimes intersect.

Another example foregrounds the role of the city as a distinct legal space with its own relationship to international law. In the US, progressive initiatives are increasingly coming from states and cities rather than the federal government. For example, CEDAW was passed in San Francisco in 2004 by a coalition: a human rights group called WILD for Human Rights, the Western office of Amnesty International USA, the San Francisco Commission on the Status of women, originally part of the city's Human Rights Commission but established as chartered department in 1994, and the Women's Foundation of California, a foundation that funds programs for women and girls in California (Diana Yoon, interview with WILD, May 2006). In the interest of developing an intersectionality approach, they added references to the convention on racism, CERD, to the convention on women, CEDAW. These groups are now trying to pass ICCPR and ICESCR as city ordinances. A similar initiative in New York City is working on a combined, intersectional CEDAW/CERD ordinance. There are also efforts in Boston, including plans to train state legislators in human rights in MA. These examples show how a geography of law framework can foreground such initiatives at the city level, which seek to join urban space with international law, bypassing the nation-state.

An important feature of spatial legal pluralism is the way pockets of legal regimes jump to new regions through transplants, global legal institutions, ratification of human rights treaties, the creation of special tribunals, and myriad other processes. One of the most important is that of vernacularization, through which global legal ideas become reinterpreted in local terms (see Merry, 2006a, 2006b). These regimes are all rooted in place rather than disembodied, but often in pockets rather than in a single contiguous territory. Their jurisdictions are often overlapping or pocked with openings where they do not apply. Rebel sections of states in civil war, territories subject to distinctive legal regimes such as Native American reservations, sections of cities subject to different rules such as embassies, all represent spatial pockets of distinct legal fields or holes within state legal fields. People move from places where they can live legally to those where they are illegal. Not only do groups change the legal regimes that govern them as they cross borders from places where they are citizens to those where they are aliens, but even those who stay in one place may find the legal nature of the place they occupy changing.

CONCLUSION

In conclusion, these examples show the value of a sociolegal analysis of international law that incorporates attention to power, intersections among systems, social networks, meaning and subjectivity, and space. Ideas of spatial legal pluralism provide one framework for thinking about these intersections. This approach does not posit sharp distinctions between international and domestic law. It recognizes transnational forms of law and gaps or holes in legal orders. It recognizes the multiplicity of law, countering the narrative of progress and increasing coherence of some international law scholars. It provides a framework for examining the varieties of legal consciousness, including differences in the awareness of and commitment to various forms of law, rather than examining only a progressive incorporation of norms. And adding the spatial dimension to the analysis of international law emphasizes overlaps, openings, gaps, and borders. This model builds on all three approaches discussed here – bottom-up lawmaking, transnational legal processes, and global legal pluralism, but emphasizes power, meaning, social interaction, and the spatial dimensions of legal fields.

REFERENCES

Benda-Beckmann, F. von (2002). Who's afraid of legal pluralism? *Journal of Legal Pluralism*, *47*, 37–82.

Benda-Beckmann, K. von (1981). Forum shopping and shopping forums: Dispute processing in a Minangkabau village in West Sumatra. *Journal of Legal Pluralism*, *19*, 117–159.

Benda-Beckmann, K. von (1984). *The broken stairways to consensus: Village justice and state courts in Minangkabau*. Dordrecht: Foris Publications.

Benda-Beckmann, K. von (2001). Transnational dimensions of legal pluralism. In: W. Fikentscher (Ed.), *Begegnung und Konflikt – eine kulturanthropologische Bestandsaufname* (pp. 33–48). Muenchen: Verlag der Bayerischen Akademie der Wissenschaften. C.H. Beck Verlag.

Berman, P. S. (2002). The globalization of jurisdiction. *University of Pennsylvania Law Review*, *151*, p. 311.

Berman, P. S. (2005a). Redefining governmental interests in a global era. *University of Pennsylvania Law Review*, *153*, p. 1819.

Berman, P. S. (2005b). From international law to law and globalization. *Columbia Journal of Transnational Law*, *43*(2), 485–556.

Berman, P. S. (2006). Conflict of laws and the challenge of legal pluralism (Draft).

Biolsi, T. (1995). Bringing the law back in: Legal rights and the regulation of Indian-white relations on Rosebud Reservation. *Current Anthropology*, *36*, p. 562.

Blomley, N., Delaney, D., & Ford, R. T. (Eds). (2001). *The legal geographies reader: Law, power, and space*. Oxford, UK: Blackwell Publishing.

Carothers, T. (2006). The rule-of-law revival. In: T. Carothers (Ed.), *Promoting the rule of law abroad: In search of knowledge* (pp. 3–15). Washington, DC: Carnegie Endowment for International Peace.

Chanock, M. (1985). *Law, custom, and social order: The colonial experience in Malawi and Zambia*. Cambridge, UK: Cambridge University Press.

Chayes, A., & Chayes, A. H. (1998). *The new sovereignty: Compliance with international regulatory agreements*. Cambridge, MA: Harvard University Press.

Cotterrell, R. (2006). *Law, culture and society: Legal ideas in the mirror of social theory*. Aldershot, UK: Ashgate.

Coutin, S. (2000). *Legalizing moves: Salvadoran immigrants' struggle for US residency*. Ann Arbor, MI: University of Michigan Press.

Dezalay, Y., & Garth, B. (2002). *The internationalization of palace wars: Lawyers, economists, and the contest to transform Latin American states*. Chicago: University of Chicago Press.

Ewick, P., & Silbey, S. (1998). *The common place of law*. Chicago: University of Chicago Press.

Goodale, M. (2002). Legal ethnography in an era of globalization: The arrival of western human rights discourse to rural Bolivia. In: J. Starr & M. Goodale (Eds), *Practicing ethnography in Law: New dialogues, enduring methods* (pp. 50–72). New York: Palgrave Macmillan.

Hagan, J., & Levi, R. (2005). Crimes of war and the force of law. *Social Forces*, *83*(4), 1499–1534.

Halliday, T. C., & Osinsky, P. (2006). Globalization and law. *Annual Review of Sociology*, *32*, 447–470.

Hathaway, O. (2002). Do human rights treaties make a difference? *Yale Law Journal*, *111*, 1935–2042.

Hoebel, E. A. (1954). *The law of primitive man.* Reissued 2006. Cambridge, MA: Harvard University Press.

Isin, E. F. (2002). *Being political: Genealogies of citizenship*. Minneapolis, MN: University of Minnesota Press.

Keck, M. E., & Sikkink, K. (1998). *Activists beyond borders: Advocacy networks in international politics*. Ithaca: Cornell University Press.

Kelly, T. (2004). Returning home? Law, violence, and displacement among West Bank Palestinians. *Polar: Political and Legal Anthropology Review*, *27*(2), 95–112.

Khagram, S., Riker, J. V., & Sikkink, K. (Eds). (2002). *Restructuring world politics: Transnational social movements, networks, and norms*. Minneapolis, MN: University of Minnesota Press.

Kingsbury, B. (2003). The international legal order. In: P. Cane & M. Tushnet (Eds), *Oxford handbook of legal studies* (pp. 271–291). Oxford: Oxford University Press.

Koh, H. H. (1996). Transnational legal process. *Nebraska Law Review*, *75*, p. 181.

Koh, H. H. (1997). Why do nations obey international law? *Yale Law Journal*, *106*, 2599–2659.

Koh, H. H. (1999). How is international human rights law enforced? *Indiana Law Journal*, *74*, p. 1397.

Koh, H. H. (2003). On American exceptionalism. *Stanford Law Review*, *55*, 1479–1527.

Koskenniemi, M., & Leino, P. (2002). Fragmentation of international Law? Postmodern anxieties. *Leiden Journal of International Law*, *15*, 553–579.

Levit, J. K. (2005). A bottom-up approach to international lawmaking: The tale of three trade finance instruments. *Yale Journal of International Law*, *30*, 125–209.

Low, S. M., & Lawrence-Zuniga, D. (Eds). (2003). *The anthropology of space and place: Locating culture*. Oxford and Malden, MA: Blackwell Publishing.

Malinowski, B. (1926). *Crime and custom in savage society*. Littlefield Adams.

Marcus, G. (1998). *Ethnography through thick and thin*. Princeton, NJ: Princeton University Press.

McCann, M. (1994). *Rights at work*. Chicago: University of Chicago Press.

Melissaris, E. (2004). The more the merrier? A new take on legal pluralism. *Social and Legal Studies*, *13*(1), 57–79.

Merry, S. E. (1990). *Getting justice and getting even: Legal consciousness among working-class Americans*. Chicago: University of Chicago Press.

Merry, S. E. (2006a). *Human rights and gender violence: Translating international law into local justice*. Chicago: University of Chicago Press.

Merry, S. E. (2006b). Transnational human rights and local activism: Mapping the middle. *American Anthropologist*, *108*, 38–52.

Merry, S. E., & Stern, R. (2005). The female inheritance movement in Hong Kong: Theorizing the local/global interface. *Current Anthropology*, *46*(3), 387–409.

Moore, S. F. (1978). The semi-autonomous social field. In: *Law as process: An anthropological approach*. New York: Routledge.

Nielsen, L. B. (2006). *License to harass: Law, hierarchy, and offensive public speech*. Princeton, NJ: Princeton University Press.

Perez, O. (2003). Normative creativity and global legal pluralism: Reflections on the democratic critique of transnational law. *Indiana Journal of Global Legal Studies*, *10*, 25–64.

Rajagopal, B. (2003). *International law from below: Development, social movements, and third world resistance*. Cambridge, UK: Cambridge University Press.

Rajagopal, B. (2005). The role of law in counter-hegemonic globalization and global legal pluralism: Lessons from the Narmada Valley struggle in India. *Leiden Journal of International Law*, *18*, 345–387.

Risse, T., Ropp, S. C., & Sikkink, K. (Eds). (1999). *The power of human rights: International norms and domestic change*. Cambridge, UK: Cambridge University Press.

Rodriguez-Garavito, C. A. (2005). Nike's Law: The anti-sweatshop movement, transnational corporations, and the struggle over international labor rights in the Americas. In: B. de S. Santos & C. A. Rodriguez-Garavito (Eds), *Law and globalization from below: Towards a cosmopolitan legality* (pp. 66–91). Cambridge, UK: Cambridge University Press.

Roitman, J. (2005). The garrison-entrepot: A mode of governing in the Chad Basin. In: A. Ong & S. J. Collier (Eds), *Global assemblages: Technology, politics, and ethics as anthropological problems* (pp. 417–437). Blackwell.

Santos, B. de S. (1995). *Toward a new common sense: Law, science and politics in the paradigmatic transition*. New York: Routledge.

Santos, B. de S., & Rodriguez-Garavito, C. A. (2005). Law, politics, and the subaltern in counter-hegemonic globalization. In: B. de S. Santos & C. A. Rodriguez-Garavito (Eds), *Law and globalization from below: Towards a cosmopolitan legality* (pp. 1–27). Cambridge, UK: Cambridge University Press.

Slaughter, A.-M. (2004). *A new world order*. Princeton, NJ: Princeton University Press.

Tamanaha, B. Z. (1993). The folly of the social-scientific concept of legal pluralism. *Journal of Law and Society*, *20*, 192–217.

Tamanaha, B. Z. (2000). A non-essentialist version of legal pluralism. *Journal of Law and Society*, *27*, 296–321.

Tarrow, S. (1998). *Power in movements: Social movements and contentious politics* (2nd ed.). Cambridge, UK: Cambridge University Press.

Teitel, R. (2000). *Transitional justice*. Oxford: Oxford University Press.

Upham, F. (2006). Mythmaking in the rule-of-law orthodoxy. In: T. Carothers (Ed.), *Promoting the rule of law abroad: In search of knowledge* (pp. 75–105). Washington, DC: Carnegie Endowment for International Peace.

Wilson, R. A. (2000). Reconciliation and revenge in post-apartheid South Africa: Rethinking legal pluralism and human rights. *Current Anthropology*, *41*, 75–98.

Wilson, R. A. (2001). *The politics of truth and reconciliation in South Africa: Legitimizing the post-apartheid state*. Cambridge, UK: Cambridge University Press.

Wilson, R. A. (2005). Judging history: The historical record of the international criminal tribunal for the former Yugoslavia. *Human Rights Quarterly*, *27*(3), 908–942.

Yngvesson, B., & Coutin, S. B. (2006). Backed by papers: Undoing persons, histories, and return. *American Ethnologist*, *33*(2), 177–191.

Zumbansen, P. (2007). Transnational law and societal memory. In: E. Christodoulidis & S. Veitch (Eds), *Law and the politics of reconciliation* (pp. 129–147). Aldershot: Ashgate.

POLICING AND THE POLITICS OF PUBLIC AND PRIVATE IN POST-KATRINA NEW ORLEANS

Adelaide H. Villmoare

ABSTRACT

During the immediate aftermath of Hurricane Katrina and the onslaught of flooding, the single most important role for government and the public sphere was deemed to be law and order, at times to the exclusion of other public responsibilities. Law and order were articulated almost exclusively as a policing matter with the emphasis on order rather than law. Policing took different public and private forms in the early days of the flooding. This chapter examines the nature of that policing and the unquestioned presence of private police as a key element of the law and order response to Katrina in New Orleans.

INTRODUCTION

Although the law and order rhetoric of the 1960s has never completely disappeared from the political scene, it surfaced with renewed vigor in post-Katrina New Orleans. During the immediate aftermath of the hurricane and the onslaught of flooding, the single most important role for government

Special Issue: Law and Society Reconsidered
Studies in Law, Politics, and Society, Volume 41, 169–185

ISSN: 1059-4337/doi:10.1016/S1059-4337(07)00007-5

and the public sphere was deemed to be law and order, at times to the exclusion of other public responsibilities. Law and order were articulated almost exclusively as a policing matter with the emphasis on order rather than law. And policing took different public and private forms in the early days of the flooding.

Understandably order was a priority after Katrina. Most foundations of an orderly society were ripped apart by the flooding and devastatingly slow and ineffective rescue efforts. Neighborhoods, families, churches, schools, jobs, the physical infrastructure, and government, including the police, courts, and jails, were either destroyed or immobilized. Douglas Brinkley's *The great deluge* (2006) describes in intricate detail the fear, death, and violence the flooding precipitated. Even in the absence of orderly routines of life, however, many concentrated on help rather than order.

People reached out to one another by using the minimal resources available them. The New Orleans Louisiana "homeboys," people who had refused to evacuate, for example, assisted neighbors they did not know (Brinkley, 2006, p. 303). They worked on saving lives and doing the best they could to support their community. When outside help was slow and inadequate, reporters in New Orleans displayed outrage at government's failures at all levels to rescue its people. The failures played out against the widely recognized "cleavage of race and class" (DeParle, 2005) that was repeatedly and graphically visualized on television. Comparisons between the suffering in New Orleans and the lack of help seen in the third world appeared with some frequency in the media (Geltzinis, 2005).

But order, not help, was the priority of many others. Calls for order involved little by way of formal law or justice and emphasized policing to protect property and counter violence. Rumors and realities of looting and violence, for instance, fueled the Federal Emergency Management Agency's (FEMA) heartless and destructive early responses. FEMA's self-imposed mandate was above all else to institute order in New Orleans. It refused offers of help from various governmental and non-governmental bodies and individuals because it had no secure way to control the organizations offering assistance. FEMA prevented rescue groups from entering New Orleans because it deemed the city too dangerous (Dyson, 2006, pp. 118–123; Horne, 2006, p. 89). FEMA's concentration on order and its own authority and control were more important than letting people get into New Orleans to help.

Policing was to be the antidote to disorder and rumors of looting, "thuggism," and violence, and policing had a confusing public and a private face. The New Orleans Police Department (NOPD), the National Guard, some US military, and privately hired security personnel all worked in the inundated city. Public and private police acted independently of one another. In the face of the breakdown of government in New Orleans, public coordination of policing did not occur.[1] And private security firms patrolled parts of the city completely on their own with no government authorization.

In the first days of the flooding the perceived need to protect property and people from looting and violence was more pressing than governmental authority as a source or resource of public order. Democratic tenets that policing, especially policing with weapons and the legitimacy to use them, should be tightly monitored by a publicly elected government did not much matter in post-Katrina New Orleans. In the chaos of the moment absent was recognition that policing, particularly private policing, could escalate violence or result in further disorder and loss of life. Such recognition has not yet figured in public discussion about the policing responses to the hurricane and flooding.

This chapter revisits issues of public and private distinctions in the context of the law and order responses, particularly the private policing responses, in post-Katrina New Orleans. The speed and ease with which private policing constituted part of the early reaction to the devastation in the city were remarkable. When private security firms moved into the city, no one asked questions about their presence, their legitimacy as a policing force, or their relationship with governmental authority. The unquestioned presence of private policing in the face of pressing law and order rhetoric may be emblematic of neo-liberal politics that readily accepts failures of government, welcomes privatization of public responsibilities, and embraces "a *multiplicity* of non-state policing agencies of diverse form" (Kempa, Carrier, Wood, & Shearing, 1999, p. 198).[2] But in a democracy private policing, especially in emergency circumstances where issues of accountability recede into the background, should provoke public discussion. And in New Orleans, where the disaster unfolded in the "cleavage of class and race," the role, power, and public accountability of private police should have been openly and explicitly examined.[3]

To make this argument is not to conclude, however, that the public sphere is necessarily orderly or just or that the private sphere is inherently unjust or anti-democratic. Public law and order have failed to overcome and continue to support inequitable and repressive policies. In the public sphere right after Katrina the police chief of mostly White Gretna, Louisiana at gunpoint blocked mostly Black evacuees from leaving New Orleans and entering its township, and the town council subsequently passed a resolution supporting his actions.[4] In the private sphere everyday understandings of law can challenge the oppression of public order and law and enable the disempowered to press for progressive political change (McCann, 1994; Ewick & Silbey, 2003; Lovell, 2006). In a democracy, nonetheless, questions of law and order should be ultimately formulated and addressed in the public sphere.

PUBLIC AND PRIVATE

Although one can draw an analytic distinction between public and private, where the public is defined by government and democratic discourse open to all, it is futile to establish crisp, permanent lines between public and private spheres (Wolfe, 1997).[5] Depending on the context it can be difficult to distinguish, for instance, public and private policing because different forms of policing are interrelated (Sklansky, 2006).[6] Public and private are seen in relation to one another, they overlap, and they fulfill some of the same societal functions (Bailey, 2002).

Despite its slippery quality the distinction remains valuable because the public, rather than the private, is politically obliged to speak to the responsibilities of democratic governance. To acknowledge this obligation is not to deny that doing politics involves the pursuit of self-interests which have no public purpose. Obviously politics can be completely self-serving. Democratic engagement should mean, however, that all sectors of society, the dispossessed and the powerful, as Carl Boggs (2000) puts it, "come together, interact, make decisions, forge citizen bonds, carry out imperatives of social change, and ultimately search for the good society" (p. 7). Searching for the larger good is an expansive and inclusive process. The public, thus, includes civil society and government working for purposes that reach beyond narrow constructions of self-interest.

Civil society, which Joe Bailey (2002) characterizes as "those collective public activities that are independent of the state's regulating, controlling, and shaping activities" (p. 21), is crucial to the ways in which the governmental sphere operates in a democracy. Media and varieties of political discourse constitute a significant part of civil society, as do the different ways in which people come together to "do" politics. Protest against public policy is as much a part of the public sphere as the policy itself. Democracy requires not only open, responsible, and equitable governance but awareness and participation on the part of those not in government. Political agendas are established by politicians, government bureaucrats, and the populace. An inert civil society diminishes the value of the public and fosters undemocratic values and policies (Macedo et al., 2005).

Values of equity and fairness have more ideological purchase in the public sphere than in the private in the US. While there are many governmental policies that support profoundly inequitable results (e.g. the war on drugs), in public there is at least a chance of engagement with the unjust consequences of such policies.[7] Decisions removed from the sphere of government and civil society have the potential for less transparency and accountability because the vehicles for demanding both are very limited in the private realm where institutionalized responsibilities to respond to such demands are often non-existent. The significance of the public sphere and open information and debate are most compelling with respect to the use of force. Privately exercised force can readily further inequality with impunity, as it historically did in the US. Although the public exercise of force is not automatically attuned to democratic values of equality and accountability,[8] there is a greater likelihood of substantial and organized outrage about and resistance to the improper use of public force than there is to private force.

"DISORDER" AND LOOTING IN POST-KATRINA NEW ORLEANS

The aftermath of Katrina in New Orleans and the lack of preparedness at all levels of government resulted in the collapse of the traditional institutions of law. With the flood both public and private sources of order evaporated. Disorder of all sorts prevailed, only part of which could be considered criminal, and even criminal actions took on non-criminal meanings in a city where people were trapped without food, water, and medicine, and where help arrived only haltingly.

The first news reports fueled law and order passions.[9] Media built on rumors and created the frenzy about lawlessness, particularly among African Americans. According to one study of reporting on Katrina, the panicky coverage even supplanted images of disorder and crime with those of a "war zone" (Tierney, Bevc, & Kulihgowski, 2006, pp. 63, 72). Most of the rumors, however, proved ill-founded. According to testimony before the Senate by William M. Lokey, Federal Coordinating Office in Louisiana:

> Throughout the early days of the response, media reports from New Orleans featured rampant looting, gunfire, crime, and lawlessness, including murders and alleged sexual assaults at the Superdome and Convention Center. Few of these reports were

> substantiated, and those that were – such as gunfire –were later understood to be actually coming from individuals trapped and trying to attract the attention of rescuers in helicopters. (The Failure of Initiative, 2006, p. 169)

There were lootings and assaults in the desperate conditions following Katrina. People did go "shopping" for electronics and other consumer goods. Brian Williams of NBC said that gangs had invaded into the Ritz-Carlton Hotel (Brinkley, 2006, p. 319).[10] Violence, including sexual assaults, occurred (Horne, 2006, pp. 115–116). But most rumors of disorder were wrong. Louisiana National Guard Colonel Thomas Beron explained that at the Superdome "bad things happened, but I didn't see any killing and raping and cutting of throats or anything … Ninety-nine percent of the people in the Dome were very well-behaved" (Brinkley, 2006, p. 193).

A counter-story to that of lawless looting was that many were seeking what they needed to survive and cope with their destitute circumstances. A Walgreens, locked, without power and where food and drinks were spoiling, was broken into; people took food and drinks (although later the store was ravaged). The police helped a group of doctors "commandeer" medical supplies from the store (Brinkley, 2006, pp. 361–362). The "Robin Hood Looters" scavenged for food to help those stranded (Rodriguez, Trainor, & Quarantelli, 2006, p. 91). The reality of much "looting" became clear to those observing events. An NBC video man witnessed police chasing and arresting a pregnant woman who had taken pampers and powdered milk for her baby (Brinkley, 2006, p. 202). Two African American men were sighted carrying supplies from Rite Aid and later distributing them to elderly people left behind in a high-rise (Brinkley, 2006, p. 378).

There was yet another counter-story – about looting that did not occur, opportunities for stealing and destruction that were not seized. Writing about his native New Orleans after the flood, Michael Lewis (2005) observed that in the Uptown areas "houses may have been violated by trees but not by looters, despite how easily they could have been entered" (p. 46). He looked at hundreds of houses that had not been touched by anything other than the storm. If looting had been a dedicated project, there were so many places that would have been invaded but were not.

Race was an integral part of the rumors about looting and disorder.[11] Most of those stranded in New Orleans were African American; most of the identified looters were African American. Two well-publicized AP photos and captions which circulated the Internet and analyses after the fact framed the racialized talk about looting. In each photo people were shown with bags and soda; the one of the African American referred to "looting," and the one of the white referred to "finding" bread and soda (Dyson, 2006,

p. 164). So, those who were "looting" were African American, and those, like the doctors, who "commandeered" were white. Looters and those involved in bullying and threatening property were labeled "thugs." These photos and the language of thuggism were emblematic of the criminalization of African Americans (Kaufman, 2005). Michael Eric Dyson (2006) observes that "Even those critics who were sympathetic to the urgent conditions of the abandoned blacks felt pressured to embrace the frame of reference of black criminality before otherwise defending poor blacks" (pp. 166–167). The need to reestablish order meant, among other things, that African Americans had to be controlled.

POLICING

Responders and observers evinced the belief that mainly what was needed was the imposition of force. Conservative commentator Peggy Noonan remarked: "As for the tragic piggism that is taking place on the streets of New Orleans, it is not unbelievable but it is unforgivable, and I hope the looters are shot." Brigadier General Gary Jones of the Louisiana National Guard said on September 2: "This place is going to look like Little Somalia. We're going to go out and take this city back. This will be a combat operation to get this city under control" (Voices in the Storm, 2005). Policing akin to military duty was being called for.

Official responses to "black criminality" and disorder were almost universal: police with guns authorized to shoot. According to Dyson (2006), Governor Blanco authorized the National Guard "to shoot and kill 'hoodlums'" (p. 114). Michael Lewis (2005) recounts this story from his stop at a gas station on his way into New Orleans: "I ran into two young men leaving in a pickup truck. They had just been stopped by the police and related the following exchange. Cops: 'Are you armed?' Young men: 'Heavily.' Cops: 'Good. Shoot to kill'" (p. 47). At one moment Mayor Nagin decided that most of the New Orleans police should cease rescuing people and arrest looters instead. While Brinkley (2006) says that this decision was made because of the "wanton violence" (p. 447), it was difficult to know how violent the city was. But the publicly stated priority on policing over rescue was made clear in this decision.[12] And police exercise of serious force, even to kill, was endorsed in many quarters.

Post-Katrina policing involved a variety of public and private forces. Police Chief Eddie Compass tried to maintain the NOPD, but many officers whose homes were destroyed found their first obligation to be to their families and left the city. The police department did arrest people and put some of them in the temporary jail at the Greyhound bus terminal. The FBI, whose local headquarters was flooded, worked alongside the NOPD (Brinkley, 2006, p. 226). Three hundred National Guard troops arrived on September 2.[13]

Private security firms streamed into New Orleans. After Katrina the increase in security firms registered in Louisiana rose from 185 to 235 (Scahill, 2005). DynCorp, Intercon, American Security Group, Wackenhut, Instinctive Shooting International, and Bodyguard and Tactical Security were guarding homes and businesses. Heavily armed, they appeared ready to use their weapons. Israeli trained Instinctive Shooting International guards, for instance, came in "Russian assault helicopters" and displayed their M-16s as they sought to "secure the perimeter" (Lewis, 2005, p. 49) of the gated community of Audobon Place (Scahill, 2005). Blaine Kern, owner of Mardi Gras World, gave the security guards he had hired permission to shoot, and they did exchange gunfire with looters (Brinkley, 2006, p. 199).

Blackwater was one of the first groups into New Orleans immediately after the hurricane. Its initial foray into New Orleans was without a government contract. According to Blackwater Vice Chairman Cofer Black, the company sent in a helicopter and crew to help. Blackwater, then, appeared to begin its policing without public authorization. Heavily armed Blackwater men patrolled streets to "join the hurricane relief effort" (Scahill, 2005). At some point they claimed to be operating under contract with the Department of Homeland Security (Scahill, 2005). Blackwater set up a headquarters above a downtown bar and said they were "securing neighborhoods" and "confronting criminals."[14] As it had in Iraq, Blackwater was acting in a public capacity even though the immediate source of its authority was – at least in the first stages of its entry into New Orleans – ambiguous. Later it did have a contract with FEMA to protect federal reconstruction projects (Scahill, 2006).

Policing may have been intended to secure social order, but the weaponry, the paramilitary and military character of those patrolling, and the lack of law were a recipe for further violence and abuse of the disempowered. As Lewis (2005) described the situation, "Pretty quickly, it became clear that there were more than a few people left in the city and that they fell broadly into two categories: extremely well-armed white men prepared to do battle and a ragtag collection of irregulars, black and white, who had no idea there was anyone to do battle with" (p. 49). The militarized forces of order were looking for a war rather than seeking to assist the abandoned.[15] The private, armed guards and few home owners remaining Uptown believed the rumors about black people with automatic weapons hunting white people (Lewis, 2005, p. 50). They prepared for armed battle between whites and blacks. There was little public constraint on unfounded rumors, racism, or the ability to use force and violence for private purposes.

Before Katrina New Orleans had a troubling crime rate.[16] One could argue that crime control was an ongoing dilemma for government in a city with great economic and racial disparities and few resources to enrich the foundations of civic order. In a city with an infestation of guns, sharp inequalities, devastating flooding paralyzing the city's infrastructure and work forces, and the media's inevitable tendency to generate "disaster myths" about looting (Tierney et al., 2006, pp. 60–61), the American recipe for a law and order panic was in place. That panic created the agenda and tone of initial actions where policing overwhelmed alternative priorities. Responding to disorder, rather than to flooding and stranded and vulnerable people, meant that policing – public and private – was the first order of business. Where disorder and the fears of disorder rather than rescue, help, or social justice define a situation, as they did in the early post-Katrina days, the use of force through policing – public and private – is often the initial political reaction. And in New Orleans it was a reaction whose political meanings were not publicly recognized or addressed.

PUBLIC ORDER AND PRIVATE POLICING

Singer (2003) observes that until lately "One area where the debate over public or private never ventured … was the military, the force that protects society" (p. 7). One could say the same about policing, but with the recent, rapid growth of non-state, private policing the "privatization of force" has been ripe for public debate.[17] While experts and scholars in the field have raised questions about the meanings of private and quasi-private policing, there has been a remarkable silence on the issues in political discourse. The US may already have crossed over to unquestioning acceptance of private policing in all its variations. Neo-liberalism has affected policing and law and order politics, just as it has other policy areas. And it has done so without careful public airing of its meaning for democratic values and possibilities of progressive politics. The policing in Katrina's aftermath should have provoked consideration about whether a liberal, democratic state can, does, or should monopolize policing forces, but it did not.

Unquestionably private policing in the US has made dramatic strides. As Elizabeth E. Joh (2005) demonstrates, "Private police now employ more people and spend more dollars than our public police agencies do. Moreover, private police are increasingly referred to as the first line of defense in the war against terrorism" (p. 575). One study, cited by Sklansky (2006), reveals that "45% of all local governments were contracting out at least some of their security work by the late 1990s – up 27% from a decade earlier" (p. 92). Private policing is not new, but its contemporary corporate character and extensive range of expertise and responsibilities are. Private policing undertakes "various lawful forms of organized, for-profit personnel services whose primary objectives include the control of crime, the protection of property and life, and the maintenance of order" (Joh, 2005, p. 577). This form of policing poses serious issues for a democracy (Sklansky, 2006).

Blackwater's swift, armed appearance in New Orleans without apparent public authority is emblematic of the issues. Few public queries were then or have been now raised about its presence.[18] There would appear to be an assumption of normalcy about a private corporation's personnel and weaponry on the streets of an American city.[19] Granted there was little normal about post-Katrina New Orleans, but the unquestioned presence of Blackwater and other private policing/military companies could and should have been at least legally and politically noticeable and notable. Even non-disaster situations in which private firms participate provoke little reaction and few political queries. Joh (2005) reports that

> ... some private agencies can rival the most sophisticated public police or military organizations. Palm Beach Gardens, a gated community in Florida, employs a five-person Special Tactical Operation Patrol; it lacks any special legal authority, but is equipped with night-vision scopes, infrared heat detectors, high-speed vehicles, and specially-trained dogs. (pp. 599–600)

In a neo-liberal society where wealth is expected to buy peace of mind and security, private security firms fit in rather comfortably with that expectation.

Certain firms, like Blackwater, do both policing and military work. Legal distinctions between use of police and deployment of military are reduced or erased when private companies train for and do both.[20] Was Blackwater acting as a police or military force in New Orleans or both? In general one could say that the distinction between police and military continues to matter in US politics. Under disaster conditions perhaps the distinction should matter less or not at all, but the governor of Louisiana and the president of the US thought it did.[21] There was public discussion about the Posse Comitatus Act which prohibits the use of US military for law enforcement purposes unless Congress approves the action or governor's request military help to support local police (rather than supplant them). But for private military firms, the discussion did not present itself in post-Katrina New Orleans. Former Israeli commandos with their Russian assault helicopters "securing the perimeter" with "guns aimed, eyes darting" in Audobon Park (Lewis, 2005, p. 49) ought to have provoked a public reaction about the rule of law, the role and authority of private police, and the ways in which force is exercised in the US.

CONCLUSION

The law and order reaction to post-Katrina New Orleans raises a number of questions about public responsibilities in policing and the role of private police especially under crisis conditions. Gretna's White police firing over the heads of mostly Black evacuees to prevent their entering their town leaves little room for doubt about the challenges public policing still poses for democratic values. And private commandos looking to secure White residences from Black New Orleanians should prompt questions about their role in a democracy. But issues of private policing have not garnered the public attention they should have. The lack of discussion about private police forces is disquieting in a society that continues to struggle with racial divides. In the public forum racism is open to legal challenge, criticism, and political resistance. In New Orleans there was no public forum about private policing; rather there was simply acceptance of private security firms as an appropriate response to the situation.

Analysts point out that in the US government exercises control over its contractors and can work effectively with and monitor private police (Sklansky, 2006; Rosky, 2004). If inequitable treatment results from privatization, the government can step in and require private companies to comply with standards of equity. But that oversight requires public dialog about law and equity, which can be minimal at times of crisis. When media, racial hierarchy, and other conditions make order the first and only priority, a discourse contesting that priority and the policing it inspires often gets little public consideration in the US. Further, as Rosky (2004) suggests, private supply warps public demand and can intensify the demand for the exercise of force (p. 955). Private military and policing firms are a growth industry, and they press for ever more contracts with government. The impetus for force, then, is not necessarily the public sphere of government, rule of law, or democratic values but rather profit and economic self-interest.

The argument about public control of contracted private police does not address the private purchase of private force, which was in play in New Orleans. When privately contracted police are as armed and ready to do battle as public police in disaster situations, the possibilities of inequitable and irresponsible use of force are real and threaten understandings of legitimate force in a democratic society. Stories of camaraderie and acceptance between private and public police indicate that police – public or private – may be more tuned in to fellow police – public or private – than they are to civilians or survivors. When Blackwater empties a private apartment to set up its headquarters as the National Guard looks placidly on, one has to wonder what the role of the public is.[22] No one questioned whether Blackwater acted with governmental authority or whether that action itself was justified.

Democracy requires a vibrant public sphere where there is vigorous, open discussion about major decisions, especially when those about the exercise of force. The law and order rhetoric of early post-Katrina New Orleans resulted in mostly unquestioned support of policing in virtually any form in which it arrived.[23] Policing as the first, effective public response to the flood indicates the need for much more and more energetic public dialog about policing and democracy. The public sphere must address concerns for order, especially those that speak from and reinforce racial hierarchy, if democratic equity is to have a chance in the US.

NOTES

1. Journalist Peter Fimrite (2005) observed that: "There are National Guard, police, and Army checkpoints every few blocks … The units often do not appear to know what the others are doing."

2. There is a substantial literature on the complexities of private policing and the relationship between private and public policing, and this literature analyses issues critical to democratic governance (Joh, 2005; Sklansky, 2006; Kempa, Stenning, & Wood, 2004; Jones & Newburn, 2002; Bayley & Shearing, 1996). But among residents of New Orleans, governmental decision makers, and private security firms after Katrina no one talked about the role of private policing. All attention turned to deploying forces to secure order.

3. Historically the movement away from private policing and toward public professionalization of police was a hallmark of democratization of urban government. Professionalization of policing in part stems from the demand for greater equal treatment by police of all residents. But, as Sklansky (2006) argues, the political isolation of a professional police force from local community control

demonstrates the limits of the ways in which policing has democratized. For an interesting and thorough analysis of arguments about privatization of policing, punishment, and military (see Rosky, 2004).

4. According to Riccardi (2005) this action was publicly and openly undertaken and supported:

> 'This wasn't just one man's decision,' Mayor Ronnie C. Harris said Thursday. 'The whole community backs it.'
>
> Three days after Hurricane Katrina hit, Gretna officers blocked the Mississippi River bridge that connects their city to New Orleans, exacerbating the sometimes troubled relationship with their neighbor. The blockade remained in place into the Labor Day weekend.
>
> Gretna (pop. 17,500) is a feisty blue-collar city, two-thirds white, that prides itself on how quickly its police respond to 911 calls; it warily eyes its neighbor, a two-thirds black city (pop. about 500,000) that is also a perennial contender for the murder capital of the US.
>
> Itself deprived of power, water and food for days after Katrina struck August 29, Gretna suddenly became the destination for thousands of people fleeing New Orleans. The smaller town bused more than 5,000 of the newcomers to an impromptu food distribution center miles away. As New Orleans residents continued to spill into Gretna, tensions rose.
>
> After someone set the local mall on fire August 31, Gretna Police Chief Arthur S. Lawson Jr. proposed the blockade.

5. Feminists have shown that much of the history of public/private distinctions systematically caused and perpetuated harm to women in the "private" realm of domestic life.

6. There is considerable variety in private policing, and distinctions between public and private policing are not always clear, as Joh (2005) and Sklansky (2006) point out. To illustrate, Sklansky (2006) writes that what Joh categorizes as protective policing includes not only store security guards who do not carry guns but also armored car drivers who do. And some of the private security personnel may exercise degrees of public authority. Security guards (e.g. Disneyland police) "can draw on legal authority beyond the powers of ordinary citizens ... to detain suspects in circumstances where a 'citizen's arrest' would be impossible." Sometimes private police who may be moonlighting police officers are "deputized by local authorities" (pp. 93–94).

7. To contend that there is a chance of challenge to unjust policies is not to conclude that such challenge occurs with any consistency or passion. For example, Marc Mauer (2006) shows there is "an attitude of complacency" about incarceration policy in the US (p. 105).

8. Lynchings crossed public/private divides because while many were done by private people and groups they were conducted with public impunity and complicity, if not outright assistance (Dray, 2003).

9. Jed Horne (2006) writes that "Caught up in what for many was the biggest story of their careers, reporters dipped their pens in purple ink. The aggregate portrait was of a city gone mad, a black city, a city of depraved men and women who would walk away from asthmatic children and leave them to die, if they didn't violate them first" (p. 108).

10. Brinkley (2006) tells of an NBC camera team videotaping the looting of a mom and pop store where some of the looters "seemed to enjoy his video presence" (p. 201).

11. Lewis (2005) writes brilliantly about the rumors: "... here is what I knew, or thought I knew: Orleans Parish Prison had been seized by the inmates, who also controlled the armory. Prisoners in their orange uniforms had been spotted outside, roaming around the tilapia ponds – there's a fish farm next to the prison – and whatever that meant, it sounded ominous: I mean, if they were getting into the tilapias, who knew what else they might do? Gangs of young black men were raging through the Garden District, moving toward my parents' house, shooting white people. Armed young black men, on Wednesday, had taken over Uptown Children's Hospital, just six blacks away, and shot patients and doctors. Others had stolen a forklift and carted out the entire contents of a Rite Aid and then removed the whole front of an Ace Hardware store farther uptown, on Oak Street. Most shocking of all, because of its incongruity, was the news that looters had broken into Perlis, the Uptown New Orleans clothing store, and picked the placed clean of alligator belts, polo shirts with little crawfish on them and tuxedos most often rented by white kids for debutante parties and the Squires Ball" (p. 48).

12. Many were working on rescue, and public groups like the Louisiana Department of Wildlife and Fisheries and the US Coast Guard did an honorable job of saving people.

13. Tierney et al. (2006) write: "By the fifth day after the hurricane's landfall in the Gulf region, the number of National Guard and active military deployed in Hurricane Katrina had tripled the number deployed within the same period following Hurricane Andrew in 1992" (p. 70).

14. According to Scahill the 82nd Airborne Division watched as Blackwater men took over an abandoned apartment and tossed its belongings over the balcony. Scahill (2006) reports that from September 8 to 25 Blackwater had a contract to provide 14 guards and vehicles to protect a temporary morgue in Baton Rouge. It appears that further contracts in the Gulf area ensued, although Scahill was unable to get access to those contracts.

15. Lewis (2005) observes: "The city on high ground organized itself around the few houses turned into forts" (p. 49).

16. The murder rate in New Orleans, which had declined in the 1990s, was climbing at the time Katrina hit. AP writer Alan Sayre (2005) noted that in 2004 when "police fired 700 blank rounds in a New Orleans neighborhood in a single afternoon," no one reported the gunfire.

17. There has been public discussion about private corrections' corporations, although the acceptance of privatization of corrections has proceeded without significant political opposition. With the Iraq war private contractors with the military have become more controversial (Glanz, 2006).

18. The articles in *The nation* by Scahill are the only ones I have found that cover this topic in the context of the responses to Katrina.

19. Rosky (2004) demonstrates that the growth of private policing is a global phenomenon (p. 899). With their remarkable geographic and cultural reach, private security firms will increasingly present themselves as a usual part of the law, order, and war configurations in most part of the world. See also Singer (2003).

20. While the US does not use private military firms to do actual fighting, it has used them in "areas critical to the US military's core missions … security, military advice, training, logistics support, policing, technological expertise, and intelligence" (Singer, 2003, p. 15).

21. Horne (2006) writes about the tension over Bush's desire to federalize the Louisiana National Guard, which Governor Blanco resisted in part for political reasons (p. 96). In the end martial law was not declared (McDonnell, 2005). Even the Pentagon was not enthusiastic about "the prospect of fuzzy-cheeked regular army units training assault rifles on the desperate and volatile storm survivors" (Horne, 2006, p. 96). The federal military commanded by Army Lieutenant Russel Honore was there for humanitarian, not law enforcement, purposes (MacQuarrie, 2005).

22. There were also tense moments of confrontation between public and private police forces in this city where coordination of policing did not exist. Fimrite (2005) wrote of an encounter between NOPD SWAT team and the military contractors the Hearst Corporation had hired to protect its journalists and the house where they were staying.

23. The one exception seems to have been the political maneuvering between the governor and the White House over whether the Louisiana National Guard should be federalized and martial law declared.

ACKNOWLEDGMENTS

Thank you to Peter G. Stillman for moving along our conversations and writing on public and private. I appreciate the thoughtful comments of the anonymous reviewers.

REFERENCES

Bailey, J. (2002). From public to private. *Social Research*, *69*(Spring), 15–31.

Bayley, D. H., & Shearing, C. (1996). The future of policing. *Law and Society Review*, *30*(3), 585–606.

Boggs, C. (2000). *The end of politics*. New York: The Guilford Press.

Brinkley, D. (2006). *The great deluge*. New York: William Morrow.

DeParle, J. (2005, September 4). Broken levees, unbroken barriers. *The New York Times*, Section 4, Column 1, p. 1.

Dray, P. (2003). *At the hands of persons unknown*. New York: Modern Library.

Dyson, M. E. (2006). *Come hell or high water*. New York: Basic Books.

Ewick, P., & Silbey, S. S. (2003). Narrating social structure: Sources of resistance to legal authority. *American Journal of Sociology*, *108*, 1328–1372.

Fimrite, P. (2005, September 9). On New Orleans' dark streets, patrols assume the worst. *San Francisco Chronicle*, p. A14.

Geltzinis, P. (2005, September 9). Katrina's wrath: Disaster shows how close we are to the third world. *The Boston Herald*, p. 5.

Glanz, J. (2006, November 14). Lawmakers seek to continue Iraq reconstruction watchdog. *The New York Times*, Section A, Column 5, p. 10.

Horne, J. (2006). *Breach of faith*. New York: Random House.

Joh, E. E. (2005). Conceptualizing the private police. *Utah Law Review*, 573–617.

Jones, T., & Newburn, T. (2002). The transformation of policing? *The British Journal of Criminology*, *42*(1), 129–146.

Kaufman, S. (2005). The criminalization of New Orleanians in Katrina's wake. Retrieved July 2, 2006, from http://www.understandingkatrina.ssrc.org/Kaufman

Kempa, M., Carrier, R., Wood, J., & Shearing, C. (1999). Reflections of the evolving concept of private policing. *European Journal of Criminal Policy Research*, *7*(2), 197–223.

Kempa, M., Stenning, P., & Wood, J. (2004). Policing communal spaces. *The British Journal of Criminology*, *44*(4), 562–581.

Lewis, M. (2005, October 9). Wading toward home. *The New York Times Magazine*, 44–51, 66, 73, 77.

Lovell, G. I. (2006). Justice excused: The deployment of law in everyday political encounters. *Law and Society Review*, *40*(2), 283–324.

Macedo, S., Alex-Assensoh, Y., Berry, J. M., Brintnall, M., Campbell, D. E., Fraga, L. R., Fung, A., & Galston, W. W. (2005). *Democracy at risk*. Washington, DC: The Brookings Institution.

MacQuarrie, B. (2005, September 11). Duties, policies of relief and rescue operations collide. *Boston Globe*, p. A18.

Mauer, M. (2006). *Race to incarcerate*. New York: The New Press.

McCann, M. W. (1994). *Rights at work*. Chicago: University of Chicago Press.

McDonnell, K. (2005, September 2). What is martial law? *Slate*. Retrieved on November 23, 2006, from http://www.slate.com/id/2125584

Riccardi, N. (2005, September 16). Katrina's aftermath: After blocking the bridge, Gretna circles the wagons. *The Los Angeles Times*, p. A1.

Rodriguez, H., Trainor, J., & Quarantelli, E. L. (2006). Rising to the challenges of a catastrophe: The emergent and prosocial behavior following Hurricane Katrina. *The Annals of the American Academy of Political and Social Science*, *604*(March), 82–101.

Rosky, C. J. (2004). Force, Inc: The privatization of punishment, policing, and military force in liberal states. *Connecticut Law Review*, (Spring), 879–1031.

Sayre, A. (2005, August 21). Murder on the rise in ill-equipped Big Easy. *Post-Gazette.com*. Retrieved on November 3, 2006, from post-gazette.com/pg/05233/556827.stm

Scahill, J. (2005, October 10). Blackwater down. *The nation*. Retrieved November 3, 2006, from http://www.thenation.com/doc/20051010/scahill

Scahill, J. (2006, June 5). In the Black(water). *The nation*. Retrieved November 3, 2006, from http://www.thenation.com/doc/20060605/scahill

Singer, P. W. (2003). *Corporate warriors*. Ithaca, NY: Cornell University Press.

Sklansky, D. A. (2006). Private police and democracy. *The American Criminal Law Review*, *43*(1), 89–105.

The Failure of Initiative. Final report of the select bipartisan committee to investigate the preparation for and response to Hurricane Katrina. (2006). Washington, DC: GPO.

Tierney, K., Bevc, C., & Kulihgowski, A. (2006). Metaphors matter: Disaster myths, media frames, and their consequences in Hurricane Katrina. *The Annals of the American Academy of Political and Social Science*, *604*(March), 57–81.

Voices in the Storm. (2005, September 9). *The nation.* Retrieved on October 24, 2006, from http://www.thenation.com/doc/20050926/chronicle.

Wolfe, A. (1997). Public and private in theory and practice: Some implications of an uncertain boundary. In: J. Weintrub & K. Kumar (Eds), *Public and private in thought and practice* (pp. 182–203). Chicago: University of Chicago Press.

REMORSE AND PSYCHOPATHY AT THE PENALTY PHASE OF THE CAPITAL TRIAL – HOW PSYCHIATRY'S VIEW OF "MORAL INSANITY" HELPS BUILD THE CASE FOR DEATH

Richard Weisman

ABSTRACT

This chapter documents how the shift in psychiatric representation from the "morally insane" perpetrator of the 19th century to the modern psychopath or person with anti-social personality disorder involves a recasting of the offender from someone afflicted with an illness whose criminal misconduct is merely a symptom of their disorder to someone whose criminal misconduct is perceived as an expression of their true character. Drawing upon recent case law, the article then shows how prosecutors deploy this modern psychiatric reconfiguring during the penalty phase of the US capital trial to persuade jurors to decide in favor of death over life without parole. Central to the building of this narrative is the reframing of the offenders' silences as well as what are taken as their unconvincing attempts to show remorse as evidence of a

Special Issue: Law and Society Reconsidered
Studies in Law, Politics, and Society, Volume 41, 187–217

ISSN: 1059-4337/doi:10.1016/S1059-4337(07)00008-7

pathology whose primary manifestation is the incapacity to feel or experience moral emotions. Applying but also modifying Harold Garfinkel's work on degradation ceremonies, the chapter shows how the pathologizing of the offender's lack of remorse involves a rite of passage in which he or she is symbolically demoted from someone worthy of life in spite of their grievous crime to someone for whom death is the only appropriate penalty.

If, as one writer has recently suggested, the criminal trial has from its inception served as a veritable "theater of contrition" (Kadri, 2005, p. 213 et.passim.) in which defendants come before court and community with humility and remorse, perhaps in no other legal arena is this drama enacted with greater intensity than in the modern bifurcated American capital trial. If the first phase of the capital trial addresses the familiar questions of culpability and intent, the second phase includes as part of its ambit not just the enumerated aggravating and mitigating factors that are more or less replicated in each of the states in which capital punishment is permitted but what is more loosely described as considerations of character. It is in this second phase of course that the jury that has already decided in favor of conviction for a capital crime reconvenes and decides between life without parole or death by execution.

Recent systematic inquiry – the prolific National Capital Jury Project above all – has amply demonstrated the prime importance to jurors of whether in their view the offender has demonstrated remorse when they decide in favor of life or death.[1] One of the major articles from this project shows that regardless of whether or not remorse is included statutorily as a mitigating factor or its absence as an aggravating factor, it plays a larger part in the actual decision-making process than all the other enunciated factors except prior history of violent crime and predictions of future dangerousness (Garvey, 1998, pp. 1560–1561) – the later of which I will argue below is not independent of evaluations of remorse. Anecdotal evidence as gleaned from the mass media supply even more dramatic evidence of how evaluations of an offender's remorsefulness contribute to the ultimate decision. To cite from just one recent example, newspaper reports of the jury deliberations in the penalty phase trial following John Muhammed's conviction for one of the murders committed during a series of sniper attacks that resulted in 10 murders quote a number of jurors as stating that it was his lack of remorse that finally persuaded them to decide in favor of the death penalty. As one juror explained, "I tried to pay attention to his demeanor the whole time … I looked for something in him that might have shown remorse. I never saw it" (Dao & Bacon, 2003, p. 1) suggesting that even with the likelihood of multiple murders, remorse stood out as the principal factor in deciding for death.

It is this raw but passionate response to the remorseless offender that reveals what is at stake in the moral performances or non-performances of capital offenders and their representation as persons who feel remorse or do not or can not feel remorse.[2] The Supreme Court in *Riggins v. Nevada* (1992) gave tacit acknowledgment of the centrality of this attribution when it ordered a retrial on grounds that the defendant had been so medicated that he was unable to show remorse. As Justice Anthony Kennedy wrote in a concurring opinion, "… as any trial attorney can attest, serious prejudice could result if medication inhibits the defendant's capacity to react to proceedings and to demonstrate remorse or compassion. The prejudice can be acute during the sentencing phase of the proceedings, when the sentencers must attempt to know the heart and mind of the offender" (*Riggins v. Nevada*, 1992, p. 1824). More recently, another Supreme Court judgment held that persons who fell in the category of the "mentally retarded" would heretofore be exempted from the death penalty in part because such defendants "are typically poor witnesses, and their demeanor may create an unwarranted impression of lack of remorse for their crimes" (*Atkins v. Virginia*, 2002, p. 2252). The significant impact of characterizations of the offender as remorseful or not to all judicial outcomes, but especially those involving capital punishment, has been quietly if selectively acknowledged within law for some time and is now supported by recent empirical investigation.[3]

But the reactions of jurors do not take place in a vacuum.[4] The character of the offender is shaped by the narratives and counternarratives that are entered or allowed entry into the legal forum. It is at this juncture that the attribute of remorse plays a pivotal role in portraying the offender as deserving of death or worthy of life. The task of the prosecutor is to somehow convince the jury that life without parole is an insufficient response to the crime that has been perpetrated. The sheer volume of appeals and counter-appeals that focus on challenging the characterization of the offender as remorseless bear witness to how crucial a contribution this designation makes to the narrative that is communicated to jurors and to the public. No item of speech in the postconviction phase of the capital trial is more likely to be contested as inflammatory or prejudicial to the character of the defendant than statements by the prosecutor and others that call into question the offender's remorsefulness for his crime. In capital cases in the past 20 years, there have been 232 separate appeals in which one of the grounds is prosecutorial use of inflammatory statements that characterize the capital offender as without remorse.[5]

At the same time, the efforts of advocates to craft a portrait of the offender as remorseful is no less critical to the process of separating the act from the person by which defense argues that, despite the gravity and severity of the crime, the offender is not beyond redemption. There are few Meursaults in the penalty phase of the capital trial – apart from those who claim to have been wrongly convicted, most offenders endeavor to present themselves as remorseful or, at the very least, as not unremorseful. It is in this sense that the modern trial for capital punishment involves a life and death struggle over how the offender will be defined and, hence, it is no wonder that interventions whether in support or in opposition to a claim of remorse are a site of intense contestation. One of the objectives of this chapter is to draw from a recent population of capital cases to show how attributions of remorse are deployed to build an identity for the capital offender that will persuade jurors to decide in favor of death.

The analysis would remain incomplete, however, without consideration of one of the most significant developments in the modern approach to remorse in law in which the absence of remorse becomes not merely a breach of expectations that invites severe moral condemnation but a symptom of an underlying pathology that marks the wrongdoer as variously diseased, impaired, or otherwise incapable of feeling what a normal member of the community would feel under similar circumstances. In the first section, I discuss the history of this shift not in order to document the gradual, circuitous evolution from the early 19th century category of moral insanity to the contemporary diagnoses of psychopathy and anti-social personality disorder as much as to place in historical relief the particular configuration of assumptions by which remorse and pathology are currently associated. Once I have identified the distinctive way in which the absence of remorse is pathologized in contemporary medical–psychological discourse, it then becomes possible to show more clearly how this approach has been translated from its uncertain and tenuous status within forensic psychology and psychiatry to its currently ambiguous and controversial status in American law.

In the second section of this chapter, I hope to bring out the representations of the remorseless offender that help to promote the intense moral indignation sufficient to decide in favor of death when life without parole is the only other option. Here I will also show the critical contribution of the pathological approach both in framing how the feelings of the capital offender are to be interpreted and in supplying a rationale for death as the appropriate punishment. In developing this analysis, I have built upon and modified the classic formulation of the ritual of public denunciation culminating in dehumanization offered by Harold Garfinkel in "Conditions of Successful Degradation Ceremonies" (Garfinkel, 1956).

My primary objective is to look at what the absence of remorse comes to symbolize about the wrongdoer and the consequences of identifying the act with the person. I want to show how the casting of wrongdoers as without remorse separates them from the community not just by virtue of their transgression but by the purported personal qualities that are embodied in the act. The pathological approach to remorse widens even further the difference between those who show remorse and those who do not even as it enlarges the population to whom the designation of remorselessness can be applied. Here the disregard of feeling rules embodied by the refusal or incapacity to express remorse is not only condemned for its rejection of the moral-emotive foundation of community but also naturalized as a psycho-biological condition from which the wrongdoer can not be rehabilitated. It is this explosive combination of moral condemnation and medical pessimism that gives added justification for imposing on the psychopathic perpetrator the most grave sanctions available in US law. That the term "monster" is not infrequently used in newspaper and popular accounts to describe persons who commit atrocious crimes with no show of remorse should not surprise us – if a working definition of the monster is someone who is dangerous, incurable, with no empathy for his or her victim, no feelings of remorse for their wrongdoing, and psychologically and perhaps biologically different from the rest of us, then this is the expectable outcome of the social practices that have been described.

1. REMORSE, PSYCHOPATHOLOGY, AND THE LAW: BUILDING THE FRAMEWORK FOR INTERPRETATION

1.1. From Affliction to Abnormality

In 1826, in his *Discussions medico-legale pour Henriette Cornier* (Georget, 1826, pp. 71–130), Dr. Etienne Georget, a French physician and one of the forerunners of modern forensic psychiatry, reported on a case that occurred in Paris and that would be retold in England, the United States, and elsewhere in 19th century Europe as representing a turning point in the history of mental disorder and the interrelationship between law and psychiatry. What was so remarkable and anomalous about Henriette Cornier was not her atrocious act of violence but the impossibility of making sense of it within the legal, medical, or psychological frameworks then available. One day, after a "singular change was observed in her character,"[6] Cornier, a 27-year-old servant, left her place of employment to visit a neighboring shop to buy some cheese for the family where she resided. She had always shown affection for the shopkeeper's daughter and so was able to persuade her to entrust her with the child for a walk. She then took the child back to her mistress' house, and, laying it across her own bed, severed the child's head with a kitchen knife. She was reported later to have felt no particular emotion – "without remorse or grief" in the original narrative as well as in subsequent published accounts – during the commission of this deed. When the mother came for her child some two hours later, Cornier informed her that "Your child is dead." The mother who did not at first believe her entered the chamber where she was confronted with "the bloody sight of the mutilated fragments of her child" (Ray, 1838, p. 220). At that point, Cornier picked up the head of the murdered child, and threw it into the street from the open window. Why did she do this, she was later asked? She replied that she wanted to attract public attention so that people might come up to her room and see that she alone was responsible for the murder.[7]

I dwell on this case because it constituted the first time a court in Europe or North America was asked to consider as a defense to criminal culpability a new category of insanity for which the primary symptom was the criminal act itself. Because Cornier demonstrated no defects in cognition – she understood the consequences of her action and was fully aware that it violated the laws of her community – she did not belong in the more familiar category of "insane" perpetrators who committed crimes in a state of delirium or who exhibited other signs of cognitive disorientation. At the same time, because the prosecution could establish no motive for her behavior that was intelligible to contemporaries – no prior history of grievance with the family of her victim to build a narrative of revenge and no hope of personal gain consistent with any instrumental objective – her act of violence could not be situated within the conventional parameters of willful criminal misconduct. Cornier presented the anomaly of someone who "knew" that her act was immoral and unlawful and yet could offer no motive for why she had done it. As viewed by her contemporaries, the only evidence of insanity in this "lucid" perpetrator was what she had done.

A decade after this much discussed trial, leading Anglo-American interpreters of the link between law and madness were still debating how to understand and categorize her affliction in the language of the faculty psychology of the period.[8] Was it a form of moral insanity – "a perversion of natural feelings, affections, inclinations, temper, habits, and moral dispositions without any notable lesions of the intellect or knowing and reasoning faculties, and particularly without any maniacal (Ray, 1838, pp. 169–170)?"[9] Or was it a disease of the will – a form of homicidal madness – in which the perpetrator demonstrated a fatal incapacity to resist her homicidal urges, as James Cowles Prichard would suggest (Prichard, 1842, pp. 19–20, 93, 95)?[10] But regardless of which faculty was affected – that of the feelings or the will – it was already clear to contemporaries that expanding the insanity defense to include those who were not cognitively impaired when they committed their wrongdoing constituted a major redrawing of the boundaries of responsibility with sweeping implications for criminal law. How would one now distinguish the cognitively unimpaired murderer whose actions were willful and deliberate from the cognitively unimpaired insane offender whose wrongdoings were caused by their affliction? It is in the crafting of this distinction that we can discern the vast changes that occurred during the 19th century in how the lucid perpetrator would be portrayed.

Early commentaries would describe Cornier whether as morally insane, or as afflicted with homicidal madness as radically different from those who belonged in the category of criminally culpable offenders. As Ray would write in 1838, the Corniers of this world were not to be classed among those who were depraved or perverse – instead, such persons had characters that were "mild and peaceable, and their days were spent in the quiet and creditable discharge of the duties belonging to their station, till a cloud of melancholy enveloped their minds, and … they perpetrated a single deed the very thought of which they would have previously shuddered with horror" (Ray, 1838, p. 275). What precipitated the atrocious act was a striking change in the conduct of the individual signaling the onset of the pathology – or, as Foucault would describe Cornier's defense at her trial – "a crack appears and there is no resemblance between the act and the person" (Foucault, 2003, p. 127). The atrocious act would cast no reflection on Cornier's character – only on her pathology.

Even her lack of grief and remorse for so horrifying an act, however "unnatural," was not the same absence of appropriate affect as that which would be exhibited by the true murderer. While Cornier had shown no emotion when her homicidal act was revealed, this was consistent with her "manie sans delire." As Esquirol[11] had written in a passage quoted by both Ray and Prichard, "the homicidal monomaniac[12] testifies neither remorse nor repentance, nor satisfaction, and, if judicially condemned, perhaps acknowledges the justice of the sentence" (Ray, 1838, p. 232). Cornier, for example, made no effort to escape custody nor to evade responsibility for her actions – not only did she make it clear that she alone perpetrated the deed but her comment to the magistrate during her examination was that she knew her crime deserved death and that she desired it (Ray, 1838, p. 221; Foucault, 2003, p. 125). "This deserves the death penalty." On the other hand, Ray continued, "the criminal either denies or confesses his guilt: if the latter, he either humbly sues for mercy, or glories in his crimes, and leaves the world cursing his judges and with his last breath exclaiming against the injustice of his fate" (Ray, 1838, p. 232). The murderer who kills willfully may repent of his crime but only for the ulterior purpose of obtaining a mercy that is undeserved – and when he or she is finally sent to their execution, their criminal character will once again be demonstrated through their anger and defiance.

Whether afflicted with homicidal madness or with moral mania, Henriette Cornier committed an act that shocked the sensibilities of her contemporaries – her brutal decapitation of her infant victim was discussed on both sides of the Atlantic. Yet, at this earliest stage of formulation, the lucid but insane perpetrator is still entitled to a measure of the same solicitude and exemptions that are granted to those afflicted with other illnesses – treatment rather than punishment is the remedy even if there was no likelihood of release from detention for acts of such brutality. In the accounts at trial as offered by the physicians for the defense and in the later commentaries, Cornier is described as herself a victim of her affliction – she is portrayed by Ray when on trial as trembling, melancholic, and in "profound chagrin" (Ray, 1838, pp. 221–222). As Prichard would suggest about the morally insane, "such persons must be admitted to be morally guilty and to deserve to suffer. But the calamity with which we know them to be afflicted is already so great, that humanity forbids our entertaining the thought of adding to it" (Prichard, 1842, p. 178). In this early representation of the cognitively lucid but insane transgressor, where the act, however despicable, does not define the person and where the perpetrator's being is still separated from their doing, there lingers the perception that but for their affliction, such persons are not so different in terms of how they feel about what they did from the rest of the community.

Yet, by the early 20th century, the cognitively unimpaired insane offender now firmly incorporated within the category of the "morally insane" would be reconceived in ways that would be much closer to contemporary formulations. Richard von Krafft-Ebing's *Text-book of Insanity*, one of the most widely disseminated manuals of forensic medicine and psychiatry, originally published in 1875 in the first of four German editions – finally translated into English in 1905 – and cited as one of the defining texts on insanity by English and American medical and legal authorities well exemplifies the changes that occurred in the intervening 50 years.[13] Profoundly influenced by the biological and evolutionist turn in psychiatry and early criminology,[14] Krafft-Ebing's work reformulates moral insanity less as an illness that is transitory than as a condition that at its worst and most frequent, is hereditary and organic, and at best, is acquired as the result of other neurologically based mental defects. In the former case, the prognosis is hopeless incurability – in the later, successful removal of the mental defect may result in remission of the abnormality (Krafft-Ebing, 1905, p. 625).

More importantly, the wrongdoing of the morally insane, whether criminal or otherwise, is conceived as a true expression of their underlying personality – "moral insanity affects the innermost nucleus of the individuality in its emotional, ethical, and moral relations" (Krafft-Ebing, 1905, p. 622). What radically distinguishes those who have this condition is what Krafft-Ebing calls a "more or less complete moral insensibility" (p. 623) by which he means that even when the morally insane are conscious of moral standards, they lack the feelings and affects that engender commitment to these standards. The best they can do is memorize the rules and codes "but if they enter consciousness they remain uncolored by feeling and affects and are dead ideas." At their core, persons who fall into this category are unable to experience or demonstrate the feelings that come naturally to persons with normal "social instincts" as evidenced by their "coldness of heart, their indifference to the lot of their nearest relatives (their absence) of scruples of conscience or repentance" (p. 623). By recasting moral insanity as no longer merely an illness but a congenital abnormality that penetrates to the nucleus of the person, the wrongful deeds of the morally insane have become an expression of their essence. In this new approach to moral insanity, act and person are now shown to correspond.

How then is the morally insane wrongdoer to be distinguished from the willful criminal if repeated and incorrigible wrongdoing is one of the primary manifestations? Here, Krafft-Ebing suggests that their "moral blindness" fails them even in their criminal pursuits. For here, their lack of judgment makes them astonishingly negligent – lacking in the "most elementary rules of prudence in committing their criminal acts." Just as the morally insane are not able to conform their conduct to legal restrictions, they are also not free to obey these restrictions – unlike the putatively rational criminal, they are unable to prevent themselves from engaging in "strange, immoral, or criminal acts" (p. 625). Their defiance of the law and their proclivity to immoral behavior differ from criminal misconduct because these tendencies are so unrestrained, so ruthless, and so contrary to their criminal purpose of benefiting from their ill-gotten gains.

In Krafft-Ebing's work, the descriptions of the morally insane reveal a stance toward the pathology that is different in tone and orientation from all the other case studies that are included in the volume. For each of these other illnesses, conditions, or impairments, no matter how transgressive the symptom, the patient is viewed as suffering from or otherwise adversely affected by their affliction. It is only when we turn to the morally insane that the language shifts to one of severe moral condemnation devoid of compassion for the offending pathology. The woman whom Krafft-Ebing uses to illustrate the abnormality is described as "impossible, very irritable, unsocial, coarse and without feeling, and inciting other patients to disobey hospital regulations" (p. 626) – what is mentioned is not how she has suffered from her condition but how the interpersonal and behavioral manifestations of her condition have adversely affected others. At the end of the case, it is noted that she was transferred to an institution for the chronic insane – that she has been judged incurable. By the time of Krafft-Ebing's work, moral insanity has been transformed from an affliction from which one suffers and which might well be temporary to an abnormality that is hereditary, untreatable, and a continuing source of danger to others. As his prescription for dealing with the condition, Krafft-Ebing writes – "these savages in society must be kept in asylums for their own and the safety of society" (p. 626). The morally insane wrongdoer has become less someone entitled to exemptions from criminal responsibility than one from whom the community needs protection. As we shall see, it is a version of this representation that is reflected in the contemporary understanding of those classed as manifesting psychopathic disorder or anti-social personality disorder who also engage in criminal wrongdoing, who are cognitively intact, and who are perceived as incapable of feeling remorse.

1.2. Contemporary Representations of Remorselessness as Pathology

In the most recent edition of the DSM (DSM-IV-TR, 2000), the first criterion for the diagnosis of anti-social personality disorder specifies "a pervasive pattern of disregard for and violation of the rights of others since age 15 years, as indicated by three or more of seven factors" among which is included "lack of remorse, as indicated by being indifferent to or rationalizing having hurt, mistreated, or stolen from another" (DSM-IV-TR, 2000, p. 706). But just as the absence of remorse serves as one of the indications of anti-social personality disorder and psychopathy, so also the meaning of this absence can only be understood in the context of these psychiatric constructs. For present purposes, I will treat the categories of anti-social personality and psychopathy as interchangeable in conformity with what I take to be contemporary usage. Despite efforts by some to confine anti-social personality disorder to what is behavioral and descriptive as distinct from psychopathy which focuses as well on those elements of character that require a greater degree of interpretation (Hare, 1996), the two dimensions of the disorder – behavioral and characterological – are intermeshed not only in DSM-IV-TR but in much of the current literature for both categories. One further caveat – I use the term representation in full recognition that this is not how authors of texts in forensic psychiatry would refer to their clinical insights and observations – my purpose in applying this concept is to bring out the interpretive work that is involved in developing these formulations while bracketing their correspondence to veridical reality. I believe that historical shifts in perception as well as contemporary debates over the validity of the category justify this bracketing of reality by demonstrating that there is variation in interpretation and therefore interpretive choice or agency in how to formulate the construct (Petrunik & Weisman, 2005, p. 77).

As indicated above, the chief defining feature of psychopathy and its antecedents is the engagement in transgressive behavior with full cognitive awareness of both the wrongfulness of the conduct and the likelihood of moral–communal condemnation. Within this larger context, for all the changes that have occurred since Krafft-Ebing's work with regard to etiology, nosology, and theories of psychopathology, at the level of clinical description, there are important similarities in what the lack of remorse has come to signify about persons placed in these categories. Most important is the perception that the legal and moral wrongdoing of persons so diagnosed are linked inextricably to deeply rooted and relatively unalterable personality traits. Whether in influential specialized texts such as Hervey

Cleckley's *Mask of Sanity – An Attempt to Clarify Some Issues about the Psychopathic Personality* (1976), reprinted in five editions between 1941 and 1982, or in more popularly oriented works such as Robert Hare's *Without Conscience – The Disturbing World of Psychopaths Among Us* (1993), or Martha Stout's *The Sociopath Next Door* (2005), the psychopath is someone whose irresponsible, destructive behavior is fully consistent with and inseparable from what Hare has referred to as the interpersonal and affective features of the condition. The examples and illustrations contained in all these works make it clear that the harm that the psychopath inflicts on others whether through material or emotional exploitation or any other form of violence is strategic, deliberate, and that the psychopath as perpetrator is at least intellectually cognizant of the relationship between action and consequence. But what is emphasized in contemporary formulations is that while the troublesomeness of the psychopath may be manifested in behavioral transgressions, the disturbance is primarily characterological. If social deviance may be one highly visible way in which the disturbance reveals itself, the core of the pathology lies in deeply rooted character traits of the individual. For the psychopath, action is a reflection of being.[15]

In what then does the disturbance identified by Cleckley, Hare, and others consist? Psychopathy is first and foremost an affective disorder – an abnormality that results in an incapacity to feel or experience emotions in a way that is central to interpersonal relations. It is as if the entire spectrum of human emotions is truncated to the point that the psychopath has access only to the most shallow and superficial of feelings whether it be anger, love, fear, or hatred.[16] But the primary locus of the deficiency is in what moral philosophers have referred to as the moral emotions or those emotions that promote or maintain ethical conduct toward others. The psychopath is someone who lacks remorse, guilt, or shame for the harm that he or she may inflict on others, feels no empathy for the suffering that he has caused, and refuses to accept responsibility for any wrongdoing. While these are separate items in the clinical profile offered by Cleckley (Cleckley, 1976, pp. 337–364) and in the psychopathy check list revised as developed by Hare (Hare, 1998, p. 106), all point to the inability of the psychopath to experience from within the feelings that restrain exploitative and callous behavior toward others. At the deepest level of character – beneath what is expressed in public – the psychopath lacks the emotive ability or capacity to attach himself to others or to the moral codes that sustain communal life.

Equally significant to the modern representation of psychopathy is its intractability as indicated by both its severity and its resistance to treatment.

Cleckley's central metaphor for psychopathy – given in the title of his book – *The Mask of Sanity* – is grounded in the paradox of appearance and reality. The condition that most resembles normality in its outward manifestations – the psychopath lacks even the social awkwardness and nervousness of the neurotic – is in actuality the condition with the most devastating prognosis.[17] Just as the least visible of aphasic disorders – semantic aphasia – is also the most disabling, the psychopath, for all his skill at mimicking sanity, is afflicted with a disturbance as intransigent and encompassing as those with the most obvious symptoms of psychological disorder. Adding to the gravity of the condition is its incurability. With few exceptions in the current literature, psychopathy is represented as a condition with an early onset that is virtually unresponsive to any of the treatment modalities currently available. Nor do the persons who fall into this category generally volunteer to be treated thereby worsening an already dismal prognosis. The therapeutic pessimism expressed by Krafft-Ebing in his case study of moral insanity is thus closely paralleled by the despairing prognosis offered for persons diagnosed with psychopathy or anti-social personality disorder today (Arrigo & Shipley, 2001, pp. 328–329). Contributing further to this pessimism is the elision of the social as a significant factor in the etiology of the condition. Clinical profiles portray persons with these conditions as demographically diverse – unaffected by considerations of class and status – and as likely to grow up in well-functioning loving families as in families with severe dysfunction.[18] Indeed, the thrust of much of contemporary research is toward naturalizing psychopathy as a condition that is correlated with physiological and neurological differences and potentially traceable to bio-genetic causes (Blair, Mitchell, & Blair, 2005, especially Chapter 3; Abbott, 2001; Hare, 1998). This casting of the psychopath into biological otherness further widens the gap between psychopathy and normality even as it strengthens the case for therapeutic pessimism.

Yet, for all the gravity of the abnormality, its recalcitrance to change, and its possible biological causation, psychopathy is evaluated as a condition that should not entitle those so designated to an exemption from criminal responsibility. Both Cleckley and Hare, for example, assert that the incapacities of the psychopath – however resistant to change – do not negate the ability to make choices and weigh consequences.[19] But if the psychopath is someone who can make choices and who is nonetheless likely to engage in criminal wrongdoing, what is the difference between willful misconduct that is a manifestation of psychopathy and willful misconduct that is merely criminal and non-pathological? In an argument reminiscent of

Krafft-Ebing, both authors, among others, suggest that there is a non-instrumental purposelessness to the criminal misconduct committed by psychopathic offenders in contrast to those who are non-psychopathic, and that, unlike those not so afflicted, they are unable to learn from experience. Indeed, Hare goes so far as to urge a rigorous separation between those who exhibit only the behavioral manifestations associated with psychopathy (heretofore to be designated as anti-social personality disorder) and those who in addition demonstrate the affective and interpersonal dimension of the disorder lest they who have only anti-social personality disorder be unfairly ascribed the dismal prognosis of the true psychopath (Hare, 1996). Hence, the criminality of the psychopath is if anything more virulent, less purposeful, and less susceptible to control through punishment than that of non-psychopathic offenders even though both are credited with free will.

The final piece in the modern representation of the psychopath is perhaps the most significant in terms of the role of remorse. Unlike the late 19th and early 20th century conceptions, the middle to late 20th century has reconfigured the psychopath as the consummate social performer.[20] Indeed, one of the signature characteristics of the modern psychopath is the ability to read the reactions of their victims or their helpers and to build trust and good will only in order to further their exploitation. What Cleckley called superficial charm and Hare refers to as impression management call attention to the ability of the psychopath to simulate emotions and feelings that he is not able to experience. The same persons whose innate sensibility is one that lacks empathy with the victim or experiences no remorse or guilt is nonetheless able to perform these emotions – to "mimic" normality in Cleckley's terms – in order to achieve ulterior objectives. The gap between appearance and reality in which the psychopath is able to mask his deep disturbance is paralleled by his extraordinary ability to appear to be moved by emotions that he cannot possibly experience. In place of the clumsy, inarticulate, and unattractive exemplars of the late 19th century, contemporary forensic psychology reconceives the psychopath as, if anything, more competent than the ordinary person in controlling the impressions of their audience.

But it is not merely the likelihood of imposture that distinguishes the psychopath from the non-psychopath. Underlying his inevitably insincere moral performance is an even more damning deficiency. The psychopath is someone who does not suffer and cannot suffer for his misdeeds. Remorse, shame, empathy, or guilt all involve some degree of emotional pain either in advance of harmful conduct toward others or as a result of having engaged in harmful conduct. Those who cannot experience these emotions do not suffer for their wrongs – nor do they even suffer as deeply as others for the punishments that may result from these wrongs. Texts on psychopathy remark on the adaptability of persons in this population to the harshness and humiliations of prison life, the low level of anxiety experienced in situations that would cause severe stress to non-psychopaths, and the general ineffectiveness of deterrents that might cause pain and suffering in others.[21] The inability to feel remorse – no matter how adept the performance – is linked to the psychopath's general immunity from the anguish of emotional pain for the harm he does and from the punishments that might follow.

In the following section, we shall see then that those who have been diagnosed as psychopathic enter the legal domain under a heavy burden not only as someone who is likely to reoffend, who is unresponsive to treatment, and who is psychologically and possibly biologically different from non-psychopaths but also as someone who can perform but not experience or suffer from the moral emotions that are used to demonstrate character. From this vantage point, we can say that contemporary representations offer a set of instructions for reading the emotions of those who have been diagnosed with psychopathy or anti-social personality disorder. The moral performance of the psychopath is framed in such a way that appearance and reality are reversed – the more convincing the performance to the layperson, the greater the proof that the performer is an accomplished psychopath. How this expert framing of the psychopath's demonstrations of remorse contributes to the death narrative will be considered below.

2. MOBILIZING MORAL INDIGNATION: CAPITAL TRIALS, PSYCHOPATHY, AND REMORSE

Below, my focus is on how the characterization of the offender as remorseless is used to mobilize moral indignation on behalf of a sentence of death. I base my discussion of these narratives on those judgments and appeals of judgments that cite as one of the grounds for the appeal the inclusion or exclusion of evidence regarding remorse during the penalty phase.[22] Where possible, I have also supplemented these texts with other accounts in books and newspapers of the same events. As mentioned above, I have drawn from but also modified Garfinkel's typology of public denunciation in identifying the different components of this process. At the core of the denunciation is a rite of passage from one status to another – a transitional process in which the person or social object is symbolically reconstituted in such a way as to demote him in the social order – in this case, from someone worthy of life in spite of his grievous crime to someone for whom only death is the appropriate penalty. It is the representation of the remorseless offender that lies at the heart of this transformation and it is toward a deeper understanding of this process that the following analysis is directed.

2.1. Reading Silences: Conceiving the Remorseless Offender

When it comes to demonstrations of remorse, there is no such thing as a non-performance. Silence, reserve, or impassivity, when judicial and communal expectations demand a visible display of feeling, are construed as signs no less revealing than the most elaborate of self-presentations. Yet, for a variety of reasons, whether strategic, principled, or simply misconceived, some among the convicted choose or are instructed to remain silent or, if willing to speak at all, exercise their right to allocution to deliberately not call attention to their feelings of remorse. In some cases, the evidence available to the prosecution is so damaging to any credible claim of remorse that arguably, the raising of it will only invite a devastating rebuttal. But other cases suggest the deeper dilemmas that confront the capital offender. It is not just that, as others have concluded, those who did not plead guilty in the first place, face insuperable hurdles in now convincing the same jury that they have moved from hope for acquittal to sincere self-condemnation (Sundby, 1998). The gravity and the intensity of the crimes are such that, from the standpoint of moral economy, the offender and their counsel may decide that since no expression is commensurate with the harm wrought by the offense, avoidance of the issue is the best option. Such calculations appear to have figured in at least one instance in which the defendant in consultation with his lawyer decided that since "this was such a grievous, horrible murder, that there is nothing I could put in front of this jury that would make them have enough mercy on me to give me life rather than death … they may feel that because, after being found guilty of this crime, if I come in here and plead for mercy, that may turn them off, and make them want to give me death" (*Shelton v. State*, 1999, p. 501). As a result, his statement to the jury merely recounted his circumstances:

> Ladies and Gentlemen of the Jury, I stand before you not to plead for my life. I feel that's wrong and improper and basically disrespectful to the victim's family and to mine. …The State has pictured me as being a monster, as being a rapist, as being a

> violent individual., but as you heard from my family, that's not so. The State only presents one side of the picture. There's two sides to every story. And the State just presents the negative side. The jury has found me guilty of these allegations, and now it's the jury's turn to render a verdict. And that verdict is either life in jail or death. That's all I have to say. (*Shelton v. State*, 1999, p. 501)

Even in cases where the defendant has pleaded guilty, silence may be a plausible strategy in light of the daunting expectations of what might be required.[23] Yet, legal forums, as do other settings for moral performances, operate on the assumption that what is not shown is also not felt. The silence of the defendant then becomes the blank slate on which the prosecutor can map the identity of the remorseless offender.

Indeed, it is this silence that will define the essence of at least some of the offenders for whom capital punishment is sought. In the following excerpt, the prosecutor addresses the jury about a defendant who chose not to testify despite his guilty plea for the crime for which he was convicted:

> I was waiting for M to express remorse, to apologize to somebody for what he had done and what he had taken. … I did not hear any of that remorse … . (*Sims v. Brown*, 2005, p. 74)

Later, in the same speech, the prosecutor continues:

> Now, at no time did I hear any remorse. Hear a tear. I mean, we have all felt guilty about things in life. It's a human reaction, but granted, we haven't killed people. We are not mass murderers. But there's no feeling of guilt. There is absolutely no feeling of guilt. (p. 75)

In another case, it is this absence that negates any other claim that the offender might make to show that he is no longer the same person who committed the crime:

> But I submit to you that there's one thing that cuts against this man having changed and become a Christian, and that is simply nowhere in this record, nowhere from that witness stand have you heard one person say that this Defendant has shown any remorse or any sorrow over the death of his wife, over what he has done. None. (*State v. Stephenson*, 2005, p. 59)

Or the absence is demonstrated at a crucial moment when the true character of the defendant is revealed:

> What did he do at the scene after he's just done this to these two people? Does he say, I feel bad? Does he say, God, what have I done? No. He's worried about himself, as he always is, first and foremost. He tells his brother T., I may go to prison for this if I'm caught … .

> Does he have a breakdown when his mom asks him, gee, son, what happened, your hands are cut? I got jumped by some Mexicans at McDonald's. He is able to say that with a straight face. Does he seem like he is feeling any remorse at that time, knowing the scene he has just left? Does he make an anonymous call to the authorities, hey, you might want to run out to the residence and take a look, so that maybe they (the victims of the murder) don't have to be discovered by a member of their own family or neighbor. He is content to just let them rot there. (*People v. Pollock*, 2004, p. 1184)

The impact of this absence lies in the contrasts to which the prosecutor calls attention. For one, these revealing moments stand out as the extreme obverse of how a "normal" member of the community would feel in a similar circumstance. Here the connection is explicit:

> I listened as the defense witnesses testified yesterday for any evidence or testimony pertaining to the victim. And there was. The defendant's grandmother testified, bless her heart, that she not only prays for (the defendant) but she prays for the victim and the victim's family. What a nice thing. What a human being. What a nice person from a nice family … .
>
> Do you see what I mean? He's not like them. He doesn't share in their goodness., he doesn't share in their compassion, he doesn't share in their humanity. (*People v. Jurado*, 2006, p. 141)

The gap between what one should feel and what the offender has shown is enough to expel them from the moral community as defined by the presence or absence of feelings of remorse – which in turn incorporates other moral emotions such as empathy and compassion – that members are expected to experience and show in similar circumstances.

But there is another contrast that is equally important to the portrayal of the defendant as apart from the moral community – the gap between his suffering and the suffering he has inflicted. Almost all the crimes for which contemporary courts seek the death penalty involve forms of violence that are grouped under such categories as brutality, heinousness, and the like – categories that by themselves already call into question the defendant's remorsefulness at the time of the murder. The prosecutor can then summon moral indignation by pointing to the imbalance between the harm wrought by the remorseless defendant and the defendant's own lack of mental anguish:

> The life in prison, is he going to spend it brooding and contemplating about the evil he has done? You think he is going to have that knot in his stomach? You think he will think about the lives he has taken? The years he has stolen? Has he yet? Has he come out and said to anyone that tearfully he is sorry for what happened, that he thinks about it every day, that can't sleep at night? That he can't eat? That he feels guilty and he can't

> take it any longer? Will he spend the rest of his life in remorse or will it be like you hear on the tape: ... me first, satisfy my needs today. (*Sims v. Brown*, 2005, p. 75)

Or, there is the contrast between the suffering that is inflicted and the fear – "cowardice" as the prosecutor calls it – of suffering the consequences:

> Is it any wonder that a person who would attack a helpless, fragile, arthritic little old lady and stab her as many times as he did, brutalize her, slit her throat, ripped her clothes off, ... any one who would do something so cowardly, is it any wonder that when he runs, he is silent after he runs? He doesn't go to the police. He isn't filled with remorse. ... Is it any wonder that that type of coward would not fess up to all the details of his confession to the police? Of course not. (*Raby v. Dretke*, 2003, p. 327)

The suffering of the innocent and untainted victim stands in stark contrast to the indifference and callousness of the remorseless perpetrator. He is separated from the rest of humanity not so much by his violent deed as by his failure to acknowledge what he has done and his unwillingness to suffer for what he has done.

Yet, as Garfinkel has stated, the project of the degradation ceremony is not just to condemn the act and the perpetrator but to render the act and the feelings that accompanied it as the embodiment of who the perpetrator is – "What he is now is what, 'after all,' he was all along" (Garfinkel, 1956, p. 422). The absence of remorse – the callousness and indifference toward the victim that was expressed in this particular crime and at this particular time – must be shown to be devoid of "contingency, accident, or coincidence." The true status passage in the movement from convicted capital offender to deathworthy capital offender is proof that the remorseless, callous, unempathetic individual who performed deadly acts of violence with no feeling for his victim is who he will be for all times and all places.

It is this transformation that is accomplished through the lay and expert invocation of the clinical categories of anti-social personality disorder and psychopathy. Consistent with contemporary clinical representations, the offender is "reconstituted" as someone whose absence of moral emotions is the defining attribute of their pathology – a pathology that had an early onset and is virtually incurable. Let us consider the following excerpt from a cross-examination of an expert witness conducted during the penalty phase:

> Q. One of the features of a person with an anti-social personality disorder is that he tends to be irresponsible; correct?
>
> A. Well, one of the features of anti-social personality can be irresponsibility. I don't know if that's necessarily a criteria that fits him. He fits a number of the other criteria ... .

> Q. They also tend to express no remorse, don't they?
> A. That's true.
>
> Q. No remorse about the effects of their behavior on other people?
> A. They often don't have insight into the effects of their behavior on themselves or on other people.
>
> Q. In other words, a lot of people who have anti-social personality disorders can't play by the rules in a civilized society, correct?
> A. True. (*Bronshtein v. Horn*, 2005, p. 718)

Or another excerpt in another prosecutor's address to the jury that similarly naturalizes the absence of remorse:

> He shoots C., and there's no remorse. Let's talk about the definition of remorse. I looked it up in the dictionary: "A deep torturing sense of guilt felt over a wrong that one has done."
>
> Which we know sociopaths can't do. He shoots C., no remorse. Killed A., no remorse. Shoots C. again, it's getting easier, No remorse. (*People v. Boyette*, 2002, pp. 454–455)

Remorse may be differentiated from empathy, shame, and the admission of responsibility on the Hare scale or circumscribed on the MMPI – but there is no indication that jurors or legal advocates work with such fine distinctions. Remorse is shorthand for a host of feelings that one should have when one does grievous injury to another – all of which are absent in the remorseless offender. The visceral loathing that remorselessness attracts is then translated into an essentialist portrait of the offender – he is literally made into something apart from the human. Consider the following representations during the penalty phase:

> But, ladies and gentlemen, his act is transparent to the neutral and critical observer such as you are and you all know that no matter what words may be used to try and convince us that this defendant feels remorse and cares for others, et cetera, et cetera, those are words. … the sadism, premeditation, and ritualistic repetition shown in these crimes are the classic trademark of the psychopath who feels no remorse and has no concern for anyone outside of himself. He's the beast that walks upright. You meet him on the street. He will seem normal, but he roams those streets, parasitic and cold-eyed, stalking his prey behind a veneer of civility. (*People v. Farnam*, 2002, p. 199)

Indeed, one must beware of his outward appearance of normality and his superior capacity to control impressions. As another prosecutor warns the jury:

> (Defendant) is a very remorseless, cold-blooded individual. … Remember, appearances can be deceiving, and he's been working on you, watching you come and go, smiling and

> waving when he's introduced to you. Appearances, ladies and gentlemen, can be very deceiving. (*People v. Boyette*, 2002, p. 434)

Identifying the capital offender as remorseless forms a crucial part in his reconstitution as a deathworthy subject. If the showing of remorse purports to reveal something deep and fundamental about the character of the defendant, so does its absence. This true mark of character when coupled with its clinical recasting as a sure sign of unalterable pathology invests the absence of moral emotions with the force of nature. Not only is the capital offender expelled from the moral community as someone who cannot conform to the most rudimentary norms of civil society – he is made into something apart from the human, appearances to the contrary. He is the carrier of a deformation that is rooted in his incapacity to feel even though its primary manifestations are in the working of grievous harm on others. His actions are anti-social – his absence of feeling unnatural. It is this absence that makes him unfit for the mercy of the jury and the court. As one prosecutor expressed it to the jury – "And it seems to me that before you consider allowing Mr. C. to live under a sentence of life without the possibility of parole, you'd ask to see at least some evidence of remorse from Mr. C. for the perpetration of these crimes" (*People v. Crittenden*, 1994, p. 146).

2.2. Reframing the Moral Emotions

But what about those defendants who do attempt to show remorse or for whom a claim to remorsefulness is made by their counsel? A demonstration of remorse that is credible is enough to interrupt the process of degradation by which the defendant is made deathworthy. The narratives that urge a jury to vote for death do not for a moment concede to the defendant – although you are remorseful, you have committed an atrocious and brutal crime for which you must still receive the death penalty. The deathworthy defendant must be shown to deserve death not only for what he has done but for the kind of person he is. The capacity for empathy, shame, and guilt – all subsumed under the signifier of remorse – tend to restore the perpetrator to membership in the moral community in spite of the grievous deed. To complete the denunciation, the defendant's claims to remorse must be countered by rebuttals by which they will be discredited or by reframing whatever evidence is put forward as not what it appears to be.

On the one hand, because of the problematic relationship between appearance and reality in deciding whether or not remorse is genuine, for every narrative that purports to reveal the defendant as incontrovertibly remorseful, there is an equally compelling counternarrative that can also be crafted from the same pool of evidence. Indeed, the polarization described by one judge in her dissent in a case in which the defendant was sentenced to death can be generalized to other capital cases in the penalty phase:

> There were essentially two narratives about D. that could be culled from the facts. … The former narrative cast D as unregenerate; the latter, as capable of redemption. Whether D's life would be saved depended in great measure on which of those narratives the jury believed. (*State v. DiFrisco*, 2002, p. 276)

For example, weighing against one defendant who went to the police and confessed to the murder he had committed is a quote from the initial interview in which he is reported to have said about his victim – "we should have just tied her up and taken her life savings and split the country" (*People v. Sakarias*, 2000, p. 645). The later statement is accompanied by the commentary – "again, a selfish concern with with his own well-being, never expressing a type of remorse –," "I'm sorry I did it, I'm sorry I caused pain." Or another defendant's statement to the jury that "I feel a lot of remorse. It was a terrible thing. And if it could be changed, it was within my power, I would change it" (*People v. Marshall*, 1990, p. 943) is rebutted by an earlier interview just after his arrest in which when asked if he felt remorse, he replied that yes – because his plans to travel were interrupted. Or the prosecutor points to a revealing moment in which a witness testifies to a conversation in which the defendant "laughed and thought it was funny" and "thought it was no big deal that he killed three people" to counter an earlier claim to remorse (*Cooper v. State*, 2003, p. 978). Or the show of remorse claimed by another defendant after her conviction is challenged as inconsistent with her earlier attempt to have her confession excluded as evidence (*People v. Mulero*, 1997, p. 460). If silence allows the state to call attention to the conspicuous absence of feelings that should have been felt and communicated, alleging that remorse has been demonstrated affords the opportunity to discredit the claim through counternarrative – by recasting what is portrayed as genuine as instead counterfeit or strategic – one identity showing the defendant to be responsive to the moral claims of community pitted against another identity in which he is cast as unregenerate and beyond redemption.

The other approach to discreditation involves reframing what might be taken as expressions or gestures of remorse in persons who are perceived as psychologically normal as having a different meaning when viewed in the context of anti-social personality disorder. Thus, for example, suicide attempts that might otherwise be construed as expressions of mental anguish or suffering consistent with remorse are reinterpreted as "gestures" that are variously "feigned" or designed to "manipulate (their) environment" or "to gain sympathy" (*State v. Daniels*, 1994, p. 289), all founded on the premise that someone with anti-social personality disorder would not be able to "feel remorse for (his) crimes and for killing his victim, but would (only) be able to feel remorse for himself." Consider, for example, the following excerpt from the cross-examination of an expert witness by defense counsel after he (the expert witness) had already testified that his client was a "sociopath." In this highly publicized case, the central issue in the appeal concerned whether the defendent's various attempts at suicide were true signs of remorse:[24]

> And in your opinion that person (some one who hypothetically has anti-social personality disorder) would not show remorse?
>
> A. Dr. G. – psychiatrist – Well, it doesn't hold true ironclad to all such individuals, but it is one of the typical characteristics, yes.
>
> Q. And you can't say, can you, Doctor, whether or not R feels remorse for these crimes?
> A. Not precisely, no.
>
> Q. You haven't examined him since July 7th.
> A. No, I have not.
>
> Q. So you venture no opinion as to whether or not he is remorseful at this time?
> A. No opinion except that I would doubt it very much. (*Harris v. Vazquez*, 1990, p. 613)

Given the incapacity of the defendant, external signs of remorse must be read in a different way. Here, expert opinion is deployed to instruct the juror to disregard appearances – to understand that behaviors that might otherwise suggest complexity or contradiction conform to the same underlying substrate of a person who is incapable of experiencing remorse. Therefore, the actions of such persons – even if they appear otherwise – are indicative of strategic or insincere expressions of remorse rather than true expressions of what the offender actually feels.

Attaching the incapacity for remorse to anti-social personality disorder also invites consideration of all the other traits associated with the condition. For example, in another cross-examination during another penalty phase trial, once the expert witness had admitted that the defendant had anti-social personality disorder, he was then asked about the other characteristics of such persons, replying that in addition to the fact that "persons with this disorder show little remorse for the consequences of their aggressive acts and blame the victims for being foolish or helpless," the condition includes other characteristics such as "a pervasive pattern of violating the rights of others," "lying, manipulation, and malingering" (*Bucklew v. Luebbers*, 2006, p. 1014). In another reframing, a defendant who claimed to feel remorse for his crime was described by the expert witness as "incapable of the kind of deep feelings for someone else implied by the word 'remorse'" (*State v. Campbell*, 2002, p. 57) by virtue of his anti-social personality disorder. Other capital cases point to strategic decisions by defense teams not to call expert evidence to corroborate a claim of remorse for fear that the expert's finding of anti-social personality disorder will not just negate the claim but place the defendant in the most unfavorable of categories.[25]

Among those who have committed grievous wrongs against the community, it is not only those who are silent or who refrain from showing remorse who are the objects of public denunciation. By means of counternarrative and reframing, the bar is raised to also include those who confess, who profess to feel remorse, even those who claim to have suffered for their wrongs. Remorse plays a critical role in this process because it supplies an instrumentalist justification for the visceral moral outrage directed at those who fail to show any feelings of empathy or inner anguish for the harm they have caused. The failure to feel remorse is not just the infuriating absence in those who do not belong to our moral community and therefore have no "humanity" to demonstrate – it is in addition a symptom of a pathology that marks its bearer as incapable of reformation and therefore a continuing danger to the community. The ritual destruction of the capital offender as a social object demands that he be condemned not only for the brutality of his crime but for the viciousness of his character and the intractability of his pathology. The remorseless offender is rendered deathworthy by proving a correspondence between the irredeemable act and the unredeemability of the person. But the thrust of this analysis is to suggest that the moral performance that results in this degradation is one that is artfully mediated by strategic considerations, the building of competing narratives, and the reframing of common sense reality.

One of the ironies of this process is that, if it achieves its purpose, the jurors will come to divest themselves of the very same qualities of empathy, suffering over the harm wrought on another, and identification with the victim that they found so conspicuously absent in the remorseless offender. The degradation process not only transforms the offender but also those who will decide the offender's fate. Ultimately, the remorseless offender who has been reconstituted as no longer belonging to human society is someone toward whom the juror has had to learn to overcome his or her own feelings of remorse in order to vote for death.[26]

3. FURTHER REFLECTIONS ON THE MORAL ECONOMY OF REMORSE

The murders for which the state recommends the death penalty by and large represent the extremity of individualized violence against others – brutal, multiple, or desecrating or all at once. Those who commit these acts but yet claim to experience remorse present the jury and the larger community with an uncomfortable paradox. How can someone who has committed acts of such grievous harm feel toward their actions the same way as do members of the moral community? The more transgressive the behavior, the more problematic it becomes to even entertain the possibility of a shared sensibility. If the perpetrator of violent crime is like us in how he sees his own actions, are we then as different from him or her as we might wish? The refusal to grant the murderer the moral capital of feelings of remorse is also a reassurance that the boundaries that separate us from the violent act also separate us from the violent person who committed the act. Garfinkel suggests that the moral indignation mobilized by the degradation ceremony generates group solidarity (Garfinkel, 1956, p. 421). Yet, in the denunciation of the capital offender as without remorse and as the abnormal, pathological other, this solidarity is as defensive as it is integrative. We unite in moral indignation against those who commit acts of extreme transgression – but we also defend against their proximity to our own inner emotional life by denying them the possibility of shared moral sentiments.

Does this mean that the moral outrage directed against those who have committed acts of grievous harm but who do not show remorse is disingenuous? That no matter how much the despised transgressor tries to show remorse, rejection and ridicule are the inevitable responses? If we take one recent capital case as illustrative, it would seem that for persons who are placed in this position, the barriers to official and public acceptance as someone capable of remorse may well be insurmountable. Even the willingness to stipulate to the death penalty was not enough to credit Michael Ross as remorseful for the murders he had committed. In this highly publicized case, Ross, who was eventually executed on May 12, 2005, had in 1987 confessed to the rape and murder by strangulation of three young women in

Connecticut. Although he had committed five other murders in New York and Rhode Island, to which he eventually confessed, he claimed to have chosen initially to admit only to the crimes committed in Connecticut because at the time it was the only one of the three states that had the death penalty. Even in cases such as this in which the death penalty is a foregone conclusion both because of the aggravating factors and the consent of the defendant, the prosecution would not allow the claim to remorse to go unchallenged, in this instance, portraying Ross as seeking publicity and notoriety through his quest for the death penalty (*State v. Ross*, 2004, p. 322). When he finally was executed, an item in the New York Times quoted the father of one of the victims that "it was just a cowardly exit on his behalf in that he couldn't even face the families." In response to the question of whether his volunteering for death was "truly out of sympathy for the victims," psychiatrists were quoted as suggesting that instead it was "a grand act of vanity" performed by "a narcissist with a need to appear noble" (Yardley, 2005, p. 1).

The destruction of the violent offender as a moral entity would appear to be as much an imperative of the death penalty as his actual execution.

NOTES

1. A continuing research project set up in 1993, the National Capital Jury Project (using a sample of 1,155 real jurors from 340 capital trials in 14 states), has been investigating how, among other considerations, jurors determine whether or not someone is remorseful. For statistical analysis demonstrating importance of remorse in jurors' decisions, see especially Garvey (1998), Sundby (1998), and Eisenberg, Garvey, and Wells (1998).

2. Garvey captures these strong sentiments when he writes that jurors are "apt to respond to the remorseful defendant not only with good will but also *without fear and disgust*, both of which tended to recede in the face of the defendant's remorse" (Garvey, 2000, pp. 58–59) (My emphasis).

3. "Quietly acknowleged" because in the fictive world of the criminal trial, evidence of lack of remorse is allowed never as "an aggravating factor but only to respond when it is offered in mitigation" (*People v. Davenport,* 1985, pp. 288–289) to quote from one frequently cited case whereas the thrust of recent research as well as above cited case law seems to recognize the aggravating impact of characterizing a defendant as remorseless.

4. In order to protect jurors' confidentiality, the responses of jurors in the National Capital Jury Project could not be analyzed in relation to specific trials. Hence we do not know from the research how jurors' perceptions of the defendant's remorse might have been shaped by the details of the crime or by how he or she was portrayed by prosecution, defense, or other witnesses. See M. Costanzo and

J. Peterson (1994) for examples of prosecutors' emphasis on remorse in their address to the jury.

5. I have relied upon Lexis Nexis to look at inflammatory statements during the penalty phase of the capital trial between 1/1/1986 and 6/30/2006.

6. See accounts by Isaac Ray (1838, pp. 219–222) and James Cowles Prichard (1842, pp. 95–102) for the most influential of the many contemporary accounts; see also Michel Foucault (2003, pp. 112–134) for highly informative discussion and analysis of case.

7. "Pour qu'on fut bien assure en montant dans la chamber qu'elle seule etait coupable" (Georget, 1826, p. 79).

8. The dominant school of psychology in the early 19th century held that the mind could be divided into the separate faculties of will, feeling, and intellect and that each of these faculties operated independently of the other two (Rippa, 1992).

9. Ray, *Treatise*, pp. 169–170. Ray is quoting from Prichard's definition of moral insanity which in turn he subdivided into *general moral mania* and *partial moral mania.* If the derangement was manifested in all the affective faculties, it fell into the former category; if it was confined to 'one or a few of the affective faculties' (p. 180), as in the case of Cornier – she was insane only when she committed the act – then it fell into the later category.

10. It may reflect the imprecision of these categories that Prichard, who had introduced the concept of moral insanity, categorized Cornier's affliction as a disease of the will whereas Ray, borrowing from Prichard, considered her affliction to be a derangement in the faculty that controlled feelings.

11. J. E. D. Esquirol (1722–1795), a founder of clinical psychiatry along with Philippe Pinel and one of Etienne Georget's teachers.

12. Early 19th century French psychiatric nosology grouped both those who were cognitively disoriented and those whose mental disorder centered on the emotions in the same category of *monomanie* whereas the Anglo-American approach was to confine monomania to delusional thinking while placing affective disorder without cognitive defect in a separate category – that of moral insanity following Prichard (1842, pp. 36–61); or moral mania, following Ray (1838, pp. 168–170). For a relatively clear formulation of these distinctions, see *Report of the Metropolitan Commissioners in Lunacy*, London, 1844.

13. Dr. R. von Krafft-Ebing's *Text-book of Insanity, Based on Clinical Observations*, 1905. Krafft-Ebing's clinical insights on moral insanity are cited by Havelock Ellis (1890, p. 229) and in Enrico Fermi (1897, p. 26) among others.

14. For useful overview of shift in meaning of category, see Nicole Rafter (2004).

15. See, for example, the opening sentence in Hare (1998, p. 105) – "Psychopathy is a socially devastating personality disorder defined by a constellation of affective, interpersonal, and behavioral characteristics, including egocentricity, manipulativeness, deceitfulness, lack of empathy, guilt or remorse, and a propensity to violate social and legal expectations and norms." Affective, interpersonal, and behavioral characteristics all contribute to the disorder. Indeed, the tendency to equate personality disorders such as psychopathy or antisocial personality with social deviance has been sharply criticized by another important contributor to modern formulations: Theodore Millon (1996) writes in (p. 429) that "I have never felt comfortable with the write-up for the antisocial personality disorder. I very much agree with those who contend that the focus given is oriented too much to the

'criminal personality' and not sufficiently toward those who have avoided criminal involvements."

16. For example, Cleckley writes in answer to the question of what ultimately distinguishes the psychopath for those with other mental disorders, "My concept of the psychopath's functioning postulates a selective defect or elimination which prevents important components of normal experience from being integrated into the whole human reaction, particularly an elimination or attenuation of *those strong affective components that ordinarily arise in major personal and social issues*" (Cleckley, 1976, p. 260) (my emphasis).

17. "His mask is that of robust mental health. Yet he has a disorder that often manifests itself in conduct far more seriously abnormal than that of the schizophrenic" (Cleckley, 1976, p. 383).

18. For example, Cleckley (1976) writes – "A very large percentage of the psychopaths I have studied show backgrounds that appear conducive to happy development and excellent adjustment" (p. 410). See also Hare (1993, pp. 174–175), "We found no evidence that the family backgrounds of psychopaths differ from those of other criminals." Or regarding the onset of psychopathy, Hare observes – "In sharp contrast (to other criminals), the quality of family life had absolutely no effect on the emergence of criminality in psychopaths. Whether the family life was stable or unstable, psychopaths first appeared in adult court at an average age of 14."

19. Cleckley (1976, pp. 423–424) maintained this position through to the last edition of his work – "For many years, I have consistently tried to emphasize my strong conviction that psychopaths should not be regarded as psychotic in the sense of being 'innocent because of insanity' of the wrongs they do. ... Whatever in the psychotic patient there is that may render him not responsible, or less than normally responsible, for crime, cannot, in my opinion, be found in the psychopath's defect." Or, similarly Hare (1993, p. 143) writes – "In my opinion, psychopaths certainly know enough about what they are doing to be held accountable for their actions."

20. On the remarkable abilities of the psychopath, Cleckley writes – "Not only can he (perhaps involuntarily) mimic sanity in superlative fashion but also moral rebirth, salvation, and absolute reform, or perhaps transformation into a super-citizen" (1976, p. 434). Or Millon (1996, pp. 445–446) –"Unconstrained by honesty and truth, they (antisocial types) weave impressive tales of competency and reliability. ... Alert to weaknesses in others they play their games of deception with considerable skill." See also Hare (1993, pp. 46–51) who offers numerous vignettes illustrating the psychopath's skill at impression management and pleasure in duping others.

21. This inability to experience painful emotions is sometimes referred to as shallowness of emotions. For example, Hare (1998) writes – "While the cognitions and interpersonal interactions of most members of our species are heavily laden with emotion, the inner life, experiences, and behaviors of psychopaths seem shallow and emotionally barren" (1998, p. 105). On superior adaptability of those with psychopathic or antisocial personality disorders to prison life, see Cleckley – "Even when under life sentence, the psychopath tends more readily than others to obtain parole and become again a social menace" (1976, p. 434). Regarding the ineffectuality of punishment, Millon observes "(Rather) than being a deterrent, it

may reinforce their rebelliousness and their desire for retribution" (Millon, 1996, p. 454). More generally, Blair et al. (2005, p. 48) report on substantial body of research about psychopath's "attenuated experience, not of all emotional states, but specifically anxiety or fear."

22. The population of cases for this analysis was generated in the following manner. Using *Lexis-Nexis*, I used the search advisor to identify judgments in capital cases in which remorse or its derivatives were mentioned at least five times in decisions pertaining to the penalty phase. The search instruction that I used was at least 5 (remors!). I selected the time period from 1/1/1990 to 6/30/2006. I chose 1990 as the starting point because it was only by this time that a substantial jurisprudence dealing with remorse in capital punishment had begun to accumulate. The data base from which I drew these cases is listed in *Lexis Nexis* as "Federal and State cases combined." I chose this data base because it has the most complete listing of published cases currently available to researchers. Since my concern was to identify how prosecutors characterized death penalty defendants to jurors in terms of the presence or absence of remorse, I selected from my population (of all capital cases between 1/1/1990 and 6/1/2006 in which remorse was mentioned at least five times in judgments pertaining to the penalty phase) only those cases in which portions of the prosecutor's address to the jury regarding the defendant's remorse was excerpted in the judgment. I ended with 147 cases that met these criteria. Since only one of these 147 cases involved a female defendant, I have used *he* as the generic pronoun in this section of the paper.

23. In another instance, the defendant had drafted a statement that alludes to other problems in showing remorse – "People say that I don't show any emotion but that is not true. When I think about what happened I do cry and ask forgiveness from the (victims') families when I am in my cell at night or think about what happened. ... I have told them that I am sorry and meant it, when I say these things to them tho, someone say's (sic) that I don't mean it or when I don't say anything they say that I don't have any remorse but the people who make these statements have not sat down with me to see what I am feeling ... ." Ultimately, on advice of defense counsel, the statement was not read to the jury (*State v. Bey*, 1999, p. 301) at 110.

24. I refer to *Harris v. Vazquez*, 1990. The legal debate over whether Robert Alton Harris' execution would be televised forms the point of departure for Wendy Lesser's *Pictures at an Execution*, 1993.

25. In *Kimbrough v. State* (2004), the prosecutor in a case in which the death penalty was imposed defended the strategy of the defense for not calling expert evidence that would have identified the offender as a 'psychopathic deviate' suggesting that had this diagnosis been available, "he would have gone into the characteristics of psychopathy, would have quoted some of the less favorable descriptions of psychopaths, and would have equated psychopathy to antisocial personality disorder" at 14. See also *State v. DiFrisco* (2002) for another strategic decision not to call potentially useful expert testimony because the psychologist consulted by the defense had diagnosed the defendant as having antisocial personality disorder.

26. For a more psychologically oriented approach to this process of desensitization or moral disengagement, see Craig Haney (1997).

REFERENCES

Abbott, A. (March 15, 2001). Into the mind of a killer. *Nature*, *410*, 296–298.

Arrigo, B. A., & Shipley, S. (2001). The confusion over psychopathy (I): Historical considerations. *International Journal of Offender Therapy and Comparative Criminology*, *45*, 325–344.

Blair, J., Mitchell, D., & Blair, K. (2005). *The psychopath: Emotion and the brain*. Malden, MA: Blackwell.

Cleckley, H. (1976). *The mask of sanity* (5th ed.). St. Louis, MO: C.V. Mosby and Co.

Costanzo, M., & Peterson, J. (1994). Attorney persuasion in the capital penalty phase: A content analysis of closing arguments. *Journal of Social Issues*, *50*, 125–147.

Dao, J., & Bacon, L. (November 25, 2003). Death sentence for Muhammed; Sniper Jury cites lack of sorrow. *New York Times*, p. 1.

DSM-IV-TR. (2000). *Diagnostic and statistical manual of mental disorder* (4th ed., text revision). Washington, DC: American Psychiatric Association.

Eisenberg, T., Garvey, S., & Wells, M. T. (1998). But was he sorry? The role of remorse in capital sentencing. *Cornell Law Review*, *83*, 1599–1637.

Ellis, H. (1890). *The criminal.* London: Walter Scott.

Fermi, E. (1897). *Criminal sociology.* New York: P. Appleton and Company.

Foucault, M. (2003). In: G. Burchell (Trans.), *Abnormal – Lectures at the College de France, 1974–1975.* New York: Picador.

Garfinkel, H. (1956). Conditions of successful degradation ceremonies. *American Journal of Sociology*, *61*, 420–424.

Garvey, S. P. (1998). Aggravation and mitigation in capital cases: What do jurors think? *Columbia Law Review*, *98*, 1538–1576.

Garvey, S. P. (2000). The emotional economy of capital sentencing. *New York University Law Review*, *75*, 26–73.

Georget, E. (1826). *Discussions medico-legale pour Henriette Cornier*. Paris: Migneret.

Haney, C. (1997). Violence and the capital jury: Mechanisms of moral disengagement and the impulse to condemn to death. *Stanford Law Review*, *49*, 1447–1486.

Hare, R. D. (1993). *Without conscience – the disturbing world of the psychopaths among us*. New York: Pocket Books.

Hare, R. D. (1996). Psychopathy and antisocial personality disorder: A case of diagnostic confusion. *Psychiatric Times*, *13*(2), 1–4. e-journal at http://www.psychiatrictimes.com/p960239.html

Hare, R. D. (1998). Psychopathy, affect and behavior. In: D. J. Cooke et al. (Eds), *Psychopathy: Theory, research, and implications for society* (pp. 105–124). Norwell, MA: Kluwer Academic Publications.

Kadri, S. (2005). *The trial: From Socrates to O.J. Simpson*. New York: Random House.

Krafft-Ebing, R. (1905). In: C. G. Craddock (Trans.), *Text-book of insanity, based on clinical observations.* Philadelphia, PA: F. A. Davis Company.

Lesser, W. (1993). *Pictures at an execution.* Cambridge, MA: Harvard University Press.

Millon, T., & Davis, R. D. (1996). *Disorders of personality, DSM-IV and beyond* (2nd ed.). New York: John Wiley and Sons.

Petrunik, M., & Weisman, R. (2005). Constructing Joseph Fredericks: Competing narratives of a child sex murderer. *International Journal of Law and Psychiatry*, *28*, 75–96.

Prichard, J. C. (1842). *On the different forms of insanity in relation to jurisprudence*. London: Hippolyte Balliere.

Rafter, N. (2004). The unrepentant horse-slasher: Moral insanity and the origins of criminological thought. *Criminology*, *42*, 979–1007.

Ray, I. (1838). *Treatise on the medical jurisprudence of insanity*. Boston, MA: Charles C. Little and James Brown.

Report of the Metropolitan Commissioners in Lunacy. (1844). London.

Rippa, S. A. (1992). *Education in a free society: An American history* (7th ed.). New York: Longman.

Stout, M. (2005). *The sociopath next door: The ruthless versus the rest of us*. New York: Broadway Books.

Sundby, S. (1998). The capital jury and absolution: The intersection of trial strategy, remorse, and the death penalty. *Cornell Law Review*, 1557–1598.

Yardley, W. (May 14, 2005). Execution in Connecticut: Final day: One view of killer's execution: "It was just a cowardly exit". *New York Times*, p. 1.

Cases cited

Atkins v. Virginia, 122 S.Ct. 2242[U.S. 2002]
Bronshtein v. Horn, 404 F. 3rd 700[3rd Cir. 2005]
Bucklew v. Luebbers, 436 F. 3rd 1010[8th Cir. 2006]
Cooper v. State, 856 So. 2nd 969[Fla. 2003]
Harris v. Vazquez, 913 F. 2nd 606[9th Cir. 1990]
People v. Boyette, 29 Cal. 4th 381[Cal. 2002]
People v. Crittenden, 9 Cal. 4th 83[Cal. 1994]
People v. Davenport, 41 Cal. 3rd 247[Cal. 1985]
People v. Farnam, 28 Cal. 4th 107[Cal. 2002]
People v. Jurado, 38 Cal. 4th 72[Cal. 2006]
People v. Marshall, 50 Cal. 3rd 907[Cal. 1990]
People v. Mulero, 176 Ill. 2nd 444[Ill. 1997]
People v. Pollock, 32 Cal. 4th 1153[Cal. 2004]
People v. Sakarias, 22 Cal. 4th 596[Cal. 2000]
Raby v. Dretke, 78 Fed. Appx.324[5th Cir. 2003]
Riggins v. Nevada, 112 S.Ct. 1810[U.S. 1992]
Shelton v. State, 744 A. 2d 465[Del. 1999]
Sims v. Brown, 2005 U.S. App. LEXIS 26806[9th Cir. 2005].
State v. Bey, 161 N.J. 233[N.J. 1999]
State v. Campbell, 95 Ohio St. 3rd 48[Ohio 2002]
State v. Daniels, 337 N.C. 243[N.C. 1994]
State v. DiFrisco, 174 N.J. 195[N.J. 2002]
State v. Ross, 269 Conn. 213[Conn. 2004]
State v. Stephenson, 2005 Tenn.Crim. App. LEXIS 208[Tenn Crim App 2005]